Subject to Ourselves

Great Barrington Books

Bringing the old and new together
in the spirit of W. E. B. Du Bois

∿ An imprint edited by Charles Lemert ∿

Titles Available

Keeping Good Time: Reflections on Knowledge, Power, and People
by Avery F. Gordon (2004)

Going Down for Air: A Memoir in Search of a Subject
by Derek Sayer (2004)

The Souls of Black Folk
100th Anniversary Edition
by W. E. B. Du Bois, with commentaries by Manning Marable,
Charles Lemert, and Cheryl Townsend Gilkes (2004)

Sociology After the Crisis, Second Edition
by Charles Lemert (2004)

Subject to Ourselves: Social Theory, Psychoanalysis and
Postmodernity, Second Edition
by Anthony Elliott, with a new foreword by Zygmunt Bauman (2004)

Forthcoming

Seeing Sociologically: The Routine Grounds of Social Action
by Harold Garfinkel, edited and introduced by Anne Rawls,
foreword by Charles Lemert (Fall 2004)

Thinking the Unthinkable: An Introduction to Social Theories
by Charles Lemert (Fall 2005)

An Anatomy of Critical Theory
by Kyungman Kim (Fall 2005)

SUBJECT TO OURSELVES

Social Theory, Psychoanalysis
and Postmodernity

Second Edition

Anthony Elliott

New Foreword by

Zygmunt Bauman

Paradigm Publishers

Boulder • London

Copyright © 2004 by Paradigm Publishers

Published in the United States by Paradigm Publishers, 3360 Mitchell Lane Suite C, Boulder, Colorado 80301 USA.

Paradigm Publishers is the trade name of Birkenkamp & Company, LLC, Dean Birkenkamp, President and Publisher.

Library of Congress Cataloging-in-Publication Data has been applied for.

Printed and bound in the United States of America on acid free paper that meets the standards of the American National Standard for Permanence of Paper for Printed Library Materials.

Designed and Typeset by Straight Creek Bookmakers
09 08 07 06 05 04   1 2 3 4 5

For Nicola
(Níor dhúirt éinne liom go mbeadh laethanta
mar seo)

Contents

Contents

Preface

Of my various writings exploring the relationship between social theory and psychoanalysis, this book has somehow managed to scoop up the most diverse readership. Inquiries from specialists working in the fields of, say, comparative literature or urban studies, as well as student requests to explain further the concept of "reflexive scanning" and why it takes off in conditions of postmodernity, have all been forthcoming over the years. So, it is especially pleasing to have a new edition of the book published.

Charles Lemert was instrumental in making this happen, and he joined with Dean Birkenkamp at Paradigm Publishers in supporting the project throughout. Elizabeth Wood, at the Centre for Critical Theory at the University of the West of England, oversaw the preparation of this work with patience and grace, and her input has been invaluable.

In many various ways, this is Nicola Geraghty's book. Again, with astonishment, I can only remark that the days got better than even the best we knew. Her influence upon my argument, along with that of the late Albert Paolini, is impossible to fully acknowledge.

Anthony Elliott
Bristol, England

Foreword

On Anthony Elliott's
Subject to Ourselves

Zygmunt Bauman

In January 1968, Hannah Arendt, taking a hint from Bertold Brecht's poem "To Posterity," described the current human condition as another experience of living "in dark times." There has been no shortage of such experiences in human history. The marks of dark times were as a rule "the disorder and the hunger, the massacres and the slaughters, the outrage over injustice and the despair when there was only wrong and no outrage." But the dark times' most remarkable and most sinister feature was that all this "took place in public," and yet "it was by no means visible to all, nor was it at all easy to perceive it." It was covered up not by realities but by the highly efficient talk and double-talk of nearly all official representatives who, without interruption and in many ingenious variations, explained away unpleasant facts and justified concerns of those whom they represented.[1]

And so it is not just because of the atrocities we hear about and the outrage they arouse, but because of the camouflage woven of public discourse—copious and exuberant, and for that reason opaque—or because (as Martin Heidegger put it) "the light of the public obscures everything," or because of the off-putting paradox of human conditions hidden through overexposure and lost somewhere in the tangle of information highways, that our times are experienced as "dark."

"In those days," says Ulrich Beck—old days, pre-postmodern days—hazards "assaulted the nose or the eyes and were thus perceptible to the senses, while the risks of civilization today typically *escape perception*."[2] In the world where life as before is local but the factors that determine its prospects and its course are global, one does not know of the dangers until they strike or unless one is told by the few people in the know that the strike is in the cards. Today's risks, unlike yesterday's dangers, can be barred from awareness by being kept in silence or glossed over; they can also be argued away from awareness by playing down the costs and playing up the bonuses. And they can be fabricated, or blown out of all proportions, so that some people somewhere can profit from staging a preventive strike against the presumed villains and gain credit for winning the war before it started. (Just recall the "millenium bug" affair, or think of the CIA and FBI vying to frighten fellow Americans with predictions of imminent terrorist attacks that could be staved off only by the unremitting vigilance of their vastly increased staffs.) Meanwhile, some other risks that are more real and less easy to handle are minimized, so that they cause not the electors' insomnia nor provoke wrath.

Never before has "the light of the public" obscured so much, and neither were the things obscured as central to human challenges and pursuits as the things that are obscured in our own dark times. Add to this, as did Dany-Robert Dufour, that most of us, the new individuals who are presumed to find private solutions to public troubles, "are more abandoned than free"[3]; and that, as Beck observed, most experts tend to "dump their contradictions and conflicts at the feet of the individual and leave him or her with the well-intentioned invitation to judge all of it critically on the basis of his or her own notions"[4]—and you'll understand why never before was there so great a responsibility on the part of the scholars and researchers who are able and bound to pierce through the dazzlingly lit public stage in order to visit and explore the areas unattainable to common experience.

A true therapy of social ills—so Pierre Bourdieu kept reminding his fellow scholars—starts "with recognition of invisible maladies, that is, of the facts of which the sick themselves do not speak, of which they are unaware, or which they forgot to mention." A true therapist of social ills is s/he who reaches to "the economic and social determinants of the innumerable attempts on personal liberty and legitimate aspirations to happiness and self-fulfilment." This is not, of course, the whole story; this is not the mission accomplished. "Revealing the mechanisms that make life miserable, even unlivable, would not suffice to neutralize them; bringing to light contradictions would not resolve them."[5] This is, we may say, neither the end nor the beginning of the end. This is, though, the end of the beginning—and a necessary condition for the end to begin.

Anthony Elliott's remarkable book may serve as an example of how that vocation can be fulfilled and its precepts followed to great effect. It may be seen as setting a pattern for all future attempts to explore and represent the conditions under which men and women in our variety of dark times struggle with the challenges of self-building, identity formation, and social placement.

Like all books destined and bound to invigorate self-reflection and enrich awareness in times of confusing signals and elusive meanings, it may be read in many ways—just as the messages derived in the course of reading can be interpreted in many ways. It is thanks to those qualities that this book is certain to set self-reflection in motion and to prod the long, perhaps infinite, yet indispensable, process of recapitulation and reinterpretation of the allegedly private life-experience whose social entanglements Elliott draws out of concealment and lays bare.

Let me repeat: Different readers, prompted as all readers tend to be by varied concerns of their own, will retrieve different foods-for-thought from the bountiful harvest of Elliott's extraordinary erudition and in-depth analyses. The great merit of the book is precisely the unusually wide range of options it puts at the disposal of an attentive reader. Personally, I particularly cherished the chance to learn about the "complex, contradictory fantasy scenarios that creatively shape, and are also shaped by, the social and cultural worlds of modernity and postmodernity" (p. 2). I learned that if modern configuration is characterized by "a mode of fantasy in which security and enjoyment are derived by attempting to control, order and regulate the self, others and the sociopolitical world," the postmodern configuration is formed by focusing fantasy on "reflective space" itself rather than on the fruits of reflection, and wrapping it around the creation "of open spaces" for "plurality, ambiguity, ambivalence, contingency and uncertainty" (p. 4). I learned also, again with considerable benefit, that our strivings are bound to remain as contradictory as the challenges they attempt to cope with and the problems they try to resolve—since in our type of society, "modern and postmodern reveries" are deployed alongside each other, simultaneously, and with mutually reinforcing effects.

Deploying the two strategies at the same time, with notoriously off-putting or infuriatingly antinomic or anomic results, is not a matter of whim. Neither is it an outcome of wrong information or a dearth of information, erroneous judgment or lack of judgment, indecision or lack of will, inconstancy of purpose or value-confusion. The causes of the endemic inconclusiveness of the fantasy-guided efforts are akin to those that underlie the "indetermination principle" in small particles physics—the more successful the effort, the more thoroughly its declared purpose is defied. Wise after the fact (and Elliott's meticulous anatomy of that new, mellowed wisdom is second to none), we know that the social reality in which we happen to operate is not a system with marginal and essentially curable malfunctions, nor a social order with similarly marginal and essentially repairable disturbances and deviations. We know that order and disorder are rather like two sides of a coin or two poles of a magnet—two equally indispensable and unavoidable aspects of the world, aspects that are born together and can be wiped out only jointly. We know, finally, that the urge to order, to regulate, and to control is itself a major cause of ambiguity, ambivalence, and contingency, just as the discomfort which the resulting uncertainty may cause is the moving spirit of the ordering/regulating drive.

Awareness that the ambivalence is endemic and incurable, and that therefore the uncertainty that accompanies human life-pursuits is here to stay, is itself an ambivalent and uncertainty-breeding wisdom. It brings little comfort. Most certainly, it won't soothe anxiety and placate fears. But it is also a sobering and ultimately salutary wisdom. It teaches that the fantasies of patented solutions, simple remedies, and shortcuts are not only the most idle, but also the most misleading and dangerous figments of the feverish imagination prompted by pains of uncertainty. This is a timely lesson and one of grave and undiminishing import, since in dark times there is no shortage of patented-remedies-peddlers and shortcut guides, while the temptation to succumb to siren songs grows together with the desire for restfulness that only the end to uncertainty can offer.

Ours, says Elliott (who goes on to demonstrate the truth of his assertion), is a "multidimensional, chaotic world," fraught with a "plurality of local rationalities and identities." This is, he insists, the source of fears, but also of hope. And it cannot be otherwise, since our fears and our hopes stem from the same soil and have no other soil in which to take root. "Under contemporary social conditions, our innermost hopes and longings are in ongoing dialogue with our most fearful anxieties and gripping terrors" (pp. 6–7). That dialogue, let me add, is our hopes' best hope and our fears' greatest fear, and I am immensely grateful to Anthony Elliott for making that dialogue more meaningful, substantive, thoughtful, sensible, and (hopefully) enlightening.

Let me repeat Bourdieu's sobering warning: Bringing contradictions to light does not mean to resolve them. But let me add as well that the chances to resolve a contradiction do not rise with its obscurity.

This book offers its readers the most valuable service a responsible author may provide. It clarifies the conditions under which its readers—men and women living in dark times—will need to act when struggling to give sense to their lives. And as the mist covering those conditions is relentlessly, page after page, dispersed—so grow that struggle's chances of success.

Introduction to the Second Edition
Psychoanalysis, Modernity, Postmodernism: Theorizing for a New Era

Psychoanalysis, the late Cornelius Castoriadis once forecast, shall be eclipsed as therapy but will prosper as theory. The Culture Wars and recent Freud-bashing tend to confirm that he was right on the first count. The current fascination in the social sciences and humanities with all things Freudian, from fantasy to fetish, also suggest the accuracy of his punditry on the second. I argue in *Subject to Ourselves* that it is primarily in our fluid, globalized, and postmodern world that the potentially reflexive and freeing impact of psychoanalysis on the way we think, theorize, and process information at an emotional level might best be approached. For Freudianism filtered through the lens of the postmodern, at least in the hands of its more innovative practitioners, allows us to glimpse what a *psychoanalysis of psychoanalysis* might look like at the level of culture and politics.

This is not to say that the postmodern rendition of psychoanalysis is everywhere supreme. Far from it. Psychoanalysis in its postmodern recasting certainly does not enter into an alliance with either psychology (a discipline which, at any rate, has now dispensed with Freud almost entirely) or sociology (a discipline which, for the most part, still struggles with modernist readings of Freud as represented in the theoretical departures of, say, Talcott Parsons or Nancy Chodorow). Nor does it fare much better within the psychoanalytic profession itself. For the psychoanalytic establishment, roughly speaking, manipulates the reception of Freudian theory through the activity of training (read: drilling) candidates into analysts eligible to pronounce on the pathologization of human subjects and daily life. That a strong modernist desire for identifying, classifying, drawing boundaries, and dividing people into psychological categories is at work here is surely all too evident. As Douglas Kirsner notes of the undemocratic spirit of psychoanalytic institutes the world over in his eye-opening study *Unfree Associations,* the profession reproduces itself through the imposition of a clear hierarchy, an authoritarian ideology, a rigid conception of truth, and contempt for conceptual innovations or departures as threatening or "nonanalytic."[1] Farfetched? Well, maybe. But even if Kirsner overstates his case, the modernist zeal of psychoanalytic institutes is beyond doubt, and perhaps repair.

Julia Kristeva has recently argued that evidence of a present-day, modernist desire for certitude is increasingly found in the practice of psychoanalysis itself. As Kristeva observes, "Today, and still more in the future, I think psychoanalysis is the art—I admit the conceit—of allowing men and women who inhabit modern, arrogant, polished, expensive, and exciting cities, to safeguard a way of life."[2] Having shed the heavy Freudian lenses she wears when interpreting various artistic processes and cultural activities, Kristeva's concern is that psychoanalytic therapy seems to do so little for the reflective and democratic aspirations of its subjects. In practice, it is as if the modernist regulating frame of psychoanalysis keeps subjects of analysis held in check—preventing men and women from moving forward, and certainly at some distance from changing the self, let alone the world.

Psychoanalysis calls such a limiting of the powers of critical self-reflection "repetition"; to paraphrase Freud, that which we cannot process at the levels of consciousness and the unconscious, we are destined to repeat. That the practice of modernist psychoanalysis has been, ironically, caught in its own logic of repetition is something not lost on other traditions of critical thought—especially constructivist approaches. For what psychoanalysts term repetition is, for some authors, nothing less than a process of social normalization. Nikolas Rose, who argues in a Foucaultian vein that the act of confession constitutes subjectivity of the self as well as identity as an object for inspection and interrogation, sees the normalizing impact of psychoanalysis in terms of an attempt to stop difference and thus kill desire for otherness. "Psychotherapeutics," writes Rose, "is linked at a profound level to the sociopolitical obligation of the modern self. The self it seeks to liberate or restore is the entity able to steer its individual path through life by means of the act of personal decision and the assumption of personal responsibility."[3]

Another way of putting this point is to say that it is through the repetitive arts of self-confession and self-interrogation that difference and otherness are brought low, leaving the self with nothing else, as it were, than an oppressive technique for monitoring subjectivity. Rose takes his cue from Foucault's account of the "psy-complex"—the idea that psychologists, psychotherapists, psychiatrists, psychoanalysts, and counsellors of all kinds are fundamentally preoccupied with the monitoring, regulation, and normalization of individual psychic functioning. In our own time, the cultural logic of the psy-complex has been shifted up a gear. We now live, Rose contends, in a confessional society. The dominance of the therapeutic has come to infiltrate most aspects of social life, especially at the micro-level of the most common and trivial aspects of human encounter. As Rose develops this point:

> Psychotherapeutic language and advice extends beyond the consultation, the interview, the appointment: it has become a part of the staple fare of the mass media of communication, in the magazine advice columns and in documentaries and discussions on television. No financial exchange need be involved, for on live radio phone-in programmes we may confess our most intimate problems for free and have them instantly analysed—or eavesdrop on the difficulties that so many of our fellow citizens appear to have conducting the business of their lives.[4]

In one fell swoop the therapeutic, it seems, has become a cure for cultural difference and our desire for otherness.

So, we live now in a society where therapeutic vocabularies rule. From the worried-well in psychotherapy to TV talk-shows and celebrity-tell-all interviews, ours is the era of a confessional revolution. Yet it still may be worth wondering why the modernist impulse to confess—especially the public confession of things privately experienced—is thought to define subjectivity in its entirety. That is to say, is confessional culture the apotheosis or the death of deliberative and reflective subjectivity?

There are indeed profound reasons for thinking not. In a sharp critique of the social constructionist position, Vivien Burr and Trevor Butt argue that social theorists such as Foucault and Rose are unable to confront the issue of the psychological experience of socially constructed identities. "We may agree," they write, "that the myriad of syndromes, pathologies, and neuroses affecting us are socially constructed, and that the therapist and counsellors to whom we appeal for help are the, albeit unwitting, figureheads of an extensive system of social control through disciplinary power. Nevertheless, the distress and misery experienced by people, framed though it is in terms of personal inadequacy and pathology, cannot, morally or empirically, be ignored."[5] Social constructionist arguments thus abolish the human experience they intend to illuminate. The passion to unearth social construction, in other words, leads in the end to a mere construction of passion. Again, let me quote Burr and Butt: "Writers such as

Foucault and Rose have not broached the issue of what our response, if any, should be at the level of the individual. Indeed, poststructuralist analyses have tended to regard the level of the social or of 'discourse' as the only appropriate one."[6]

All this raises the question of whether psychoanalysis enables the human subject to explore and tolerate alternative constructions of self—the kind of imaginative wanderings that Freud unearthed in the process of "free association"—or whether it simply exchanges one socially constructed identity for another that is, at least on one reckoning, equally pernicious. Now, interestingly, what distinguishes Kristeva's critique of psychotherapy from that of social constructivist theorists is her strong emphasis on *affective investments underpinning psychotherapy as ritual* in order to "safeguard a way of life." It is worth wondering, says Kristeva, what kind of affective resistance it requires within psychotherapy or psychoanalysis in order to effect a freezing of critical self-interrogation and self-reflection. This critique, let me repeat, Kristeva actually launches from the vantage point of psychoanalytic theory itself—a kind of psychoanalysis of the limits or dead ends of psychotherapeutic practice and of psychoanalysis as ritual. As such, this critique can be used to confront Burr and Butt's concern with "psychological experience of socially constructed identities." There may of course be little point in insisting on the conceptual advantages of such an approach—social constructivists, to be sure, can always make the retort that "affective investments in identity" are just further constructions, and on and on in an infinite regress—and yet I do believe that close engagement with the ongoing affective dimensions of our personal and social lives is a crucial task of social theory. And it is a task that leads us to confront some of the core social dilemmas of the age—the search for rearticulating identity in the global frame of interpersonal interconnections and dependencies, the postmodern hunger for cultural difference and otherness, as well as individual and collective desires for human autonomy.

One of the defining characteristics of contemporary culture has been a longing for cultural difference, for a sufficient sense of otherness—in the way we define individual freedom; in ideals of creativity, beauty, and art; in the desire for and demands of multicultural communities; and in the pursuit of spontaneous living. One of the most interesting developments in much cultural theory at the present time is its underscoring of the degree to which the pursuit of difference and otherness infiltrates a whole range of psychological and political vocabularies, and of how these vocabularies are necessarily transforming our relationships to both the past and the present. The idea of cultural difference moves on the frontier between identity and nonidentity and is thus preoccupied among other things with the relation between self and other, homogeneity and fragmentation, consensus and plurality. What has happened to the fabric of everyday life and social relations of late, or at least this is so according to one influential version of postmodern cultural theory, is not only that this pursuit of difference has become locked in an ongoing battle with more traditionalist, structured identities and identity structures—ranging from family values to religious fundamentalism to neo-fascism. It is rather that difference is now promoted as a markedly contradictory psychological and political aim in itself, to which individuals and groups can only do sufficient justice through incessant self-critique, repeated reflexive mappings, and the transgressive tracking of both identity and geopolitical axes on which the field of culture plays out. Even so, the politics of difference is clearly a risky undertaking—both at the level of self-identity, where otherness is located as regards the psyche and interpersonal relationships, and at the level of radical politics, where otherness is addressed in terms of the whole society. Too much toleration for difference and you run the risk of fragmentation; too little and you are left with a spurious (modernist) homogeneity.

If the pursuit of difference as a political goal captures the contemporary social imagination, then this tells us as much about the modern as it does about the postmodern condition. And one thing it tells us, I argue in *Subject to Ourselves,* is that there is now, for many people, a kind of cultural benchmark against which the excesses and eccentricities of modernism and modernity can be measured. There is, I argue, a deep fear of enforced uniformity and uniform sameness, of not having enough psychic and cultural space to develop the uniqueness of self, of repression of idiosyncrasy in the name of security and safety. To put it in a nutshell: People are increasingly suspicious today of the fates of those who believe themselves identical to the images they have of themselves. For postmodern men and women of today's polished, expensive cities, it's recognized that the desire to make others in the image of oneself involves a destructive and debilitating denial of difference and otherness. From our experiences, or indeed from our inherited or acquired knowledge, of traditional family arrangements, of patriarchal gender codes, of bureaucratic hierarchies and rigid work routines, and of deadening institutional party politics—we are fearful of modernist compulsions, summed up elegantly by Zygmunt Bauman as the desire for "clean order and orderly cleanliness" as well as "reason-dictated rules and regulations."

From a psychoanalytic point of view, such self-reflective attempts to grasp the creative powers of difference, otherness, pleasure, and transgression depend, in turn, upon profound emotional transformations. When cast in a suitably expansive, heterogeneous, and other-directed cast of mind, the postmodern imaginary can be seen as one open to multiple perspectives, coupled with a high tolerance of ambiguity and ambivalence. By "postmodern," I refer, in the most general terms, to the contemporary philosophical standpoint that rejects epic narratives, solid metaphysical foundations to knowledge and everyday life, universal values, self-identical subjects, and on and on. Postmodernism has been among other things a way of linking the personal and the global at a time in which the texture of everyday life is being profoundly reshaped by the activities of transnational corporations, the culture industry, and the communications sectors. Yet from within this philosophical tradition, postmodern theorists have had remarkably little original or compelling to say of the transformed psychic experiences of human subjects, nor for that matter of the altered dynamics of interpersonal relationships. It is, of course, true that there remain general pointers. Jacques Derrida thought that deconstructive concepts of difference and dissemination were not limited only to the interpretation of texts, and that a widening appreciation of diversity was on the rise everywhere. Jean-Francois Lyotard, by contrast, highlighted the breakdown of modernist encodings of human strivings or unconscious drives and conducted inquiries into the open structures of libidinal economy. Nonetheless, these remain highly abstract critiques. Ways of feeling and forms of psychic representation are largely divorced from questions of culture and politics in postmodern conditions.

Enter the relevance of psychoanalysis, which has had a great deal to say about the production of human meaning and emotion in a postmodern world preoccupied with conspicuous consumption, global economic shifts, and new information technologies. In fact, a number of innovative psychoanalysts and psychoanalytic critics have produced work of incomparable value on the nature of contemporary living and our postmodern emotional dilemmas. The pioneering insights of psychoanalysts including Thomas Ogden, Jessica Benjamin, Christopher Bollas, Charles Spezzano, Julia Kristeva, and Jean Laplanche are of major importance in this respect. So are the path-breaking psychoanalytically informed works of cultural critique by Judith Butler, Slavoj Zizek, Jacqueline Rose, Stephen Frosh, Lynne Segal, Joel Whitebook, and Jane Flax. Many of the ideas of these psychoanalysts and critics have deepened and enriched the debate over postmodernism, partly due to the insights offered on the transformed emotional characteristics of "post-individual identities" or "postmodern nomads." Certainly, where contemporary psychoanalysis has been most arrestingly original—at least in terms of the discourse of postmodernism—lies in its stress on the emotional contradictions of attaching meaning to experience in a world which revolves increasingly around image, information, and consumption.

In one sense, psychoanalysis has put flesh on the bone of the postmodern recasting of identity. Contemporary Freudianism has given us valuable insights into the emotional transformations that underpin everyday life in a postmodern world of fragmentation and fracture. One could thus attempt to deepen the postmodernist emphasis on difference, diversity, and otherness by drawing upon a range of concepts in contemporary psychoanalysis that underscore the profoundly imaginary and creative capacities of the psyche in its traffic with culture, from Kristeva's evocation of "open psychic systems" to Castoriadis's spontaneous "radical imaginary." Yet while this critical excavation of enlarged emotional capacities for processing social differences in current cultural conditions has undeniably been a useful supplement to postmodernism, perhaps the more enduring contribution of psychoanalysis to contemporary theory will be its insights into the intriguing new emotional dilemmas of individuals attempting to process information in a world overburdened with sound bites and telecommunications. From this angle, the postmodern celebration of a world that ushers in hyper-reality, cyborgs, and the posthuman condition looks decidedly uncritical or apolitical, such is the aversion of much of this discourse to considering the emotional consequences of transformations in culture, communication, and capitalism. Even so, these are concerns which contemporary psychoanalysis treats with full seriousness, shifting the debate firmly back to the ethical domain.

In *The Life of the Mind,* the political philosopher Hannah Arendt wrote of a "frailty of human affairs." Through a powerful extension of Kant's philosophical reflections on judgment, Arendt expanded the terrain of positive rationality and politics to include taste, intuition, aesthetic judgment, and imagination. Deeply attuned to the accelerated progress of technology, and with her political theory framed against the backdrop of twentieth-century totalitarianism and death camps, Arendt calls us to reflect seriously upon the precariousness or vulnerability of political communities founded upon pluralities of narrative. In her highly original conception of narration, she suggested that public space can be constituted as political—as a self-actualizing site of power—only when lives can be recounted or narrated and thus shared with others, who, through memory, speech, and symbolic persuasion, give localized expression to such acts of narration and thus make history into a historically specific, condensed sign—what Arendt terms the revelation of the "who." Kristeva, in a powerful psychoanalytic study of Arendt's political thought, conceptualizes the location of frailty or vulnerability in human affairs thus:

> Judgment is clearly vulnerable. That vulnerability, however, is precisely what enables it to provide a place for *The Life of the Mind* as the revelation of a 'who' and to avoid getting stuck in a 'system' governed by intrinsically totalitarian values. ... Seduced and yet bogged down by the 'frailty of human affairs,' Arendt gives her attention to the two pitfalls that threaten judgement—pitfalls that appear to coexist with the linear existence of human time in the process of life and, by implication, in the modern practice of politics: irreversibility and unpredictability.[7]

What has long intrigued followers of Arendt's political theory is her unflagging commitment to language, especially poetry, as an indispensable medium for the institution and flowering of civil society. In the hands of Arendt, poetry was no longer defined as the opposite of the political, the discursive, or the public; poetry, she argued, is "the most human of the arts." Poetic language, symbolism, the aesthetic—such cultural forms permit the public sphere to operate as a discursive space reflecting both shared interests and conflicting agendas. And yet critics of Arendt claim that her various attempts to aestheticize political judgment are a radically contradictory affair, if only because the principle of a general aesthetics of imagination in which an equilibrium of the general and the particular, of the individual body and the plural domain of politics, is not pushed far enough. Kristeva, for example, while affirming the correctness of Arendt's attempt to expand the concept of the political to include aesthetic judgment, taste, intuition, and imagination, nonetheless argues that the recovery and flowering of public political life depends on a creative narrativization that cannot but reflect the psychic splitting of the subject—something Arendt's political theory was unable to comprehend due to her failure to theorize the repressed unconscious. As Kristeva develops this critique of Arendt:

> We can simply note that relegating the body to an uninteresting generality, simply because it is biological and is an obstacle to the uniqueness of the 'who,' allows Arendt to do away with psychology and psychoanalysis. Compared to medicine and physiology, which are interested in what our organs have in common, as she believes—certainly that's true, but they study more than that!—Arendt condemns them together: 'Psychology, depth psychology or psychoanalysis, [reveals] no more than the ever-changing moods, the ups and downs of our psychic life, and its results and discoveries are neither particularly appealing nor very mean-

ingful in themselves.' The expression 'neither particularly appealing' is undoubtedly the most revealing here: not only is psychoanalysis 'not appealing,' it is frightening. It frightens *her*.[8]

There can be little doubt that Kristeva sympathizes with Arendt's pluralist political position, rooted as it is in concepts such as narrative, language, and public space. And yet, more perhaps than Arendt, Kristeva is attuned to the emotional contradictions of frailty, vulnerability, affection, intimacy. From her revised post-Lacanian conceptual standpoint, Kristeva contends that the telling of narratives fractures as much as it unifies identity; she asserts that language is, crucially, an emotional holding operation against the disruptive subjective impact of lost loves, repressed pasts, displaced selves.

What might such "lost loves, repressed pasts, displaced selves" look like in terms of our contemporary cultural condition? Love objects lost, cherished cultural ideals eclipsed: modernism, colonialism, imperialism, patriarchy, and on and on. Pasts repressed are often enough thought buried, destroyed—and yet we see resurgence of guilt everywhere in the polished, expensive cities of the West, as if the dethronement of European imperialism is at some level shameful, too embarrassing. Thus the nostalgia for yesteryear, when identities were solid, durable, built to last. This may be, as Zygmunt Bauman suggests, the reason postmodernism fits hand in glove with the social and mental habits of contemporary women and men, mesmerized by the prospects of breaking free from an exhausted modernity and yet always harboring a pathology distinctively modernist in design and compulsion—as though one might just actually bid farewell to modernist impulses for structured order and orderly structures once and for all. Society as factories of meaning, to paraphrase Bauman's designation of the liquid stage of the late modern world, takes on postmodern qualities to the degree modernity turns back on itself, monitoring its cultural conditions and psychological illusions. And yet still we could ask: What might the evocative blend of pluralized narrative or language on the one hand, and the globalization of public political space on the other, look like from the vantage point of a postmodern culture mourning the loss of modernist dreams for orderly structures and certitude?

The postmodern version of psychoanalysis that I seek to promote in *Subject to Ourselves* is one more committed to the emotional processing of cultural difference and affective celebration of otherness than to cognitive certitude or rational mastery. In the pursuit of political demands for appreciation of cultural differences and otherness, there are values embedded in psychoanalytic theory that are of vital importance— especially regarding the unique particularities of individuals and also our equal rights to participate in the self-shaping of the future direction of society. For psychoanalysis starts from the premise that people have to learn to reckon into account their own emotional limits and dependencies—not simply as a kind of brake on narcissism and omnipotent thought, but for creative engagement with others and for the prospects of human autonomy. To genuinely recognize another's difference and autonomy thus requires acknowledgment of the contingent ground of social things, of biological structure, of human need, of emotional desire, of Eros and sexuality in various forms of social association. Such an ethics of self-constitution, as Arendt and Kristeva after her affirm, is one concerned with human frailties and vulnerabilities.

The incessant search for some kind of balance in personal and social life between creative self-making and imaginative cultural production on the one hand, and recognition of the profound ontological implications of frailty and vulnerability on the other, lies at the heart of desires for human autonomy. Where there are demands for autonomous society, to return to Castoriadis once more, these are the fruits of action undertaken by individuals seeking *ontological opening*. The pleasure of finding such openings beyond the highly regulated informational, cognitive, and organizational closures of the late modern epoch lies precisely in engaging with self and world in a fundamental way, beyond instrumentally orientated fantasies of technoscientific control. Engagement with a cluster of basic moral and biological issues of human life—the nature of love and passion, the impact of illness, human existence, and death—can allow individuals to become deeply aware of the self-making of their world, of the role of imaginary constructions in their interpersonal relationships, and of the contingency of social things more generally. "Autonomous society," writes Castoriadis, "is that society which self-institutes itself explicitly and lucidly, the one that knows that it itself posits its institutions and significations, [and] this means that it knows as well that they have no source other than its own instituting and signification-giving activity, no extrasocial 'guarantee.'"

The self-reflexivity of such a state of social affairs—that there is, contrary to the ideological proclamations of modernity, "no extrasocial guarantee"—is precisely the promise of the postmodern: the splitting of meaning, representation, and signification into deconstructed and reconstructed objects of reflection. Postmodern dismantling of the self-institution of meaning or signification is, of course, a radically ambiguous affair—as it is as difficult to truly grasp one's "own instituting and signification-giving activity" as it might be to imagine an alternative to it. All in all, if the postmodern declaration of autonomy involves a radical dismantling or deconstruction of the social world it-self, this is because postmodernity (as a series of global transforma-tions in institutions, sociality, and culture) nurtures in some sense the existence of individuals with rationally and emotionally articulated capacities for self-interrogation and self-reflection. The achievement of such a state of mind, it might be added, raises in turn the thorny issue of what kind of good it might do us—individually and collec-tively—to emotionally grasp, tolerate, and reflect on the loss of a mod-ernist "extrasocial guarantee" (that is, the illusion of omnipotence generated and sustained by Enlightenment rationality, technoscience, religion, and on and on).

"Postmodernity," writes Bauman, "perhaps more than anything else is a *state of mind*. More precisely a state of those minds who have the habit (or is it a compulsion?) to reflect on themselves, to search their own contents and report what they found."[9] In pursuit of the postmodern celebration of reflexivity, difference, otherness, and au-tonomy, there are values inherent in the tradition of psychoanalysis that are of vital importance. The psychoanalytic aesthetic—ranging from free association through reverie to toleration of the depressive position—is in this sense a proto-postmodern cultural theory, one that both deconstructs and reconstructs modernist discourses of subjectiv-ity, truth, reason, and freedom. Equally valuable, psychoanalytic theory underscores the powerful emotional pressures and limits of the mind that threaten and potentially defeat the goal of autonomy, and there-fore offers insights into the corporatist strategies of instrumental ra-tionality, which must be challenged and contested.

Fantasy, Modern and Postmodern

How are we to conceive of fantasy in relation to contemporary social and political processes? What is the location of fantasy in shaping the 'world picture', in Heidegger's sense, of modernity and postmodernity?

One way of approaching the political stakes of fantasy is to trace the creative and coercive implications of unconscious imagination at the level of selfhood, interpersonal relationships, culture and society. The specific delineation of such an approach depends, for the most part, on which school of psychoanalysis is deployed to unearth the relations between self and society; for the split subject speaks a plurality of heterogeneous fantasies, symptoms and identifications, as Melanie Klein, D.W. Winnicott, Wilfred Bion, Heinz Kohut, Jacques Lacan, Julia Kristeva and many others have impressively shown.

Let us begin, however, with some speculations offered by Freud in his 1924 essay, 'A note upon the "mystic writing-pad"'. In this work, Freud discusses a child's writing apparatus in which text appears on a celluloid surface, registered through the impression of marks made upon an underlying wax pad. This mystic writing-pad offers an endless capacity for the taking of notes since, as a consequence of temporarily lifting the celluloid from the wax, a fresh surface can always be obtained. What especially interests Freud in this writing instrument are the impressions that remain on the underlying wax. He suggests that these impressions, in psychoanalytical terms, can be likened to fantasies which are located at the level of the repressed unconscious. For, like unconscious fantasy, these hidden impressions beneath the celluloid script branch out in all directions; they are

1

fragmented, multiple, discontinuous; they continue to influence, and at times distort, succeeding scripts; they remain 'legible in suitable lights', says Freud.[1] Moreover, these hidden traces, or fantasies, suggest the filtering effects of culture and society in psychic experience, accounting for how the subject's communication with itself and others comes into being, changes, and persists over historical time.

Freud's argument concerning the unconscious link between fantasy and meaning gains the strongest support in Jacques Derrida's deconstructionist reading of psychoanalysis; however, Derrida stresses – against Freud's occasional biological tendencies – that fantasy is an active order where a constant shifting is in process.[2] Fantasies are not copies, says Derrida, but unconscious constructions and reconstructions. From this angle, the registration or storing of experience, whether on a mystic writing-pad or in the life of the mind, is an active creation; an elaboration of fantasy that is central to the making of personal and social worlds.

Such a focus raises the issue of the relationship between fantasy and the existing social order – the world of late modernity or postmodernity. The aim of this book is to analyse the nature of these interconnections and to develop a novel account of the implications of internal conflict and psychic division for the current debate over modernity and postmodernity. I propose to develop a critical assessment of the complex, contradictory fantasy scenarios that creatively shape, and are also shaped by, the social and cultural worlds of modernity and postmodernity. The book proposes that without a psychoanalytical concept of fantasy – of the representational expression of desires and passions – we are unable to grasp the inseparability of society and subjectivity in the late modern age.

The psychic crisis of subjectivity is at the core of this book, but it is understood in an unconventional way. Taking a temperature check of current social and cultural theory, it is indeed tempting to see this crisis as solely the product of a compulsive drive for a rationally designed social order (a drive intrinsic to modernity itself), or as an outcome of the collapse of grand narratives, which tends to be described in terms of the fragmentation or dislocation of postmodern culture. But the specific tensions of modernity and postmodernity – and this is crucial – are never free from the psychic dispersal of subjectivity, fantasy and sexuality. That is to say, fantasy – as a realm of psychic conflict and division – frames our contemporary social and political worlds from the start, and it is therefore essential for an understanding of the trajectories of both personal and cultural life.

In this book, fantasy is understood as a creative realm of inter-changeable places, multiple entry points, rolling identifications; and it will be invoked to conceptualize that point of division between self and other, identity and difference, desire and history, sexuality and politics. It will also be used to articulate the multiple couplings and splittings of modernity and postmodernity. As Zygmunt Bauman writes:

> Postmodernity does not necessarily mean the end, the discreditation of the rejection of modernity. Postmodernity is no more (but no less either) than the modern mind taking a long, attentive and sober look at itself, at its condition and its past works, not fully liking what it sees and sensing the urge to change.[3]

Self-reflection on modernity is part and parcel of that 'turning back against itself' that comes into existence with the advent of postmodernity. Yet an adequate understanding of the psychic and subjective underpinnings of contemporary culture demands breaking with current understandings of 'fragmented selves' in social and cultural theory – or so I want to propose. As such, I argue that postmodernity is a self-monitoring modernity that promotes a 'mapping' or 'scanning' of the fantasmatic dimensions of self and society. Postmodern subjectivity is constituted through a turning back of fantasy against itself in order to embrace the ambivalence and uncertainty of mind and world. This means proceeding in personal and cultural life without absolute guidelines and definitive authority, tolerating uncertainty and confusion, and attempting to think the unthinkable within the turbulence of contemporary social processes.

This fantasmatic dimension of identity, society, culture, and poli-tics is precisely what frames the enquiry of this book into modernity and postmodernity. To establish this connection, I will begin with a general consideration of the modernity/postmodernity debate in chapter 1, linking the discussion to a psychoanalytical examination of the status of the human subject. I will then turn to analyse the generative role of fantasy in shaping the modern drive for order, boundaries, classifications, laws. Chapter 2 assesses this modernist drive for control and certitude by examining the tension between creative imagination and formal reason in the writings of Freud, with a particular focus on the location of typologies, classifications and boundary maintenance in psychoanalysis. Chapter 3 considers con-temporary institutional transformations in politics and world affairs, tracing the impact of reflexivity on relations of knowledge and power, thereby opening the way for a consideration of the recent horrors in Bosnia-Herzegovina.

I will then explore the cultural background to postmodernity as a decentred, fragmented social order, considering the role of fantasy in shaping the intense postmodern fascination for plurality, ambivalence, ambiguity, uncertainty and contingency. Chapter 4 examines some core psychoanalytic themes in this decentring of self and society, with particular reference to the postmodern social theory of Fredric Jameson and Jean Baudrillard. Contesting the idea of the dominance of dislocation and fragmentation, the chapter considers alternative personal and cultural possibilities opened in the postmodern, with clinical illustrations offered to substantiate these claims. Finally, through a detailed appraisal of the connections between identity and fantasy in chapter 5, I argue that postmodernity promotes a reflexive mapping of ourselves, a mapping of selves multiple, other and strange. Presenting a set of diverse case-studies, including the cultural uses of media in the O.J. Simpson trial and the psychic implications of living with global political catastrophe, I consider changing experiences of selfhood, desire, interpersonal relations, culture and globalization that are promoted in conditions of postmodernity.

The purpose of this book is to contribute to the ongoing conversation between three core discourses of contemporary Western thought: psychoanalysis, social theory and the modernity/postmodernity debate. The hope that guides this study is that a critical understanding of fantasy can (and indeed already does) make a difference in coming to terms with crises in contemporary culture. In what follows I shall develop a theorization of two essentially contrasting object-relational configurations, one that is linked to modernity and the other to postmodernity. The object-relational configuration of modernity suggests a mode of fantasy in which security and enjoyment are derived by attempting to control, order and regulate the self, others and the sociopolitical world. The object-relational configuration of postmodernity suggests a mode of fantasy in which reflective space is more central to identity and politics, the creation of open spaces to embrace plurality, ambiguity, ambivalence, contingency and uncertainty. A central argument of the book is that contemporary society, not without certain tensions and contradictions, deploys modern and postmodern reveries simultaneously. It is this fantasmatic dimension of modernity and postmodernity that frames the psychoanalytic and political purpose of *Subject to Ourselves*.

1

The Ambivalence of Identity

Between Modernity and Postmodernity

Postmodernity is modernity coming of age: modernity looking at itself
at a distance rather than from the inside, making a full inventory of its
gains and its losses, psychoanalysing itself, discovering the intentions it
never before spelled out, finding them mutually cancelling and incon-
gruous. Postmodernity is modernity coming to terms with its own
impossibility; a self-monitoring modernity, one that consciously dis-
cards what it was once unconsciously doing.

Zygmunt Bauman

Contradiction, conflict, spiraling, reconciliation, a dissolving of
achieved reconciliations, new resolutions of dissonances – these are at
the center of life and the mind's life.

Hans Loewald

Imagine a global pain map. In crude form, we might designate on this
map pockets of collective rage, hate and negativity (describing polities
from the Middle East to Bosnia), emotionally charged fields of gender
domination and oppression (from the asymmetry of sexual difference
to child sexual abuse), the uncertainty and fear that comes into play
when considering our possible collective futures (including anxieties
which focus upon ozone depletion, the greenhouse effect and overpopulation), the personal and ethical problems about the present
plight of sexual relationships and family life (such as the risk of
AIDS), as well as the broader emotional dislocations of identity and
selfhood in contemporary society (such as disturbances in creating
personal meaning and self-continuity). Dread, fear, anxiety – it is easy
enough to recognize such emotional states of pain on this map, even
if the concerns listed are somewhat selective.

Nevertheless, I make this inventory of personal and cultural problems to underscore the deep strains of modern living. I emphasize

discontinuities and negativities within the psychological roots of social, cultural and political life because it is precisely here that we confront the furthest extremities, or disturbances, of today's world. Under contemporary social conditions, our innermost hopes and longings are in ongoing dialogue with our most fearful anxieties and gripping terrors. Yet the ambivalences of modern living – expectant hopes and fearful anxieties – are certainly not closed in upon themselves, sealed off from the social-historical world. On the contrary, society enters fully into the construction of our most personal hopes and dreads. Social phenomena or trends are not just incidental to the forging of personal identity; they in some part constitute the inner texture of self-experience (as can be gleaned from the foregoing account of contemporary anxieties and fears). That is to say, there is a mutual penetration of inner and outer worlds, from which the criss-crossings of fantasy and culture are fabricated and sustained.

At a broader level still, this brings us to issues concerning the 'emotional agenda' of our times. What is truly contemporary about the links between selfhood and society, personality and culture? According to many, from newspaper commentators to academic theorists, our era is one of radical transition. Changes in social organization that have occurred in recent decades are said to be incomprehensible within existing general theories and conceptual frameworks. A dazzling variety of social, political and cultural transformations are highlighted in this regard. Globalization, transnational communication systems, new information technologies, the industrialization of war, the collapse of Soviet-style socialism, universal consumerism: these are the core dimensions of modern institutions and social affairs. Yet what are the connections between changes at the level of social institutions and those in everyday life, the domains of personal and aesthetic reflection? How do contemporary social processes affect the personal domain?

There are two very different ways of thinking about the relations between contemporary institutional transformations on the one hand and personal and cultural experience on the other, in recent social theory. These discussions concern the ideas of modernity and postmodernity – as a diagnosis of the contemporary epoch – and both offer powerful and compelling frameworks for social and cultural analysis.

The modernist argument is that personal and cultural experience in the contemporary world involves various tensions and ambiguities, the distinctive characteristics of which involve contradiction, fluidity

6

and fragmentation. These instabilities are directly connected to processes of modernization. Modernity is a post-traditional social order, involving the continual overturning of previous collective assumptions, traditions and customs. The globalized world of institutional interconnectedness in which we now live, marked as it is by rapid technological and industrial change, is experienced by people ambivalently – as exciting opportunity and threatening risk. An openness to the social world can mean the opportunity for experimentation and renewal, personal transformation and autonomy. Equally, however, it can mean the risk of personal and cultural turmoil, the disintegration of things thought solid and secure. Hence, the central modernist dilemma: to attempt to reach some kind of personal balance between security and risk, opportunity and danger.

Postmodernism, on the other hand, recognizes something different in contemporary cultural experience. It reacts against the tiredness of the modernist negotiation of risk and uncertainty by attempting to dissolve the problem altogether. Postmodernism suggests that cultural ambivalence cannot be overcome, that ambiguity and discontinuity cannot be straightened out, that social and cultural organization cannot be rationally ordered and controlled. Postmodernism denies that there is any repressed truth to the paths of modernity, and as such recasts society and history as *decentered*; there are only images of the past framed from different points of view. From this perspective, the multidimensional, chaotic world of global communication ushers in a plurality of local rationalities and identities – ethnic, religious, sexual, cultural and aesthetic. In a postmodern frame, this giddy proliferation of discourses opens individuals and collectivities to other possibilities and ways of experiencing the world. In short, postmodernity opens the way for a liberation of differences.

It is a commonplace of recent social theory to view contemporary personal and cultural life as increasingly marked by dislocation, dispersal and fragmentation. Yet exisiting social-theoretical discourses about modernity and postmodernity raise important issues about the nature of personal and social experience, issues which are usually neglected, sidestepped, displaced. How can one make sense, psychologically, of recent fragmentations and dislocations of subjectivity whilst also recognizing that people experience their 'identity' as something central to the texture of their day-to-day lives? What does selfhood and identity mean today? How are we connected and related to each other in contemporary culture? In this chapter, I consider the

7

problems that emerge – the tensions and reconciliations – when selfhood is viewed against the conceptual backdrop of modernist and postmodernist theory. The chapter will thus draw out the significance of contemporary social transformations in relation to psychic structure and self-identity, and especially of what identity comes to mean. It will draw these things out through an examination of modernity and postmodernity from the standpoint of developments in psychoanalysis – a theoretical hermeneutic which, parallel to much modernist and postmodernist thought, emphasizes the *ambivalence of identity*, the tension between self and other, desire and lack, life and death, consciousness and the unconscious. It will be argued that psychoanalysis uncovers aspects of contemporary experience as creations of the unconscious imagination. It will also be argued, against fashionable pronouncements on the disintegration of human subjectivity, that postmodernity ushers into existence a *radicalization of human imagination*. Focusing primarily upon the global opening of self/other boundaries, I argue that postmodernity deals in a wholly new way with psychic containment, turbulence and autonomy.

Modern hopes, modern fears

Broadly speaking, the term 'modernity' can be taken as referring to that set of social, political and economic institutions brought into existence in the West some time during the eighteenth century, and which have become worldwide in influence in the twentieth century. Max Weber characterized the emergence of modernity as a process of 'rationalization' and 'disenchantment'.[1] Today, at the turn of the twenty-first century, however, there is a marked and profound disenchantment with the emancipatory promise of modernity itself. The political theorist Claus Offe says of this contemporary disenchantment:

> [it] is not so much that the gaze is turned away from either 'the others' or from history and toward one's own contemporary and structural conditions, but rather that the situation of 'modern' societies appears just as blocked, just as burdened with myths, rigidities, and developmental constraints, as modernization theory had once diagnosed to be the case for 'pre-modern' societies.[2]

Current debates about modernity focus on the relation between the nature of social rationalization on the one hand, and aspects of cultural reproduction and identity on the other. In this connection, the following issues are raised. How have contemporary social processes of rationalization affected the personal and cultural spheres? What has been the impact of the institutionalization of rational calculation, mastery and control upon human subjectivity?

As a first approximation, it can be said that the social structures in which contemporary selves are constituted are profoundly different to cultural forms of the premodern world. In contrast to traditional types of social organization, in which tradition, custom and status held a legitimizing force, modernity radically transforms the intensity, dynamism and extensionality of social relations and processes. The development of modernity has involved a rejection of the certainties of tradition and custom – the world-view that there is an essential, internal order to culture. Against the sociological backdrop of capitalist economic development, industrial upheavals, urban expansions, the creation of parliamentary democracy, mass movements and the like, modernity has produced stunning technological transformations in the experience of space and time, the generation of information and knowledge, and the widening of human experience. The culture of modernity is a form of world-construction marked by the rejection of fixed, traditional boundaries.

This dissolution of traditional frameworks of meaning, however, has only been achieved at a substantial psychological cost. In the critical theory of the Frankfurt School, modernity is linked to the 'decline of the individual'.[3] Anticipating current debates about mass society and narcissistic pathology, the Frankfurt School regarded the logic of capitalist economic exploitation as penetrating the deepest recesses of human subjectivity. In this perspective, the psychic costs of modernity are the end of autonomous individuality and the emergence of passive, decentred consumerism. In Fromm's gloss, capitalist modernity generates 'individuals wanting to act as they have to act'.

The most influential recent view in social and cultural theory draws attention to the rise of large-scale bureaucratic institutions, and the associated impact of depolitization as it affects the personal domain. In this perspective, the rationalization of public life is said to weaken and drain the personal sphere, such that the individual subject recedes into the shadows. Selfhood and personal identity become increasingly precarious in conditions of modernity, as the individual loses all sense of cultural anchorage as well as inner reference points. Thus Christopher Lasch detects a 'culture of narcissism' at the heart of capitalist modernity, a culture in which selfhood contracts to a defensive core.[4] The result is that personal life turns inward upon itself: a narcissistic preoccupation with self becomes central to psychic survival, a preoccupation which reinforces capitalist consumption and manipulation. Another, more sophisticated, variant on this position is Jürgen Habermas's thesis of an 'inner colonization of the life-world' by technical systems.[5] Modern social life, according to Habermas, has become increasingly subject to administrative and bureaucratic control, and this has led to a crushing of individual creativity and autonomy.

For many theorists, however, such accounts of modernity appear too one-sided. The critique of social institutions and the public sphere as primarily invasive and destructive of personal life has been interpreted as a kind of conceptual closure in the face of the sheer intensity and scale of contemporary social processes. This closure, as Cornelius Castoriadis has argued, is an instance of the failure of social and political thought to address the imaginative opportunities ushered into existence by modern social institutions and their worldwide spread.[6]

By contrast, Marshall Berman's treatise, *All that is Solid Melts into Air*, is representative of another line of thought concerning the cultural possibilities and limits of modernity.[7] Berman's book, published in 1982, is a provocative, polemical intervention into the debate concerning modernity and the consequences of modernization. Berman is little concerned with charting the sociological trajectories of Western modernity, and instead traces the divisions in intellectual thought regarding the nature of modern experience itself. The cultural ambivalence of modernity, he says, is echoed throughout social and political thought, with its schizoid splitting of contemporary social life into either pure affirmation and idealization or condemnation and denigration. 'Modernity', writes Berman, 'is either embraced with a blind and uncritical enthusiasm, or else condemned with a neo-Olympian remoteness and contempt.'[8] In particular, the conceptual contrast between the iron cage of bureaucratic technique, from Max Weber to Herbert Marcuse, and the energetic vitality attributed to modern sensibility, from Walter Benjamin to Marshall McLuhan, parallels a division between constraint and empowerment which is intrinsic to modernity itself. The problem, as Berman sees it, is that contemporary social processes are increasingly portrayed from only one side of this divide. An either/or logic can thus be said to haunt the field of modernity.

In place of such 'rigid polarities and flat totalizations', Berman attempts to recover a sense of the ambivalence of modernity. To move beyond the barren binary impasse in theories of modernity, Berman considers the intrinsic ambiguities of modern city life. In this cultural field, he locates the simultaneous fragmented and liberated sense of contemporary urban living, its bizarre blending of personal isolation and loneliness on the one hand and intense social proximity and cultural interconnectedness on the other. Turning to the great modernists of the early twentieth century, in particular Goethe, Baudelaire and Marx, Berman argues that the very dislocations of the social process which modernity brings into existence, such as isolation and the loss of connection, paradoxically serve to create a new world of cultural possibilities and pleasures. That is to say, Berman theorizes the ambivalence of modernity *positively*. As he observes:

> To be modern is to find ourselves in an environment that promises us adventure, power, joy, growth, transformation of ourselves and the world – and, at the same time, that threatens to destroy everything we have, everything we know, everything we are. Modern environments and experiences cut across all boundaries of geography and ethnicity, of class and nationality, of religion and ideology: in this sense, modernity can be said to unite all mankind. But it is a paradoxical unity, a unity of disunity: it pours us all into a maelstrom of perpetual disintegration and renewal, of struggle and contradiction, of ambiguity and anguish.[9]

Modernity, according to Berman, is a double-edged phenomenon. Instead of assigning persons to preordained social roles, as in premodern cultures, modernity succeeds in leading human subjects into a creative and dynamic making of self-identity and the fashioning of life-styles according to personal preference. Such a transformation in the social fabric leads to vastly greater opportunities as concerns freedom and autonomy. But the modern way of life also has a darker side. Attempts to legislate rational order this century have regularly been at the cost of destroying individual particularity and human life. In the wake of Nazism, the Holocaust, Hiroshima, Stalinism and other social-historical catastrophes this century, the veil of illusions which underpin the moral and political practice of modernity has been lifted for all to see.

Central to modernity is the abandonment of any fixed social status and rigid hierarchy of power relations. This dissolution of communal traditions and customs, says Berman, carries major implications for the individual self, and especially the expression of personal identity. In brief, modernity opens up spaces for continuous individualization, it opens up positive possibilities for self-modification in regard to our emotions, desires, needs and capabilities. In this way, anxiety comes to replace the certainties of tradition and of habit. This is an anxiety that is at once deeply disturbing and exhilarating, an anxiety that frames the freedom of the self in its dealings with the social world. The premodern world, the ordered world of role-hierarchy and local tradition, has dissolved, leaving uncertainty and ambiguity. Self-definition begins anew, this time more in step with the hopes and dreads of emotional life.

Seen from this angle, modernity is about the celebration of dynamism, an ever-expanding acceleration of personal and cultural life. This acceleration is expressed as a multiplication of the possibilities of the self on the one hand, and of self-dislocation by global social processes on the other. Construction and deconstruction, assembly and disassembly: these processes interweave in contemporary societies in a manner which has become self-propelling.

The account of selfhood implicit in the work of Berman is one that suggests that individuals develop an emotional framework for handling the troubled waters of the culture of late modernity. In a post-traditional society, identity – as a forging of self-continuity – becomes something that has to be 'worked at', intersubjectively negotiated, reflected upon and thought about. This necessarily brings the self into an engagement with the wider world, and the ravages operating within modernity. But self-experience and interpersonal relations, in this reading, are nevertheless of meaning and value. Individuals more or less are involved in the recognition of the difficulty of creating meaningful experience, and of building relationships based on trust, intimacy and love, against the backdrop of the terrors and anxieties of modernity. The fashioning of self-identity is therefore intimately related to wider social processes that are worldwide in their impact: person–planet/planet–person, as Theodore Roszak has argued.[10] People handle risks, and the fears and anxieties associated with them, in terms of the expansion or compression of identity, the opening out or shutting down of the self to an enveloping outside world.

Self and desire in psychoanalysis

The ambiguities and contradictions of contemporary culture sketched in the foregoing section make the theory of modernity fertile ground for exploring the problem of identity and subjectivity. For, implicit in the foregoing theories of modernity, there is the suggestion that individuals have within themselves an authentic capacity for self-definition and the subjective organization of meanings. In each person there is the struggle to negotiate the opportunities and dangers of modernity in terms of an ongoing, enduring sense of self; to respond to the continuities and discontinuities of contemporary social processes in terms of one's own distinctive subjectivity. In psychoanalytic terms, this self-organization is refracted through unconscious processes of fantasy, drive and affect, an organization which provides core emotional linkages from one subjective state to the next. There is no experience of ourselves or others which is free of sexuality or the unconscious, as there is no cultural process untainted by the libidinal and aggressive drives in and through which society is fashioned. It is precisely at this juncture, between unconscious sexuality and social meaning, that the discourse of psychoanalysis recasts the relations between self and society, showing that fantasy and desire are deeply intertwined with the law and social order.

Freud's elaboration of the interplay between libidinal passion and self-control, outlined in his structural model of the psyche in *The Ego and the Id* (1923), is the psychoanalytic blueprint which perhaps best prefigures the foregoing images of modernity as a world of contradiction and ambivalence. Freud pictures internal conflict as the psychic clash among libidinal drives (id), regulatory functions of self-control (ego), and moral injunctions (superego). To hold with Freud that the id is constitutively unconscious is to claim it as a realm of inner impulse, of drives, wishes, desires; an indestructible enterpoint of radical imagination. The ego, by contrast, is a direct outcrop of these chaotic passions, a kind of defensive internal registration of the id's ceaseless demands for pleasure, but coupled with a painful awareness of the difficulties of human survival in the external world. The relation between id and ego is therefore one of tension and anxiety, as the latter seeks to contain the unstructured energy of the former by attempting to reconcile such passions with external cultural pressures for self-control. Yet if the outside world forcefully exerts its presence upon psychical life at the level of the ego, it does so to an even greater extent at the level of the superego. For Freud, the superego is the remainder of the human subject's attempt to master the Oedipus complex. A primary splitting of the ego, the superego is the internalization of Oedipal desires and taboos, wishes and prohibitions. Superego development is thus a taking in of the 'external world', and most particularly the moral prohibitions of culture as a whole, into parts of the self.

Ambivalence thus has its roots in the clash among unconscious drives, ego-anxiety and superego guilt in the individual. Personal continuity and discontinuity are envisioned in Freudian psychoanalysis as the struggle to maintain the tension between contrasting and conflictual desires and self-organizations. Psychoanalytically, the investment of desire in self–other relationships and cultural representations is a key part of self-identity, because it forms the emotional backcloth for any experience of a stable external world. In the object-relational terms to be explored more fully later, selfhood is a plural, shifting organization, patterned around constructive and reparative object relationships, and derived from different interpersonal contexts. In this vision, we are all negotiating a complex, contradictory subjective sense of self, and our experience of the world involves multiple perspectives of unity and fragmentation. But neither selfhood nor the object relationships from which self-organization derives are free from unconscious anxiety. For constructive and loving interpersonal relationships necessarily open the self to anxieties concerning loss, pain and destructiveness. Stephen Frosh expresses this well:

> For tragedy to be possible, for destructiveness to be meaningful and loss appreciated, there has to be something that can be identified with, something that can love as well as lose, hope as well as be betrayed. In this something, this self, there is enduringly the spark of an optimistic resistance, a potential to respond in a humanly worthwhile way to the mess that is all around.[11]

These emotional capacities, derived from multiple relational configurations, are deeply interwoven with the institutional settings of society and culture. That is to say, the human capacity to respond to 'the mess that is all around' is a response to the ambiguity of modernity, its mixture of opportunity and danger. Individuals develop a subjective sense of self designed to handle simultaneously the stunning opportunities and destructive terrors of the late modern age. In Freud's vision, such a negotiation demands a strong ego, an ego of rational self-control; a state of mind capable of struggling with anxieties generated internally and externally, and capable of repressing, displacing or sublimating threatening unconscious drives and asocial desires. This is the classical Freudian image of modern culture as repressive, the global diagnosis that modernity denies the true expression of sexuality and personal desires. As Marcuse develops this point, the real turbulence of modernity is that of 'surplus-repression' – a repressive, political structuring of the psyche which produces intense personal misery and emotional suffering.[12] Yet unconscious desire is not, as Marcuse and other Freudian radicals have argued, exclusively tied to the repressive anchoring constraints of culture. One of the most substantial insights of Freudian psychoanalysis is that desire, which splits and disperses the human subject, is always caught up in the process of symbolic representation. That is to say, the unconscious, through condensation and displacement, is a force always pressing for wish-fulfilment. It is this ceaseless pressure of the unconscious, represented in dreams and fantasy, which leads the late Freud to the view that the task of analysis is itself interminable.

It might be claimed, then, that there is a more full-blooded imaginary – a realm of fantasy and affect that is essentially creative – in Freudian psychoanalysis.[13] Fantasy, dream, identification, symbol, representation: these are not ordered, cognitive experiences of ourselves, but rather aspects of unconscious mental life which are absolutely other and deliciously indeterminate. The unconscious, Freud comments, knows nothing of time, contradiction or closure. Beyond the structures of instituted logic, the unconscious 'does not think, does not calculate or judge in any way at all'.[14] Moreover, it is from this crafty ambivalence – the fabrication of unconscious wishes which are intrinsically contradictory and mutually incompatible – that the multiple contradictions of subjectivity develop. Significantly, there is a potential subversiveness here as concerns the connections between self and society. There is for Freud another place, another mode of time, a mode of otherness which subverts and derails the impersonal decrees of the social order and law. Again, the temporal specificity of the primary libidinal process should be noted. 'The timelessness of the unconscious', Jacques Derrida writes, 'is no doubt determined only in opposition to a common concept of time, a traditional concept, the metaphysical concept: the time of mechanics or the time of consciousness.'[15] Another way of putting this point is to claim that there is a subtle flaw at the heart of the social process, the negativity or perversity of unconscious sexuality and desire, an imaginary realm outside of time which thwarts and transforms the reality principle of daily life. Wishes that escape from time: this is for Freud the turbulence of the unconscious, as culture and desire continually displace one another.

It is thanks to unconscious ambivalence, to the polysemic richness of human passion, that Freud could elaborate a theory of human subjectivity as fragile, split, multiple, heterogeneous. One of the major contributions of psychoanalysis to reframing the concept of the autonomous individual, a central ideal of modern Western culture, lies in its vision of the subject as *decentered*. As Freud puts this, 'the ego is not master in its own house'.[16] The discovery and underlining of a hidden world of unconscious desires and fantasies was itself a dramatic challenge to modernist ideologies of rationality and objectivity. For Freud, examination of the hysterical and obsessional discourse of his patients revealed forbidden (sexual) wishes underneath the specious surface of consciousness. Significantly, this psychoanalytic rehabilitation of irrationality at the heart of rationality both captures and reflects the darker side of the project of Enlightenment – of the terror generated in and through modernist ideals of knowledge, economic growth, and scientific and technological progress. It undercuts the perpetual condensation of autonomy as unfettered activity, showing the modern impulse of instrumentality to be the imagined product of an unbearable anxiety. By the same token, the psychoanalytic excavation of unconscious desire deconstructs contemporary ideological oppositions – between the cognitive and affective, reason and desire, order and chaos, masculinity and femininity – as a set of compromise formations designed to keep ambivalence and contingency at bay.

But let us comment that Freud's self-understanding of the subterranean forces of the unconscious was also deeply coloured by his scientific vision, in particular those elements of his thinking that privileged Enlightenment rationality and objectivity as the bearers of sure knowledge. The primary aim of exploring the unconscious for Freud was principally to overcome the dislocating effects of fantasy and primary process alterity. 'Where id was, there ego shall be': analysis aims to appropriate distorting unconscious fantasy in the interests of rationality and autonomy. In this sense, as will be discussed more fully in chapter 2, Freud's understanding of the ego in terms of rationality (secondary process) was a means of escaping the radical otherness of unconscious desire, and thus doing away with the discomfort of anxiety.

With respect to the social and cultural dimensions of modernity, the same orientation towards mastery and control can be found. Creation of a world free of ambivalence, the rationally structured lifeworld of uniformity and hierarchy, is central to the self-containment of modernity. Science, technology and bureaucratic expertise all play a fundamental role in this respect: imposing co-ordination upon otherwise plural, multidimensional aspects of human experience, crushing difference in the name of order and control, ordering reality into the structured space of social interaction. The idea that modernity is associated with instrumentality, an instrumental logic which denies difference, particularity and otherness, is familiar enough. What is being stressed here, however, is the impact of these cultural and social factors upon psychic structure and self-organization. Psychoanalysis suggests that modern selves are, in part, constituted through a repudiation of difference and heterogeneity; a denial which leads to the privileging of self-control over desire, actualization over reflection, reason over emotion. The most influential recent psychoanalytic account of the pathologies of self-mastery is to be found in Jacques Lacan's theory of the creative and coercive effects of the phallus. Phallic mastery, says Lacan, involves narcissistic fantasies of oneness, of ecstatic plenitude, of unlimited power and authority. This is the imaginary component of phallic mastery, that non-gendered realm of primary narcissism which reunites the subject with that obscure object of desire, the lost maternal object, in immensely powerful ways. Here there is no division or gap between self and other, internal and external experience, desire and satisfaction. In Lacan's thought, however, the phallus also has a symbolic status: it is a signifier, a master signifier, which mediates the relation between human subject and object-world, that something beyond the self which Lacan designates as 'Law' or the 'Name-of-the-Father'. Hence, the phallus is a predetermined marker for the entry of sexualized subjects into the symbolic order, an order understood as a formal structure of language which represents and defines sexual difference. Imagined mastery, power and self-unity; symbolic decentering, difference and loss: these are two sides of the psychical effects of the phallus, and they are expressed in complex, contradictory ways in the reproduction of late modern society.

To summarize all this, the experience of modernity is double-edged, generating both progressive and defensive paths of self-discovery. The discovery of the self, in conditions of modernity, involves an opening out to internal and external forces of multiplicity, contradiction and division. Modernity displaces twice over: the radical otherness of the unconscious, a strangeness within, coupled with an awareness of the otherness of the Other, the globalized world of shared experience. The counterpart of displacement is self-mastery. The dislocations of modernity can be experienced as extremely threatening and overwhelming; in fact, so much so that individuals develop rigid defences against the intensity of human experience. Such a repudiation of experience is achieved through narcissistic fantasies of omnipotence, self-control, ordering, mastery.

Postmodernity: theory, identity, society

The 'project of modernity', as has been seen in the preceding pages, is in part characterized by an institutionalization of unilinear history and meaning. Science, bureaucracy and technological expertise serve in the modern era as an orientating framework for the cultural ordering of meaning. A conception of history as having a single direction, the endeavour to develop a rational programme of collective emancipation, the grounding of all human experience and representation in reason: these are some of the key criteria of modernity. Paradoxically, though, it is precisely such modernist aims for self-mastery and control that fall victim to the very social processes they seek to colonize. Recent decades have powerfully shown that the ethos of modernity has come to haunt us. From the awesome destructive potential of nuclear arms to the massive risks of ecological catastrophe: the world in which we live today is fraught with dangers and risks, many of which arise directly as a consequence of the successes of science and the drive for progress. Such threats have powerfully served to highlight the gross limitations of modernist aims and perspectives, generating in turn the emergence of a new social and political agenda that seeks to counterbalance these oppressive features of modernity. This sphere of awareness is that of postmodernity.

Postmodernity confounds identity, theory and politics in a scandalous way, with its levelling of hierarchies, its dislocating subversion of ideological closure, its interpretative polyvalence, its self-reflexive pluralism. The world of postmodern culture is heterogeneous. On the one hand, postmodernism refers to certain currents of cultural and critical discourse which seek to deconstruct the ideological affinities of totalizing thought, the operations of power, the legitimating functions of knowledge and truth, and the discursive practices of self-constitution.[17] On the other hand, however, postmodernism penetrates well beyond the boundaries of theory, at once inaugurating and designating new forms of personal and cultural experience. From a radical viewpoint, postmodern theories seek to demonstrate that the interconnections between self and society no longer depend upon the epistemological and ideological categories of modernity. Although it is admitted that we are still living in a time of extraordinary social and political transformation, there is no longer a blind faith in metadiscourses of scientific knowledge and technological legitimation. Our growing appreciation of the limits of rationality, it is

argued, has led us to abandon the epistemological illusions of emancipatory declarations made in the name of Freedom, Truth, Equality,
Liberty and so on. There has been, in short, a breakdown in the
metanarrative of Enlightenment. For, as Lyotard puts this in *The
Postmodern Condition*, postmodernity is defined as an 'incredulity
toward metanarratives'. The grand narratives that unified and structured Western science and philosophy, grounding truth and meaning
in the presumption of a universal subject and a predetermined goal of
emancipation, no longer appear convincing or even plausible. Instead, the anti-totalizing, postmodern perspective reveals the generation of knowledge as singular, localized and perspectival.
Knowledge is constructed, not discovered; it is contextual, not
foundational. In this vision, truth-validation is itself explicitly recognized as entering into the pragmatics of intersubjective transmission.

Social transformations are understood to be of central importance
in this erosion of the grand narratives of the modern era. The
globalization of social institutions and, especially, the proliferation of
transnational communication systems introduce a qualitative transformation in the experience of space and time, the result of which is
a dramatic acceleration in the turmoil and flux of personal and
cultural life. The overall effect is one of a blurring of the boundaries
of cultural life itself; or, as Baudrillard argues, there is an *implosion*
of all boundaries, an erasure of the distinctions of high and low
culture, of appearance and reality, of past and present. The postmodern, in this view, is the abandonment of the modernist goal to
find an inner truth behind surface appearances. Postmodernity is thus
inherently decentred and dispersed: everything is of the same value,
which means that nothing much counts in terms of meaning, distinction, hierarchy. On the contrary, postmodern culture, with its dislocation of structure and surface-obsessed profusion of style, supplants
authenticity with copies, reality with images. Images and copies,
'simulation' in Baudrillard's terminology, in fact constitute
postmodernity as *hyperreal*. 'The real', writes Baudrillard, 'becomes
that of which it is possible to give an equivalent reproduction –
the real is not only what can be reproduced, but that which is
always already reproduced, the hyperreal.'[18] From the aesthetically
commodified images of pop art to the media spectacle of the Gulf
War: the postmodern world is a circuit of transient signs.

This situation, however, is not only a purely cultural affair. With
the development of globalization and mass communication technologies, the fragmentation of social space and dislocation of historical time press in deeply upon self-organization. The world of mass

media and brilliant technology in which we now live is captivating and mesmerizing, not only because it offers new textures of social experience, but because this global network of signification penetrates deeply into psychic structure itself. That is to say, the excess or overloading of cultural meanings in postmodernity impacts upon the psychic space of the subject as disorientation, discontinuity and fragmentation. The drama of individual human life is increasingly bound up with the dislocation and dispersal of postmodern social space. Significantly, this dislocation is itself located in fairly specific, if somewhat elusive, social, economic and political contexts. The social and economic world in which the postmodern subject is constituted is, as Fredric Jameson has argued, the world of late, multinational capitalism. The immense communicational and computational networks of late capitalism, with its plurality of surplus-generating forms (from the stock market to the industrialization of war), derail the symbolic framing of reality, the grasping of psychic experience, the mapping of social space between self and other. As Jameson comments:

> If, indeed, the subject has lost its capacity actively to extend its protensions and re-tensions across the temporal manifold and to organize its past and future into coherent experience, it becomes difficult enough to see how the cultural productions of such a subject could result in anything but 'heaps of fragments' and in a practice of the randomly heterogeneous and fragmentary and the aleatory.[19]

Anticipated by the Frankfurt School, the dissolution of the bourgeois ego is today a reality in postmodern society.

Yet it should not be thought that this collapse of the centred, self-determining ego leads to a disintegration of subjectivity itself. On the contrary, there is a dramatic intensification of libidinality, an intensification fully wrapped within the circuits and signs of the postmodern. The postmodernism which celebrates the random intensities of the subject, now drained of psychological depth and significance, highlights the exhilaration of forgetting, the addiction of mindlessness, and the pleasure derived from the surface, the immediate, the particular.

The combined effect of all these transformations in theory, identity and society is that postmodernity comes to be seen as a culture permeated by fragmentation and dislocation. It is this vision which is generally conveyed by the characterization of postmodernity as anti-historical, relativist and negative. In this view, postmodernity is defined entirely by absences, the dissolution of inner experience and received social meanings. It is possible to make sense out of this apparent disorientation, however, provided that we grasp the irreducibility of the plurality of human worlds. The recent theoretical work of Zygmunt Bauman is especially significant in this respect. On the basis of a thorough-going study of modern and postmodern social practices, strategies, world-views and orientations, Bauman argues that postmodernity represents a new dawning, rather than a twilight, for the generation of meaning. 'Postmodernity', Bauman writes, 'is marked by a view of the human world as irreducibly and irrevocably pluralistic, split into a multitude of sovereign units and sites of authority, with no horizontal or vertical order, either in actuality or in potency.'[20] This emphasis on plurality and multiplicity highlights that postmodernity involves a rejection of the typically modern search for foundations, absolutes and universals. Postmodernity is a self-constituting and self-propelling culture, a culture which is increasingly self-referential in direction. From cable TV to the information superhighway: postmodern culture is a culture turned back upon itself, generated in and through internal systems of technological knowledge. Pluralism, contingency, ambiguity, ambivalence, uncertainty: these features of social life were assigned a negative value – they were seen as pathologies to be eradicated – in the modern era. For Bauman, however, these are not distortions to be overcome, but the distinctive features of a mode of social experience which has broken with the disabling hold of objectivity, necessity, law.

Bauman's discussion of the interconnections between modernity and postmodernity is extremely persuasive. He is critical of those who celebrate the postmodern as a mark *beyond* modernity. Any such reading of postmodernity as a cultural phase beyond modernity, he argues, is itself an exercise in self-contained ordering. Rather than attempting a historical periodization of the modern and postmodern eras, Bauman argues that contemporary culture, not without certain tensions and contradictions, deploys both orders simultaneously. Contemporary society revolves around a modernist impulse for creating order, boundaries and classifications as well as a postmodern tolerance for plurality, difference and uncertainty. Contemporary society, it might be said, embraces and avoids ambivalence in equal measure. There is something in all of this which is deeply disturbing and problematic: the more society generates pluralism and ambivalence, the more this rebounds as a loss of orientation and meaning. To become more aware of personal and cultural contingency is to be break with the hold of social-historical fixation and to court vulnerability. But this seemingly contradictory, and often confused, state of affairs is, in fact, one of the supreme values of postmodernity. 'Postmodernity', says Bauman, 'is modernity that has admitted the non-feasibility of its original project. Postmodernity is modernity reconciled to its own impossibility – and determined, for better or worse, to live with it. Modern practice continues – now, however, devoid of the objective that once triggered it off.'[21]

This leads directly to Bauman's central thesis: *postmodernity as modernity without illusions*. Postmodernity is an opening out to the complex, contradictory realm of human and social experience, in all its wonder and insecurity. The end of codes equals an encounter with experience, pure and unrestrained. The postmodern subject is pre-occupied, among other things, with creative and pragmatic living, free of the distortion of unrealistic hopes and aspirations, of unrealizable goals and values. The ethical distinctiveness of the postmodern age is well expressed by Bauman:

> What the postmodern mind is aware of is that there are problems in human and social life with no good solutions, twisted trajectories that cannot be straightened up, ambivalences that are more than linguistic blunders yelling to be corrected, doubts which cannot be legislated out of existence, moral agonies which no reason-dictated recipes can soothe, let alone cure. The postmodern mind does not expect any more to find the all-embracing, total and ultimate formula of life without ambiguity, risk, danger and error, and is deeply suspicious of any voice that promises otherwise. The postmodern mind is aware that each local, specialized and focused treatment, effective or not when measured by its ostensive target, spoils as much as, if not more than, it repairs. The postmodern mind is reconciled to the idea that the messiness of the human predicament is here to stay. This is, in the broadest of outlines, what can be called postmodern wisdom.[22]

Beyond the self-mastery of modernity there exists a postmodern, cultural space which calls for, and indeed celebrates, difference and otherness. Rejecting the supra-individual authority of blank technologism, rationality, economic progress, causality and system, postmodern culture transmutes the foundations of identity and society as fluid, ambivalent and radically contingent.

Contemporary psychoanalysis, postmodern identities

The dislocation and dispersal which characterize the postmodern age seem radical and novel in social and cultural theory, but the psychic fissures which they serve to promote can be found in many approaches and in many forms throughout contemporary psychoanalytic literature. Melanie Klein, D.W. Winnicott, Wilfred Bion and Jacques Lacan, and in recent years such psychoanalysts as Julia Kristeva, Cornelius Castoriadis, Christopher Bollas and Thomas Ogden, have radically reconceptualized the creative and empathetic capacities of psychical life – especially rudimentary thought processes, primitive fantasy and the interactional matrix which sustains the evocation of affect. Each of these psychoanalysts, in one form or another, has sought to undo the repressive stamp of modernist epistemology within psychoanalysis (particularly the polarization between primary and secondary process, fantasy and reality, nature and culture, and femininity and masculinity), and hence shift psychoanalysis to a more complex, post-Enlightenment understanding of psychical life and human subjectivity.

Classical Freudian psychoanalysis, exploring the affective sensibility of modernity, encouraged self-control, the renunciation of unconscious passion. Jürgen Habermas, in *Knowledge and Human Interests*, sees Freudian psychoanalysis as a self-reflective, reconstructive hermeneutic which, in uncovering the disabling effects of psychic censorship and repression, generates a capacity for the rational control of the self.[23] In this modernist reading of Freud, psychoanalysis aims at making the unconscious conscious. But emancipation from unconscious repression is no longer the central issue in postmodern times. In recent years, psychoanalysis in Europe and the United States has increasingly defined contemporary personal and cultural experience not only as an encoding of repression, but as shot through with depletion, lack and emptiness. Winnicott, for example, points to the prevalence of patients who complain of 'not feeling real', of 'being unable to feel' and of 'never saying what they mean but rather just mouthing the words of others'.[24] For these patients, the experience of subjectivity is fragmented or lacking; the self being disconnected from social experience and discourse. Personal meanings, which individuals need to experience as real and authentic, are felt to be non-existent. In an age of globalized media images, it seems as if everything is a copy of something else: the self simply mouths the words of others.

Some of the most provocative elements in recent discussions of postmodernity have been in those areas of social and cultural theory which have explored the splintering, surface facets of contemporary selfhood. The direction of this literature has been to link the cultural eclecticism of postmodernism to the demolition of psychic interiority and personal meanings. Postmodernity, in its displacement of discursive meaning with glittering surfaces and libidinal intensities, is seen as producing a fragmentation of the individual self. The most important psychoanalytic concept through which these ideas have been developed is that of Lacan's 'mirror stage', with its claim that the ego is a 'fiction' because it is frozen as an image of something which does not exist. For Lacan, the ego represents an imaginary world of wholeness and plenitude; it is a psychic defence aimed at masking the painful contradictions of desire itself. Significantly, Lacan's theory provides an account of how something outside and other – a mirror-image – is taken inside subjectivity. Yet there is no interiority or depth in Lacan's conceptualization of the mirror. One cannot get behind the mirror because it is pure surface, a flattened image which has its roots in otherness. In this respect, the links to the surface manifestations of postmodern culture are compelling. Postmodernity transmutes the social world into a wilderness of mirrors. The Lacanian decentred self, now recast as fully representative of postmodernism, is simply a copy of another, and that subject of another and another. Hence, nothing of selfhood exists beyond the surface, the immediate, the spectacle.

But to portray matters in this way demands a particular sorting of the relations between subjectivity and knowledge. It is important in this context to highlight the modernist epistemological understructure of Lacan's 'mirror stage', given that much of this book is a critique of the limits and obstructions produced by present-day integrations of Lacanian and postmodernist theory. I have in mind here the realist assumptions which underpin Lacan's delineation of the subject of imaginary misrecognition. Misrecognition in relation to what? The force of reality, and particularly the reality that desire is overwhelming because it is inscribed in lack. Although Lacan seeks to problematize the theoretical status of reality, his own writings continually emphasize the fantasy/real dichotomy. Lacan elucidates the self as a copied distortion, a filter which is played off against disfiguring perspectives of reality. Reality, in the Lacanian perspective, is that which derails the self in imaginary and symbolic terms, generating in turn further distortion and misrecognition.

The polarities fantasy and reality, which psychoanalysts from Freud to Lacan have employed to reach an objective interpretation of unconscious processes, show a characteristic of thought which belongs to the ideology of the Enlightenment, with its emphasis on mimesis and dichotomy. In contemporary psychoanalysis, by contrast, there has been a radical shift away from such realist aspirations to scientific objectivity, coupled with a rejection of the view that the clearest form of understanding occurs when secondary-process thinking is divorced from the unconscious imagination. With post-traditional psychoanalysis, the creative power of human imagination is given explicit attention. Analysts today are increasingly interested in the process of meaning-construction and of the imaginary fantasies and symbolic representations in and through which a world of inter-connecting signification is created. What is involved in contemporary psychoanalytic practice, at least in principle, is a gradual transition from reactive despair to the creation of personal meaning. In developing alternative and different experiences of subjectivity and intersubjectivity, psychoanalysis is concerned to (re)collect the terrors of the postmodern age and to recast experience within a shared, affective space. This is a matter neither of denying nor celebrating the chaotic dislocations of postmodern society, but of developing and nurturing a sense of creative meaning and value within symbolic representations of the self, of others, and of the social world. Yet whereas modernist psychoanalysis strived for clarification, renunciation and sublimation, post-traditional psychoanalysis founds itself upon the paradoxes of postmodernism by fully considering the nature of psychic ambiguity, ambivalence and contingency. Confusion and contradiction are thus no longer cast as ideological obstructions to creative living. On the contrary, in contemporary psychoanalysis, through 'mirroring', 'containing' and 'holding', subjects are encouraged to explore disturbing and painful unconscious fantasy as the basis for a revised narrative of their torn selves.

In traditional Freudian psychoanalysis, the recovery of unconscious desire is primarily traced along cognitive and developmental lines, through the reconstruction of subjective narratives of the past. But in contemporary psychoanalytic theorizing, the core capacity for encountering unconscious knowledge is located in the transmission of affect, and especially of primitive affective states that underlie the process of meaning-construction. Consider Winnicott's account of maternal mirroring, which he designates as the basis for the split between true and false selves. Winnicott proposes that the image through which the infant first begins to gain a sense of itself as a human being is its mother's face. He suggests that the mother acts as an emotional mirror for the child: through responding to the infant's needs and wishes, she communicates feelings of love and connectedness; through tolerating and containing the infant's destructiveness, she communicates an acceptance of feelings of fear and hatred. For Winnicott, and this is where he parts company with

Lacan, there is both creative identification and dislocating division in the process of mirroring. The mother, as mirror, when good enough, assists the infant in the development of its capacities for feeling, understanding and connection with others. The infant's own needs and wishes are recognized and responded to by the mother, from which feelings of spontaneity and aliveness develop. Where the mother fails to establish an emotional sensitivity to the infant's needs, however, the infant will withdraw into itself, learning to want only what the mother provides. Such experience of compliance Winnicott terms the 'false self'; an inauthentic sense of self which compulsively anticipates the expectations and reactions of others. Significantly, both authentic and inauthentic experience take place within an interpersonal field of interactions.[25] Yet it is the degree of immersion in the other person, particularly a mindfulness for the feelings and emotions which are being experienced, which distinguishes the authentic from the inauthentic.

Winnicott points to the crucial importance of a sense of mutual understanding and shared feeling in the achievement of both identity and differentiation in psychical life. In 'Transitional objects and transitional phenomena', Winnicott argues that psychic growth and development unfold through the creation of a transitional zone, a certain blending of fantasy and reality, of internal and external worlds. The child's construction of a transitional or 'not-me' object – a teddy bear or blanket, for example – is experienced as an extension of the mother, but also as a separate part of the child's mind. Such transitional objects facilitate transactions between internal and external worlds in terms of playfulness and creativity. Significantly, transitional space is also the fundamental means for a mature, reflective involvement in social and cultural life, since it allows for the exploration of fantasy and affect in symbolic terms. Thus, in Winnicott's theory, human subjectivity is forged not through a polarization of opposites, but through a creative, transitional zone which links self and other, internal and external experience, fantasy and reality.

What knits self and other together, therefore, is a responsiveness to experience, which is a matter more of affect than of reason. There is something in the primitive processes, the intense passions and anxieties of the unconscious, which at once defines and delimits the self–other boundary. The importance of primitive processes in the development of intersubjectivity is that the unconscious announces itself in feeling *before* it can be thought about or reflected upon. The experience and meaning of our subjective needs, sensations, affects, representations and fantasies are forged through a linking with the other. The theoretical consequence of this is that immersion in other people, in psychological terms, lies at the root of self-reflective consciousness and understanding. This is especially clear in Melanie Klein's theory of the paranoid-schizoid position, in which the infant entertains fantasies of tearing the maternal body to bits as well as incurring delusions that this body will in turn devour it. Notwithstanding that such fantasies represent a kind of self-disintegration, the Kleinian argument is that the paranoid-schizoid mode of generating experience, with all its destructive elements, can be emotionally modified by maternal containment in the early months of the infant's life. Through the elaboration of projective and introjective identification, the channelling of fantasized parts of self into the other or the incorporation of aspects of the other into self, the infant establishes connection with the mother's mind. As such, by functioning as a container for the infant's projections of destructive fantasy, the mother helps the infant to tolerate and manage those projections. The mother takes these negative, destructive fantasies into her own, internal world, dealing with them in terms of her own characteristic patterns of organizing emotional experience; and, by continuing to be emotionally available and receptive, she communicates an acceptance of the turbulence of human relatedness.

In the terms of the post-Kleinian analyst Wilfred Bion, maternal receptivity is achieved in and through a state of 'reverie'. 'Reverie', writes Bion, 'is that state of mind which is open to the reception of any "objects" from the loved object and is therefore capable of the reception of the infant's projective identifications whether they are felt by the infant to be good or bad.'[26] In the earliest pre-verbal relations between infant and mother, the child rids itself of feelings that cannot be tolerated by projecting them into the mother. In states of maternal reverie, the mother, by accepting these projections, contains (and thus remains related to) her infant in a way that makes emotional pain and anxiety more manageable and acceptable. Particular emphasis is given here to the emotional capabilities of the mother to tolerate and reflect upon the infant's unwanted feelings. Through intersubjective, unconscious transactions, the mother can offer these feelings back to the infant, after a period of containment, in a form which is more meaningful and less threatening to the infant. This state of emotional receptivity to the other is also considered central in post-Kleinian psychoanalytic treatment; in particular, the idea that the analyst should use, and reflect upon, their own feelings as information about the unconscious contents of the other's mind.

Here the patient communicates unconscious fantasies to the analyst through projective identification, the placing of sectors of unconscious experience into the analyst's mind. If the analyst can take in and remain open to these unwanted fantasy communications, holding the patient through containment, and reflecting upon these unconscious representations as meaningful, then new experiences of insight, awareness and creativity are likely to emerge. Where containment is not achieved, either because the individual cannot accept aspects of their unconscious experience or because the mother/analyst is not sufficiently capable of reverie, the subject will increasingly ward off pain and anxiety through projective identification. Significantly, where psychical pain and frustration become too great, the subject may rid itself not only of bad feelings and experiences, but also of that part of the mind which registers thinking itself. The inability to tolerate any form of confusion is what Bion terms 'anti-thought', a process in which significatory elements are 'stripped of their meaning and only the worthless residue retained.'[27] Such an emptying out of the mind of terrifying, persecutory objects, when coupled to the expulsion of thinking and reflectiveness, can lead to extreme psychological disturbance, such as psychosis.

There is something broader, relating to the cultural conditions of postmodernity, which should also be considered at this point. The contemporary self, as we have seen, has been characterized by some commentators as narcissistic, illusory and brittle, and by others as decentred, disorientated and fragmented. Kleinian and post-Kleinian theory profoundly questions these descriptions of the prevailing sense of self. The unconscious process of meaning-construction, in Kleinian and post-Kleinian accounts, is one characterized by an inmixing of self and other; the migration of subjective meaning into the other, tangled and confused, through the mechanisms of projective and introjective identification. The idea of emotional receptivity – of 'holding' and 'containing' the other – is recognized as central to discovering and understanding self-experience; struggling with something other, tolerating it and reflecting upon it, is fundamental to attaining an authentic sense of personal relatedness. Similarly, it might be suggested, there is a remarkably fluid and reflexive encounter with otherness generated under the cultural conditions of postmodernity. The Western world of postmodern culture – with its circuits of technology, networks of interlinking computational systems, and media simulation – restructures the local/global intersection, and hence our experience of otherness. Through the communicational conveyor belt of mass media, from news coverage of regional wars and famines to information concerning ecological and nuclear crises, the local becomes global and/or the global becomes local. In this context, interpersonal communication is projected into larger national and global spaces. Postmodern culture creates new possibilities as regards the extensional links between self and other: immersion in the other, and particularly fantasized aspects of the other, is continually invoked and negotiated through the key role of media simulation.

Once again, however, it must be stressed that this kind of communicational linkage between self and other, refracted through transnational media systems, would appear resistant to clear and ordered articulation. In post-Kleinian terms, the articulation of such mediated experience of the other becomes possible only through an immersion, an incorporation and working through, of the imagined fantasies and symbolic representations created. A toleration of confusion and disorder, as the globalized screening of otherness impacts upon the self, is necessary in order to discover new ways of thinking and new domains of personal experience. Indeed, in the light of Jameson's thesis regarding the disintegration of the 'cognitive maps' of individual and collective identities in postmodern culture, it seems likely that it is increasingly necessary to tolerate and reflect upon emotional states of uncertainty generated by the cultural conditions of the late modern age.

What is important about this reflectiveness upon self-organization and unconscious experience is not only a containment and toleration of the other, but the *searching* of fantasy life itself. It is here, tracking psychic identifications with self and others, that the idea of new imaginary structures of subjectivity has most importance. What seems to be involved is that which concerns coming to terms with the self-legislating power of fantasy itself. How much can subjective experience *take in* of imaginative perception? Or, to put the issue slightly differently, how much is left of identity once the subject turns back upon its own mental activity? This idea of reflexive fantasy connects with Cornelius Castoriadis's claim that psychoanalysis is the discovery of psychical imagination, of psychical creation *ex nihilo*: the constitution and reproduction of imaginary forms in and through which men and women image themselves, and each other, in daily life.[28] Significantly, inquiry into the process of fantasy production involves what I have previously called 'rolling identification', an unconscious interchange across the self–other boundary.[29] Rolling identifications, which entail a 'representational wrapping of self and other', permit the constitution of identity as a relation to the self-as-object and preobject relations, both of which are central to pre-Oedipal development.

Much of this recent emphasis on the power of fantasy and imagination has been developed within feminist psychoanalytic thinking. For Julia Kristeva, to take a particularly powerful integration of psychoanalysis and feminist social theory, the human subject's capacity for creativity and autonomy is deeply intertwined with the repressed maternal, a 'semiotic' connection to the maternal body. By the semiotic Kristeva means a heterogeneous play of unconscious forces – of drives, affects and representations – which exert a pulsional pressure within language itself, and which can be discerned within the rhythm, tone and disruption of speech. Kristeva argues that the primordial *jouissance* of the child/mother dyad is smashed apart by, and is repressed through reference to, the Law of the Father, the symbolic cultural structure. Semiotic connection with repressed maternal drives remains, however, symbolized in the rhythms, fractures and dislocations of social significations. Kristeva argues that contemporary psychoanalysis has become increasingly concerned with the complexities of semiotic disruptions, the overflow of unconscious representation into the confined, patriarchal space of the symbolic order. This pre-Oedipal, semiotic experience of the maternal body functions as a point of otherness – an otherness which is experienced, in fantasy spaces such as dreams and day-dreams, as a remembering of the imaginary bliss of the maternal sphere itself. The semiotic is the scene of something other, an otherness central to the fluidity of the 'subject-in-process'; an otherness which underlies the multiplication of fantasy as it intersects with received social meanings.

One way of understanding this continual remembering of the maternal body is in terms of the alterity, the strangeness and uncanniness, of human subjectivity. For Kristeva, the trauma of primitive psychic separation from the maternal body renders us subjectively divided, internally strange. This is a strangeness which is at once alluring and threatening. It is alluring in so far as it acts to neutralize otherness, rendering self and world pseudo-rational through fantasies of narcissistic completeness. Yet it is threatening because of the fragility of psychic repression, a fragility which returns the sense of strangeness to conscious experience. In fact Kristeva, developing upon Freud's work on uncanny strangeness, portrays subjective experience of otherness as central to the development of human creativity and autonomy. 'The sense of strangeness', writes Kristeva, 'is a mainspring for identification with the other, by working out its depersonalizing impact by means of astonishment.'[30] This astonishment, linked to unconscious anguish, leads to a *destructuration of self*: as the fragile boundaries between self and other break down, psychic identity is put into question and there is a dissolution (and regeneration) of imaginary structures. Strangeness, for Kristeva, is essential in the very production and formation of psychic space and imagination. As she develops this point:

> Also strange is the experience of the abyss separating me from the other who shocks me – I do not even perceive him, perhaps he crushes me because I negate him. Confronting the foreigner whom I reject and with whom at the same time I identify, I lose my boundaries, I no longer have a container, the memory of experiences when I had been abandoned overwhelm me, I lose my composure. I feel 'lost', 'indistinct', 'hazy'. The uncanny strangeness allows for many variations: they all repeat the difficulty I have in situating myself with respect to the other and keep going over the course of identification-projection that lies at the foundation of my reaching autonomy.[31]

Postmodernity and otherness, or respacing self and world

How do these trends in psychoanalytic theorizing relate to postmodernity? Let me approach this question from the inside, the domain of imagination, and then move out, to consider the ways in which contemporary psychoanalysis sheds new light on society at large. Contemporary psychoanalysis, notwithstanding its heterogeneity, is profoundly occupied with the complexity of fantasy itself, as a process of self-construction and other-directedness. 'The bridge supporting connection with others', writes Stephen Mitchell, 'is not built out of a rationality superseding fantasy and the imagination, but out of feelings experienced as real, authentic, generated from the inside, rather than imposed externally, in close relationship with fantasy and the imagination.'[32] Fantasy zones of transitional space, reverie, containment, semiotic forces, rolling identifications: imagination constitutes human subjectivity and the unconscious to its core. The realm of unconscious imagination, I claim, is a *generative space*. It is a space in and through which the subject creates meaning in the moment of differentiation of self to other. It is an affective, representational space in which to think the limit of subjectivity: the struggle of placing the 'subject' in question.

What, though, of the boundaries of personal, unconscious meaning? Are we talking here of a communicational immediacy between self and other; or of a world of multiple meaning and codes; or perhaps of a schizoid dissolution of identification and signification into an imaginary hall of mirrors? Again, the current state of psychoanalytic thinking is instructive. The contemporary subject, as experienced in therapy and represented in theory, continually moves along emotional paths of not-knowing on the one hand, and the generation of symbolic meanings, demands and representations on the other. A disconnection from symbolic representation is viewed as a precondition for the generation and reconstruction of meanings. The suspension of preconceived thoughts, coupled with an immersion in the unfolding of ambiguity, is a central means for the transformation of unconscious experience into interpersonal communication. This is a subjectivity, then, of multiplicity and fluidity; a narrative reconstruction of identity without beginning or end; a conception of the imaginary and the imagination which, following Kristeva, can be called a 'subject-in-process'. It is important to note once again the reflexive form granted to the intersubjective space of analysis – particularly transference and counter-transference – as concerns the exploration of unconscious fantasy. The experience of containment and holding in the analytic situation – the receptivity of the psychoanalyst to all of the patient's feeling-states, from anxiety to the projection of destructiveness and hate – is crucial for any reclaiming of those torn or split-off dimensions of subjectivity, and for their potential reintegration into self-experience. In Bion's terms, the reverie of the therapist or analyst acts as a container for an exploration of psychic processes prior to and underlying self-organization. Taking in, holding and making sense of fragmented experience, and returning unconscious communications as meaningful: this is a creative, intersubjective process of containment, a process which underscores the affective, reflexive resources of subjectivity in a powerful and provocative manner.

Of course, none of this is straightforward as regards self-experience. The reflexivity of selfhood, as elaborated in intersubjective settings, is filtered through that crisis in representations and legitimations which postmodern culture ushers into existence. Simply put, the self-experience of intersubjective meaning and containment is continually rendered problematic in postmodern contexts of cultural fragmentation, political dislocation and the economic interchangeability of commodities, objects and persons. But if creative and reflexive psychic organization underpins the construction of subject-positions and identity, then alternative avenues for personal and cultural development must exist. The problematizing of psychic boundaries of subjectivity, as both Kristeva and Castoriadis point out, is always carried on within the tangled frame of the repressed unconscious – the heterogeneity of radical imagination, the disruption of semiotic functioning.

The nature of postmodernity, or so I want to propose, promotes a reflexive involvement with human imagination: through an 'opening out' of the cultural sphere there are also many points of personal engagement which offer the possibilities for *revised imaginary space*. Recognizing the irreducible character of fantasy means living with uncertainty, ambivalence, otherness and difference. Our day-to-day activities – in so far as they are increasingly influenced by instantaneous global communication – have become focused around otherness. Today the centrality of the other, whether in terms of sexuality, race or nationalism, refocuses relations between identity and difference, subjectivity and politics. Thus, for example, the refashioning of sexuality and intimacy in the light of AIDS is directly bound up with research that has been conducted on a global scale, and which has influenced perceptions of security and danger in the sphere of gender relations. In an era of ambivalence and uncertainty, the social imaginary has become less and less encumbered with the rigid hierarchies and flat rationalizations of the modern era. In certain respects, this has led the postmodern subject into a void, as the self is now left to feel the full force of its inner pain, loneliness and anxiety. Postmodern selfhood we might thus describe, following Baudrillard, as anchored in nostalgia – 'Playing with the pieces – that is postmodern.'[33] But, crucially, this is only one side of the story of postmodernity. One of the most distinctive aspects of the interconnections between postmodernity and the personal domain, though certainly one of the most neglected in recent discussions, is the capacity of human subjectivity for imaginative elaboration, symbolized by new representations of self and world. The global spread of cultural production in the mass media, the pluralization of local histories and cultures, the transformation of sexuality: we witness in this pluralistic world an intensification of symbolic, intersubjective linkages, as well as an increasing awareness of the creativity of fantasy itself. At such times, we are exposed to a reordering of the symbolic codes of society, not as Law or the Name-of-the-Father, but rather as a form of openness to *ourselves*.

Various institutional developments, in the era of postmodernity, mark this multiplication of fantasy and imagination as regards human subjectivity. As we have seen in the preceding pages, post-

modernity is characterized by institutionalized ambivalence, pluralism and contingency – all of which modernity uncovered and disowned in equal measure. Postmodernity, in this sense, refers to the
dissolution of centralized perspectives and authorized identities; the
end of 'grand narratives', to recall Lyotard. However, postmodern
identity is not simply a phase of development beyond modernity.
Rather, as identities without illusions (in Bauman's sense), postmodern subjectivity is a subjectivity seeking to come to terms with, to
accommodate, the multiple identifications of culture and politics.
Contemporary identities, and this plural form is basic to the framework of postmodern experience, create reflexively organized 'narratives' (or case-histories) in respect of the cultural diversity of self and
other; representations fabricated out of sexual, cultural, ethnic, religious, political and aesthetic influences. Postmodern identities trade
in complex, contradictory networks of intersubjective meanings;
questioning fantasy, or perhaps more accurately seeking to turn fantasy back upon itself, in order to glimpse the creative workings of
unconscious desire.

The links between this new cultural experience and psychic reor-
ganization, briefly sketched in the foregoing paragraphs, are premised
upon a confrontation with the decentredness of the subject. As the
contextual supports for fantasy become increasingly self-referential in
postmodern times, human subjects become more and more aware
of the *constructedness* of selfhood, relationships and society itself.
'Decentring' here is understood not as a separation of the ego from
the subject in Lacan's sense, but rather in terms of *representational
contingency*, by which I mean the filtering of self and other through
the flux of unconscious imagination. In conditions of postmodernity,
people become profoundly aware of the contingency of meaning
and of the sign; they see that meaning is not fixed once and for all,
but rather that signification is creatively fabricated and negotiated.
In this sense, fantasy is located at the root of our traffic with
meaning.

Yet this contingency of fantasy, as mediated through symbolic
representation, often resists being brought over into reflexive awareness and thinking, the result being instead an immersion in unconscious denials, disavowals and negations. Personal confusion and
dislocation – the feeling that nothing makes sense – is reflective of the
immense emotional difficulties of sustaining any form of meaningful
experience in the late modern age. One way of interpreting the
existence of such dislocation is in terms of the disturbance and
pathology of postmodern society itself. Under postmodern con-

ditions, the fragmentation of social processes penetrates fully into the psychic world, deconstructing and fracturing subjectivity in one stroke. 'Postmodernism', writes Jameson, 'is not merely a liberation from anxiety but a liberation from every other kind of feeling as well, since there is no longer a self present to do the feeling.'[34] The human subject, in this reading, suffers from a kind of psychic burnout. This burnout signals an end to the ideological mirage of unified subjectivity, as well as the depersonalization of affect. Self-experience as integral and continuous is displaced in favour of schizoid desire and random libidinal intensities; hence the cynical erasure of subjectivity in certain currents of post-structuralist and postmodern social theory, an erasure which involves a wholesale transmutation of the subject into a subjectless world of images and surfaces, abstract signifiers and disembodied communications.[35]

Yet while the oscillation and fragmentation of selfhood is certainly a phenomenon of increasing significance in the postmodern age, there are good reasons for supposing that this disintegration of the subject in contemporary theory is substantially inadequate. To begin with, much contemporary theory displays a lack of interest in the internal dimensions of psychological fragmentation, reducing issues of emotional abandonment and psychotic unhinging to the cultural and ideological imperatives of power as such. As a result, the pain and terror of psychotic disconnection is completely sidestepped.[36] Significantly, the euphoric celebration of psychotic fragmentation and libidinal intensification in some currents of critical theory betrays, I think, a strong affinity with those older, modernist conceptions of subjectivity it claims to overcome. That is to say, the post-structuralist deconstruction of subjectivity into fragmentation takes the form it does because it is principally a reaction to – an intellectual defence against – modernist pressures for self-control and mastery.

What happens if this dominant conception of postmodern dislocation and dispersal is rejected? What happens if we reject the linkage of fragmentation and subjectivity in postmodernity, and replace it with a conception of our psychic capacity for imaginative elaboration of self and world, a conception which suggests the possibility of some more facilitating agency in the reproduction of postmodern cultural forms? In the view I wish to develop, postmodern selfhood signifies *open-endedness*, not irrevocable fragmentation. Postmodernity, it might be said, breaks down the symbolic order of society as Law or Reason, and reconstitutes it as a form of openness, a space for radical imagination. In such circumstances, an awareness of fantasy pro-

cesses as self-constituting becomes central, not only in the reproduction of social institutions, but also in framing the fluid and ambiguous field of self–other relations. Inside and out, at the level of
psychic interiority as well as that of the outside world, living
in postmodernity means living with an awareness of the overdetermination of personal and cultural worlds by fantasy. Fantasy, as
a creative flux of the unconscious, is bound up in a direct way with
both knowledge and experience of the world; it cannot be avoided or
overcome. Such postmodern awareness of the no exit from fantasy,
however, opens the possibility for challenging the terms of intersec-
tion between human imagination and social processes. The passage
from the modern symbolic, as a mode of ordering and mastering
fantasy eruptions of otherness, to the postmodern symbolic, an
awareness of the tension and anxiety embedded in the sites of fantasy,
produces new possibilities for personal and cultural life.

Radical imagination, the deconstruction and reconstruction of fantasy positions, becomes a central psychological and political issue
with the development of postmodernity. Applied to society and culture, the exploration of fantasy as a means of intrapsychic and
intersubjective communication, as a deconstruction of the fixed positions of the past, is especially important. Postmodernity, as we have
seen, is marked by ambiguity, contingency and ambivalence, all of
which fuse to produce an openness as regards contemporary social
processes. For many, this situation is something to be welcomed; it
generates excitement and hope. At the same time, however, the uncertainty of postmodernity promotes anxiety and fear as well. This is,
perhaps, the central postmodern challenge for personal and cultural
life: the creation of subject-positions in which unconscious flux and
fluidity on the one hand, and symbolic representations and meanings
on the other, are directly related to each other. The meaning and
potentialities arising from an awareness of uncertainty and contingency, however, need also to account for the anxiety which such a
state of mind produces. It is, above all, personal meaning, knowledge
and creativity which are at stake here. Psychic transgression can
produce with equal ease, or equal difficulty, an opening or closure of
imaginary possibilities. A radical encounter with uncertainty, in my
view, must extend to an engagement with the 'catastrophic' – the
subject-in-process experiencing itself as 'coming apart at the seams'.
In Kleinian terms, such an encounter with the disturbing demands a
shift from the paranoid-schizoid phase to the depressive phase, with
despair being properly owned and explored. Or, in the post-Kleinian

terms of Bion and Meltzer, personal authenticity and creativity require a capacity to tolerate inner disorder, a catastrophe within.[37] It is out of this confusion and turbulence of passion that creative living can occur.

This brings the discussion back to issues raised by Kristeva. An exploration of the representations, affects and meanings invested in fantasy sites, says Kristeva, necessarily involves a dimension of uncanniness, of strangeness, of otherness. 'The sense of strangeness', writes Kristeva, 'is a mainspring for identification with the other, by working out its depersonalizing impact by means of astonishment.'[38] This sense of astonishment, as previously noted, revolves around a confrontation with the unknown. Each time unknown experience is confronted, notes Kristeva, there is a deconstruction and reconstruction of self, and especially of infantile desires and fears of otherness. Constructed positions of self and other, and their organization in the symbolic order itself, are explored and, by implication, questioned. But there is something more significant at work in these unconscious interpretative procedures, as concerns both fantasy and postmodernity, and their mutual implication in each other. The sense of depersonalization activated by strangeness of which Kristeva speaks is, I suggest, structured by the social and political dislocations of postmodernity. Experience of otherness and uncanny strangeness becomes more and more apparent in conditions of postmodernity. In a globalized world of political, economic and military relations, the encounter with otherness is continually evoked in and through mass media and generalized communication. Newspaper headlines of mass death and torture, snippets of the plurality of cultures on television, sexual imagery deployed in advertisements: these may all activate a sense of otherness within – of desire and fear, oppression and power, sexuality and dissolution.

Such otherness is problematic. In the face of our deep-seated psychological longing for the familiar, consciousness of internal otherness – destructive, fearful, empty, desiring, lacking – cannot be guaranteed. As regards traditional boundaries of displacement and repression, self and world can appear so fixed that it seems impossible to think, feel or act differently. Indeed, the rejection of otherness, as Bion has shown, can often lead to an elimination of the psychic capacity for thinking itself. Anti-thought, the blocking out and elimination of experience and affect, opens the way for a translation into action of fearful and destructive psychical states. Excessive projection, paranoia and psychotic splitting can be unleashed when symbolic space is violently excluded; and, under contemporary ideological authorizations of the expenditure of hatred, this often leads to the dehumanization, and actual murder, of others.

Individually and collectively, however, it is at the strange borders of otherness that the fixed positions of the past can be questioned and reshaped. Contemporary psychoanalysts such as Kristeva and Castoriadis (but also post-Kleinians like Bion, Meltzer and Ogden), in showing that the unconscious experience of subjectivity is deeply interwoven with otherness, ambivalence and imagination, help us to see that the postmodern world opens new zones of engagement for being with ourselves and others. In the postmodern society of transnational communication and the plurality of cultures, imagination makes personal and cultural reflexivity possible, and underlies this ceaseless psychic construction and deconstruction of self and world. Thus, in contrast to the prevailing characterization of the 'death of imagination' in contemporary theory, postmodernity is better characterized, I argue, as a culture of imagination without illusions, a cultural space which admits the provisional and contingent form of imaginary structures. Postmodernity is a reflexive world, a world in which we are increasingly *subject to ourselves*.

2

Contradictions of the Imagination

Freud in the Stream of Modernity

Our best hope for the future is that intellect – the scientific spirit, reason – may in the process of time establish a dictatorship in the mental life of man. The nature of reason is a guarantee that afterwards it will not fail to give man's emotional impulses and what is determined by them the position they deserve.

Sigmund Freud

Freud, who from the beginning to the end of his work in fact spoke of nothing but the imagination, of its works and its effects, obstinately refused to thematize this element of the psyche . . . To take imagination into account seems to Freud incompatible with the 'project for a scientific psychology' or, later, with a 'scientific' psychoanalysis – as for Aristotle, perhaps, and certainly for Kant, the imagination ultimately had to be put in its place, a place subordinate to that of reason.

Cornelius Castoriadis

'The closest human love', William James wrote, 'incloses a potential germ of estrangement or hatred.'[1] The romantic ideal of a benign love as the ground of communal understanding, this suggests, is an illusion. Love and hatred are at once interacting and opposing feelings. The human subject can never make love entirely its own: it will be caught in a constant series of exacerbating trade-offs or tactical negotiations between the unstable dynamics of love and hatred, sexuality and aggression. Feelings of love and intimacy may be flooded quickly by the impulse to destroy, fearful modes of thinking, or the sadistic pressures of the superego.

Psychoanalysis, as we have seen in chapter 1, tirelessly interrogates this battle and dramatizes its internal consequences for human subjectivity. The delicious plenitude of unconscious enjoyment, as Freud conceived it, is a realm of competing libidinal drives, irreconcilable investments and desires, incompatible agencies or instances. Psychical life is revealed as fissured in psychoanalysis in so far as it is about endless *fantasmatic* production. Fantasy, drive, affect, dream, symbolism, condensation, displacement: unconscious desire not only drives the individual subject in different directions, it is also constitutive of the representational activity of subjectivity itself – to, for example, people's core sense of identity.

Just as this is true of human subjectivity, so it is true of conceptual knowledge. That is to say, the discourse of psychoanalysis, too, is caught up in the ceaseless contradictions and dissonances of unconscious desire. Freud's theory of the human psyche, for example, is at once informed and disturbed, instructed and derailed, by the primitive unconscious substratum. To be sure, the female hysterical patients Freud treated in late Hapsburg Vienna helped lead him to uncover an essential element of psychoanalytic treatment: free association. Listening to the subtexts of the narratives told to him by his patients, Freud sought – through interpretative intervention – to bring hidden sexual conflicts into the open, transforming free association into the 'talking cure'. Moreover, he sought to press this clinical experience of hysteria and neurosis into a comprehensive hermeneutic system, a system turned towards desire as a privileged road to scientific knowledge. The scaffolding of this system, as we will see, encompasses 'mechanisms', 'apparatuses', 'modes of functioning' and the like. However, contrary to appearances, such explanatory devices were to prove incapable of grasping the primary stuff of unconscious fantasy. For the unconscious, as Freud and others after him were to discover, has an uncanny knack of thwarting theoretical classification, ordering and hierarchy. All in all, it can be said that the search for the laws and structures of psychical life has been continually defied by the overdetermination and dispersal of the repressed unconscious.

There are a number of detailed historical studies of the concept of the unconscious, one of the most important perhaps being Whyte's *The Unconscious before Freud* (1962).[2] The unconscious, conceived as a productive force of the imagination, had been granted a central role in European thought since Aristotle's treatise *De Anima*. So too, Kant located the productive imagination as of core importance to psychical reasoning and understanding in his *Critique of Pure Reason*. The unconscious as a source of creative imagination was also pivotal to Romanticism – a point often stressed by Freud himself.

Nonetheless, the question of the originality of the Freudian unconscious remains. As Malcolm Bowie observes:

> The history of the unconscious in late nineteenth- and early twentieth-
> century Europe is a ramifying tale of scientific originality lost and
> found, of intellectual legitimacy claimed and disputed. 'How original
> was Freud?' is still a question of seemingly inexhaustible historical
> interest. A characteristic sequence of answers and counter-answers
> might go like this: (1) he was not original, other than as a publicist,
> because the unconscious had come and gone in European thinking
> since antiquity and had become positively fashionable during the
> period of Freud's early maturity; (2) but Freud differed crucially from
> his predecessors in that he was a thorough-going systematist, and
> promoted the unconscious only in so far as the psychodynamic system
> of which it was part could explain mental facts; (3) but the very notion
> of 'system' that Freud resorted to was a commonplace of the new and
> topical evolutionary biology that he grew up with, and even when he
> repudiated biological science in favour of a supposedly 'pure' psy-
> chology, he was still adhering to a biologically inspired theoretical
> mode; (4) but in doing this he was exploiting biology for his own
> purposes, not remaining subservient to it: all spectacular paradigm
> shifts in the history of science begin with a switching or mixing of
> metaphors; (5) but this is exactly the problem with Freud: he
> metaphorized science; (6) but . . .[3]

Bowie's comments alert us to a central issue concerning the status of
the unconscious in psychoanalysis: that clinical and epistemological
issues are inextricably linked. What is at the heart of human subjectivity, the passions and representations of unconscious fantasy,
and what is the truth of intersubjective space, the analysis, need to
be approached simultaneously. The contemporary controversy surrounding the scientific status of Freud and psychoanalysis, notwithstanding the fundamental issue of the fracturing of knowledge
produced by the unconscious and its difficulty, has functioned however as a kind of conceptual displacement or closure.[4] This limiting of
the scientific field of psychoanalysis, in my view, concerns above all
Freud's discovery of psychical imagination.

One of the purposes of this chapter is to explore the theory of
psychical imagination – and especially of fantasy – uncovered (and
required) by Freud. Another is to examine some of the mechanisms by
which Freud displaces this location of the creative and self-instituting
capacity of the unconscious imagination. In what follows, I explore
Freud's attempt to locate the foundations of psychical life in terms of
a specifically modernist tension between imagination and rationality;

a tension that pervades much of Freud's work. In particular, I focus upon Freud's foundational (though unfinished) text, the 'Project for a scientific psychology'.[5] The argument that will be developed is that the continuing significance of Freud's work for contemporary theory rests precisely in its uncertainty over fantasy and the unconscious imagination, an uncertainty which shifts between the boundaries of inside and outside, anxiety and control, psychic flux and scientific authorization. The final sections of the chapter turn to consider the relation between imagination and specialized knowledge in the realm of modernity.

Inner conflict, outer certainty

The 'Project for a scientific psychology' of 1895 is a text marked by Freud's desire for mastery, an attempt to subject the workings of mind to the laws of motion on the physiological basis of neurology. The psyche, in this protodraft of psychoanalytic theory, is conceptualized as an 'apparatus', one made up of various subsystems and mechanisms. The study of hysteria and of neurotic disorders led Freud to grant the psyche a neuromechanical logic of its own, a mode of action that receives, transforms and discharges energetic excitations. Freud's aim is to understand the laws of psychical economy, to master them, to render them transparent. The opening declaration of the 'Project' is indeed full of self-masterful zeal and scientific certainty: 'The intention is to furnish a psychology that shall be a natural science: that is, to represent psychical processes as quantitatively determinate states of specifiable material particles, thus making those processes perspicuous and free from contradiction.'[6] Freud's multisystemic 'psychical apparatus' is theorized as interlocking agencies of excitation homologous to physical energy – hence the grounding of psychology in natural science. Freud argues for the development of a quantitative framework in order to grasp, and thus also to colonize, the nature of mental functioning – thus rendering the secrets of psychical energy 'free from contradiction'.

Yet whilst the introduction of this quantitative viewpoint derives much of its impetus from modernist procedures of enframing, ordering and mastery, the 'Project' is also rich in speculative insight about the imaginary contours of the primitive libidinal substratum. Repression and defence, the libidinal drives with their competing forces of energy, ego-organization and memory: these ideas are all present in, and inform, the account of mental life sketched in this text.

What is perhaps most immediately striking about the 'Project' is the manner in which Freud argues that the psychical elaboration of sexuality is to be found not in some free-floating realm of images and scenes, but rather in the objective determinism of energy and forces. The heart of the matter is conceptualized by Freud as the transformation of energy or quantity (abbreviated as Q) into perceptual and instinctual stimuli within a neuronic framework. The psychical apparatus is a complex network of neurones, a network which follows the general laws of motion. The dynamics of force, attraction and defence, Freud argues, dominate the mental apparatus. Through a blending of the ideas of Hermann von Helmholtz and J.F. Herbart, neurophysiological concepts are brought to bear upon the functioning of desire and pleasure.[7] Quantity dominates the psychical apparatus from start to finish in the 'Project': it is conceptualized as an energetic current which fills or drains, charges or discharges, neurones. The powerful intensities of energy thus function as the primary source of psychical excitations, what Freud describes as a 'cathecting' of neurones.

If it is the motions of energy which bring a psychical movement or action about in the first place (through the charging or discharging of neurones), then the registration of experience, including the capacity to store memories, should vary according to the flow of quantity available at any particular moment. Yet Freud's account of energy as the primary motor-power of psychic functioning rejects this possibility, and instead connects the nature of quantity to what he calls 'neuronic inertia', or, more commonly, the 'constancy principle'. The principle of constancy means that the psychic apparatus tends to reduce its own accumulation of energy to zero, to divest itself of force and tension. 'The mind', as Richard Wollheim writes of Freud's 'Project', 'tries to expel all energy as and when it enters the system.'[8] The psyche, then, works to defuse the impact of energetic excitations, to maintain the existing level of quantity as low as possible – and in so far as Freud's thought grants the psyche a determining power at this stage of his thinking, which will become clear when we turn to consider the relation between energy and its psychic registration, it can be said that the creative function of such differentiation is itself central to the mental constitution of human beings.

The elimination of energy from the psychic apparatus, however, turns out to be not so simple. Freud's conception of the energetic filling of neurones, and of the principle of inertia (that is, the draining of such quantity charges), only goes so far to comprehend the manner in which the psyche receives stimulation from the outside world, as with the nature and function of perception. The difficulty which arises is that the psychical apparatus cannot escape from, it cannot eliminate, the voracious energy of internal demands (such as the needs of hunger and the desires of sexuálity) in the same manner. As a result of internal demand, which produces an accumulation of energy, the psychical apparatus, Freud says, 'must learn to tolerate a store of quantity sufficient to meet the demands for specific action'. In other words, the mind must be able to register feelings and thoughts in such a way as to bring together internal demand with the objective conditions of discharge. In this way, when the mind is stimulated by certain thoughts, feelings and wishes, it will be able to respond with an appropriate action, and not some random response. What this involves, at such a level of analysis, is a meshing of psychical enjoyment with the lived immediacy of self–other relations. As Freud puts this:

> At first, the human organism is incapable of bringing about the specific action [of satisfaction]. It takes place by *extraneous help*, when the attention of an experienced person is drawn to the child's state by discharge along the path of internal change. In this way this path of discharge acquires a secondary function of the highest importance, that of communication, and the initial helplessness of human beings is the *primal source* of all *moral motives*.[9]

Crucially, the question of energy and the path of its discharge is inseparable from the question of communication, the dynamics of intersubjectivity. Seen in this light, energy is at once anchored in and the guarantor of intersubjective space.

But what of discharge? The ultimate and central means in which this is now explored – the problem of energy and the internal world – is through the pressing of quantity into the mode of operation of the psychical itself. Freud separates the sensory neurones into two types: φ-neurones and ψ-neurones. An exegesis of the differences between these two classes of neurone is something that has already been well accomplished in the psychoanalytic literature.[10] In general terms, the φ-neurones receive stimulation from the outside world (as in perception), whereas the ψ-neurones receive stimulation from the internal world (such as the needs of hunger). In Wollheim's gloss, 'the φ-neurones are totally permeable, they offer no resistance to the flow of quantity through them, and, consequently, are totally unaffected by it, whereas ψ-neurones are to some degree or other impermeable, they offer some resistance to, and hence retain permanent traces of, quantity as it flows through them'.[11] The psyche in this conception is defined not by whether or not energy is eliminated, but by the maintenance of a certain level of tension in order for discharge. And discharge, Wollheim writes, is understood by Freud as a process of psychic repetition: 'if a given quantity recurrently follows one specific path through the ψ-system, then it is safe to assume that this is the path along which relief, for that quantity, is to be found'.[12]

There remains, however, the need to discriminate between the relief of discharges as regards the primary and secondary functions of the psyche, once it is granted that there is an originary productive dynamism at this energetic level of human functioning. The category of tension, in the 'Project', is linked to a regulatory mechanism that Freud calls the 'pleasure–unpleasure series'. Simply put, Freud postulates an equivalence between the experience of unpleasure and a rise in tension on the one hand, and the experience of pleasure and a decrease in tension on the other. The psyche for Freud functions according to the avoidance of unpleasure; and pleasure, as indicated, is understood in terms of the sensation of discharge. At this point, however, a modification to Freud's energetic model, and in particular to the functioning of the secondary processes, necessarily imposes itself. In order to understand how the pleasure–unpleasure combination achieves registration within the psychical apparatus, Freud introduces the concept of consciousness, which is conceived as an inhibiting system of bound energy that functions at a constant level. Consciousness is conceptualized in the 'Project' through the positing of a third class of neurone: ω-neurones. What changes everything in the discussion of the psychic apparatus at this point is that, although consciousness and reality-testing can be understood as determined by quantity, Freud insists that the flow of energy as such never enters the ω-system of neurones. Instead, Freud speaks of a transformation from quantity to quality with the mediation of an 'indication of reality'. Subjective experience of the outer world requires an inhibition of libidinal energy; and this is an inhibition that is central to the capacity to distinguish between a desire for an object and the object itself.

An inhibition of quantity thus takes place in the psychical translation from the primary to the secondary process. Freud asserts that, as quantity flows through the ψ-system and is influenced by the memory of pleasure or pain, paths of discharge will be sought that bring internal needs into line with reality-testing. That is, the psyche can either seize upon, or defend against, the power of wishes as they intersect with interpersonal relationships. Meanwhile, the ego enters directly into this task of discrimination, pressing back memory images of the 'wished-for' object in the primary process, and pressing toward 'indications of reality' that will permit a specific action to be carried out in line with internal demands and external requirements. As Freud puts this: 'Where, then, an ego exists, it is bound to inhibit primary psychical processes.' This inhibiting function of the ego involves a shift from energy as free-flowing in the primary process to energy as bounded in the secondary process. This shift also informs Freud's view that the ego can assert its rule over unconscious conflict and division; a reclaiming of subjective control in the name of rationality.

If the capacity for discrimination between imagination and reality is what sustains reflexive selfhood, however, it is also implicated in the realm of pathological defence. The nub of the problem, as the 'Project' continuously reminds us, is quantitative. Excessive quantity conflicts with these regulatory functions of the ego; it outweighs the ego's activity of inhibiting; indeed, in an act of violent incorporation, excessive libidinal eruptions can fuse a memory image of a wished-for object with perception itself. In this case, memory will be confused with reality, as happens with the conversion of affective intensities in hysteria, displacements of energy in obsession, and so on. The eruption of excessive quantity lies at the root of emotional pain, leaving the subject overwhelmed and anxious; and it also leaves its mark in the form of permanent memory traces. Such an overflowing of energy is damaging because its path of release is illusory – discharge is sought through hallucination, not reality.

Seen in this light, the quantitative focus in Freud's 'Project' redramatizes the relationship between libidinal desire and reality-testing, particularly in the characterization of memory (that is, the memory of an experience of pleasure–unpleasure) as a condition in which the sense of reality is constituted. 'Unpleasure', Freud writes in a sentence which anticipates the *Weltanschauung* (or world-view) of psychoanalysis, 'remains the sole means of education.' (There is a close tie, it should be noted, between the negativity Freud attributes to 'unpleasure' and the development of notions such as 'frustration' (Bion) and 'lack' (Lacan) in post-Freudian theory.) It is this linking of unpleasure and reality, this crushing of the narcissistic self-unity of the psyche, from which Freud locates autonomous subjectivity as the capacity of the mind to distinguish between imagination and memory on the one hand, and indications of reality, through perception, on the other. The creative mastery of this discrimination not only under-writes our mental capacities for attention, understanding and cognitive thought, but it also leads to a critical distance from the disabling influence of primary process regression.

It will be apparent from the foregoing commentary that the psychical apparatus as detailed by Freud in the 'Project' is fixed on a mechanical register – quantitative, deterministic and operationalized by three types of neurone. Indeed, in a letter to his friend and mentor Wilhelm Fliess, Freud says of the 'Project': 'Everything seemed to mesh, the gear mechanism fitted together, one got the impression the thing now really was a machine that would shortly go by itself.'[13] A mental machine whose mechanisms are to function free from distorting contradictions: the determinism, and its guiding fantasy of control, is particularly evident here. In this quantitative psychology of desire, the transition from physical tension to a properly psychical elaboration is one of excitations that enter into the interconnecting pathways imprinted in the neuronic framework. In many respects, Freud's unyielding search throughout the 'Project' for the quantitative foundations of psychological behaviour drew its animus from his deep faith in science, reason and objective knowledge. With such a faith, Freud deployed a litany of mechanistic metaphors – 'charges', 'quantity', 'apparatus', 'system' and the like – in the search for a truly *scientific* psychology. Indeed, the 'Project' is a text that maintains the hopes and ambitions of positivism throughout, modifying the logic in operation at every point in which psychical life resists classification; squeezing the heterogeneous flux of desire, with Freud's characteristic relentless determination, into the design of an established scientific world-view. Freud's deep conviction that the psychical dimensions of human experience are open to codification by science is itself subject to repetition throughout this text: with further modification to or tinkering with the system, sure knowledge lies around the next corner. In fact, even in the *Outline of Psychoanalysis*, written during the last year of his life, Freud expresses the hope that the psychoanalytic contribution to knowledge may one day 'exercise a direct influence, by means of particular chemical substances, on the amounts of energy and their distribution in the mental apparatus'.[14]

However, it is now time to assess the central tension in Freud's work – a tension which runs throughout the 'Project' – between rationality and knowledge on the one hand, and imagination and fantasy on the other. This specifically modernist tension is inscribed in Freud's division of psychical functioning between reality, logic and the pleasure–unpleasure series. A number of important problems arise at this point. What, exactly, is the relationship between imagination and reality? What is left of imagination after the subject perceives an 'indication of reality'? How do energy quantities shape psychical qualities? And is this a process of translation, or of mediation? Freud's answer to this dilemma, as we have seen, is that energy, as the life-blood of imagination, marks, structures, and indeed invades in mental disturbance, the functioning of the psyche:

> Wishful cathexis carried to the point of hallucination and a complete generation of unpleasure, involving a complete expenditure of defence, may be described as 'primary psychical process'. On the other hand, those processes which are only made possible by a good cathexis of the ego and which represent a moderation of the primary processes may be described as 'psychical secondary processes'. It will be seen that the sine qua non of the latter is a correct exploitation of the indications of reality and that this is only possible when there is an inhibition on the part of the ego. – We have thus put forward a hypothesis to the effect that, during the process of wishing, inhibition on the part of the ego leads to a moderation of the cathexis of the object wished-for, which makes it possible for that object to be recognized as not being a real one.

The objectivistic consequence of this description is one that derives from Freud's formalistic separation of imagination and logic, a separation in which imagination is subordinate to reason. Freud stamps the ideology of the Enlightenment on to this mapping of the psyche by insisting that an indication of reality is constituted when thinking is divorced from the processes of imagination – an 'inhibition of the process of wishing'. Let it be noted, however, that there is nothing in this description which accounts for the transformation of psychical energies into ego inhibition and discrimination; a difficulty which is all the more compounded by Freud's uncoupling of consciousness from imagination in this passage.[15] Note too, there is nothing in this perspective that suggests why excessive energy should overwhelm the subject in such a manner as to produce permanent memory traces.

But Freud maintains throughout the 'Project' that the question of subjective meaning is an economic or quantitative one. For Freud, the quantitative build-up of tension is the pure point of energetic origin in the constitution of psychic functioning. However, as Paul Ricoeur has argued, the relation posited between 'quantity' and 'quality' soon outstrips itself, taking Freud's deterministic hypothesis in the 'Project' to breaking point. In this respect, the question which arises is this: what brings 'quantity', or energy, *into relation* with 'quality', or psychic meaning? Demonstrating the difficulty of coming to grips with this question, within the energetic framework posited in the 'Project', can be done by considering the nature of fantasy and, for our purposes here, especially the founding of fantasy. The construction of fantasy, as various traditions in psychoanalytic theory make clear, involves the child in perpetual image-constructions of its world. Fantasies are constituted through a transcription of the tension of biological need into the representational 'expression of wishes and passions', to invoke Isaacs' definition.[16] What this means is that when a longed-for object (initially the maternal breast) is found to be missing (through, for example, the unavailability of the mother), the child hallucinates it in its absence. In doing so, the breast is represented – and actually experienced – in fantasy, even though the mother is not present in material reality. Now, even from the points raised thus far, it will be clear that there are immense conceptual difficulties in fleshing out the structure of fantasy in terms of the quantitative model offered in Freud's 'Project'. What emerges most strongly, perhaps, is the impossibility of assigning some energetic origin to something, namely fantasy, which posits an object both as existing and as non-existent – the founding fantasy is in itself a kind of 'playing' with the unavailability of the mother. What this seems to suggest is that, in making something out of nothing, in the creation of a mental image, the psyche is located in an imaginary function which exceeds anything suggested by the quantitative aspects of Freud's theory.

What is in question, in other words, is the whole concept of the representational dynamics of energy itself. The representational status accorded to the psyche in the 'Project' is that of the registration of perceived reality, of the perceptual apparatus. Perceptual stimulation, in the charging of neurones, is at the root of the construction of psychic reality and of fantasies. (This proposed intersecting of reality and imagination is further expanded in a letter to Fliess in which Freud comments that fantasy is 'derived from things that have been heard but understood [only] subsequently' – a formulation to which Freud adds that 'all their material is, of course, genuine'.)[17] In these proto-psychoanalytical formulations, fantasy is viewed by Freud as a reproduction of something already perceived, an integration of elements which have been pressed into the internal world from elsewhere, whether the outside world (that is, of 'things heard') or the neuronic system itself (through the discharging of energy). Backing away from the glimpses of the creative and dynamic nature of the unconscious that he had had in his clinical work, it is as if

Freud is anxious to be done with the problem of subjectivity, experience and meaning. Fantasy in this view is a derived, or secondary, phenomenon. Yet it is precisely in the realm of fantasy, in the fantastic creations of the unconscious imagination, that the psyche outstrips biological need as well as the imprint of external reality.

The seductions of psychoanalysis

It is with the 'Project for a scientific psychology' that Freud first maps the psychical world, a world of free and bound energy, hallucinatory wish-fulfilment and delayed thought, disruptive affect and amassed excitation. As regards the erotic powers of unconscious imagination, this account of the psyche is to provide a skeletal structure for Freud's subsequent theoretical formulations on repression and defence, on the drives, on the primary process mechanisms of condensation and displacement, and on the timelessness of infantile wishes. The 'Project' is thus Freud's response, as a first approximation, to the problem of the turmoil of primitive mental life upon perception and thought. It is a model that offers an access route to the distinctive features of normal mental functioning – that is, the inhibition of the primary process in the separating out of hallucination and perception. This separating out, or reality-testing, is what secures planned action or agency in the intersubjective world – imagining, perceiving and reasoning is how the human subject gathers its bearings. But it is also a model that recognizes the seductive power of instant gratification and hallucinatory wish-fulfilment – the hallmarks of the unconscious. It is a model that encounters the uncompromising and distorting realm of repressed desire; a conceptual structure that trades with terrifying hallucinations and traumatic inhibitions (a trade informed by the pathogenic experiences of the hysterics Freud encountered in the fashioning of psychoanalytic treatment). The 'Project' is therefore rooted at once in observed reality and theorization. It presents a path which leads from the physiological substrata of the mind, which enters and travels through the troubled waters of unconscious affective life, and which then returns to the conceptual shores of scientific certainty – or, at least, this would have been so had Freud completed the text.

However, within this framework it is actually impossible, as we have seen, to think about the productive work of the psyche, the creative indetermination of imagination and thought. The profound tension here is that Freud's 'Project' uncovers and brings to light the powers of imagination (hallucinatory wish-fulfilment and ego-inhibition frame the discontinuity of human subjectivity), while simultaneously denying the full-force of desire in the name of science, rationality and objectivity. Freud reaches towards the self-instituting capacity of unconscious imagination, yet caught up in the established mastery of science, he displaces this element in favour of the psyche as a black box of energetic inputs and outputs. What this brings into focus is the incompatibility, within the cultural, historical and scientific context of Freud's world, between imagination and science, desire and objective knowledge. And yet, as the 'Project' itself demonstrates, the subordinate place that the imagination occupies to reason refuses to be contained; it comes to invade and outstrip the colonizing power ascribed to rationality. The disruptiveness of the primary process in this text works in part, then, to derail the language of science – resisting the enframing and classification to which it has been submitted.

It is for this reason, perhaps, that Freud was to abandon the 'Project', failing to request the return of the manuscript from Fliess (to whom it was dispatched for criticism), and also omitting any mention of it in his autobiographical writings. The 'Project' can therefore be understood to function as a displaced text, a kind of founding act of repression in the constitution of psychoanalysis itself. From this point of view, it can be said that Freud banishes the 'Project', a text scarred by the scientific world-view of the late nineteenth century, in order to respond more effectively to his discovery of the unconscious imagination. Indeed, this banishment functions as a powerful form of liberation for Freud. For it was precisely at this point of his career that Freud abandoned his 'seduction theory' – the notion that every neurosis conceals a history of real sexual seduction and actual trauma – and replaced it with a more critical interpretation of the relation of psychic life to the outer world. Central to this shift in Freud's approach was a radical revaluation of the internal processing of external reality, and especially of how individuals interpret, frame and fantasize experience (including memories of sexual experiences in childhood). Retracting his seduction theory, Freud wrote to Fliess of his 'certain insight that there are no indications of reality in the unconscious, so that one cannot distinguish between truth and fiction that has been cathected with affect'.[18] But if the unconscious fantasy life of the individual is not merely a copy of objective reality, then this significantly increases the autonomy of the imagination in its dealings with the social world. As John Toews comments:

The collapse of the seduction theory in the fall of 1897 was marked by a collapse of Freud's confidence in his ability to use evidence from his patients' fantasies in reconstructing the real history of event sequences . . . [B]ut this collapse was transformed into a 'triumph' by his recognition that fantasies might be read a different way, as signs of the unconscious intentions that produced them rather than as the forgotten events to which they referred. From this perspective the 'embellishments' and 'sublimations' of fantasy were not so much outworks to be demolished as obscure revelations of a different kind of truth, the truth of unconscious psychical activity. They were openings into a hidden world of 'psychic reality' that was not passive and objective but active and subjective, a world of unconscious psycho-sexual desire.[19]

Once Freud granted fantasy an active and subjective dimension, therefore, the psychic realm no longer functioned as a mirror to objective reality.

'Freud democratized genius by giving everyone a creative unconscious',[20] writes one commentator of this recasting of the process of psychic investment. But what emerges in Freud, throughout various formulations and explanations, is a conceptual recognition of the location of desire that outstrips even this 'active' or 'subjective' component of fantasy. This amounts to saying that Freud's uncovering of the creative unconscious is at once imperative and displaced, given that it is precisely this fantasmatic dimension of human experience that captures the impasse between the inside and the outside, between the troubles of the life of the mind and the troubles of the social world. It is central in so far as Freud takes unconscious fantasy as the stake of meaning, deconstructing the radical otherness of the sense-making process, all the way from moral prohibitions to psychological disturbance. Dreams, of course, provide Freud's key reference point here in the attempt to put desire in its proper place; not merely in the sense of explaining desire and its difficulty away, but also in understanding the ambiguity and undecidability of wish-fulfilment in its encounter with the primary processes of condensation, displacement and distortion. Seen from this angle, the attachment of meaning to experience can be traced to unconscious wishes and intentions, and this for Freud forms part of the detective work of psychoanalytical practice.

There is, however, another Freud, sometimes explicit, sometimes less so, on the limits of psychoanalytical interpretation. This is the Freud who questions the nature and limitations of scientific knowledge within Western culture, and, in particular, it is the Freud who locates a hidden world of unconscious impulses and fantasies as dislocating the scaffolding of psychoanalysis itself. This emphasis stresses that scientific knowledge, even in the sphere of psychoanalysis, cannot provide protection from anxiety as regards living with the turbulence of desire. It cannot protect from anxiety because of the matchings and misalliances of passion and knowledge, fantasy and rationality, which inevitably recur, and which also mark the impossibility of limiting the space of psychoanalytic interpretation. That is to say, desire at once confers and exceeds meaning, locating the human subject at a point of otherness which is both ecstatic and intolerable. Consider, for example, Freud's comments on the 'blind spot' of dreams, a point that is always-already beyond the control or mastery of any shared, intersubjective knowledge:

> We become aware during the work of interpretation that . . . there is a tangle of dream-thoughts which cannot be unravelled and which moreover adds nothing to our knowledge of the content of the dream. This is the dream's navel, the spot where it reaches down into the unknown. The dream-thoughts to which we are led by interpretation have to, in an entirely universal manner, remain without any definite endings; they are bound to branch out in every direction into the intricate network of our world of thought.[21]

In other words, the creative unconscious (branching out in all directions of mind and world) is that which plays tricks with explanation and rationalism.

The domain of imagination, as I emphasized earlier, was never fully integrated with the core suppositions of psychoanalytic theory – it was left by Freud as a kind of splitting or rupture of the inside and the outside. The balance of this inside/outside dualism tipped in different directions throughout Freud's career, and I have previously connected these strands of thinking to a modernist and postmodernist Freud on the powers and limits of the human imagination.[22] Freud, the modernist, is forever attempting, implicitly or otherwise, to enframe and master the laws of psychic processes, to lock the radical otherness of unconscious experience within the determinable. From this angle, the inventor of psychoanalysis is in the last resort colonizing the realm of desire and of pleasure in order to know it, to make subjectivity more manageable. The 'seduction' of trauma, the 'secret' of dreams, the 'sway' of reality over the pleasure principle, the 'phylogenesis' of Oedipal rivalry: psychoanalysis revolves around creating conceptualization, classification and boundaries. And yet Freud's metapsychology also works against itself, acknowledging the limits of science in favour of fantasy and the imagination. Representation, symbolism, hallucination, fantasy, omnipotence of thought: Freud refuses the human subject an easy relation to itself or the outside world. Questioning the enlightened values of the scientific tradition, this is the Freud who speaks of the fantastic creations of the unconscious imagination, of the 'dark continent' of feminine sexuality, of the uncanny in sexuality and in language, and of psychoanalytic interpretation as interminable.

Something similar goes on in contemporary psychoanalysis. The creative power of unconscious fantasy is at once embraced and denied within a range of psychoanalytic traditions, as if the split in Freud between knowledge and imagination is condemned to repeat itself. The key strands of psychoanalysis that attempt to understand something about the self-instituting dimensions of fantasy range from the libertarian Freudianism of Herbert Marcuse, through the Kleinian and post-Kleinian tradition (with its strong emphasis on creativity and the aesthetic process), and are now perhaps best represented in the French psychoanalytic feminist work of theorists such as Julia Kristeva and Luce Irigaray. Here there is the explicit attempt to think of fantasy as a realm of indetermination, as central to a certain state of human relatedness, a generative space in which the capacity for feeling and thought develops, and the primary basis for the transformation of human relationships.

There is, however, another strand in post-Freudian psychoanalysis which has sought to reduce the space of radical imagination in subjectivity and the social process. Sometimes this has been quite explicitly addressed to the stakes of knowledge and self-mastery, especially in the American school of ego-psychology which tends to side-step questions of sexuality and desire in order to upgrade the powers of the ego along the normative paths of rationality and social adaptation. Sometimes it has also been done in more radical schools of psychoanalysis – Lacanian theory, for example, flirts with a structuralist advocacy of the colonizing role of language in the constitution of desire, a standpoint which arguably displaces many of Freud's core insights into the creative figurability of fantasy and sexuality. Whether expressed in the name of rationalism or structuralism, however, the underlying aim here is the attempt to oppose knowledge and structure (as objective reality) to subjectivity and fantasy; and to wipe out the creative, self-instituting realm of representation and passion in which subjectivity and history interweave.

Pushed to an extreme, this reintroduction of reality leads to a rigid externalization of psychical space – that is, back to Freud's 'seduction' hypothesis that psychic process mirrors objective reality, pure and simple. And, indeed, this is precisely the charge that Jeffrey Masson makes against Freud – challenging him on rejecting the actuality of seduction in favour of fantasy and the Oedipus complex – in his book *The Assault on Truth: Freud's suppression of the seduction theory*:

> By shifting the emphasis from an actual world of sadness, misery, and cruelty to an internal stage on which actors performed invented dramas for an invisible audience of their own creation, Freud began a trend away from the real world that . . . is at the root of the present-day sterility of psychoanalysis and psychiatry throughout the world.[23]

The act of fantasy or memory for Masson is instead one that recalls real experience and actual trauma; there is, as it were, a one-to-one correspondence between the trauma of abuse or seduction and mental disturbance. Yet it is exactly this point of 'correspondence' – or, more accurately, the wish for a direct fit between mind and world – that reveals most forcefully the distorting element in Masson's discourse. Without in any way denying the devastating psychic and social consequences of child abuse and trauma, it seems to me that Masson's rejection of fantasy is made in the name of establishing certitude and transparency. It is as if Masson believes that subjectivity, once stripped of fantasy, can operate without ambiguity and ambivalence; a uniform, standardized communication can take place between self and society; and mental disturbance or illness can be seen as the result of similar or identical instances of actual trauma. Seen in this light, as Jeffrey Prager writes of the contemporary attack on Freud and psychoanalysis:

> Masson [expresses] nostalgia for a pre- (or early) Freudian world . . . a world where things are precisely as they appear, always reflecting a hard, obdurate reality that can be easily and readily perceived. No interpreting self, no unconscious one. What happens happens, and there is no mystery as to how one processes, interprets, and gives meaning to those occurrences.[24]

The relation between imagination and rationality documented thus far has been primarily considered from a psychoanalytic perspective. We need, however, to consider the broader social, cultural and political influences shaping the core features of the imaginary in the contemporary epoch. We also need to consider the impact of specialized, expert knowledge upon the domain of imagination, and of the pathologies this produces.

The psychologization of desire

Perhaps the best way to approach the broader sociological implications of the foregoing argument is to consider the linkage between the origins of psychoanalysis and modernity. One prominent interpretation points to the erosion of authority and community in the light of the waning of tradition, custom and habit. Such a viewpoint is perhaps best expressed in the writings of Philip Rieff.[25] Rieff argues that psychoanalytic theory and therapy become 'culturally appropriate' with the shift from traditional 'positive communities', which anchored belief-systems and symbols in stable social networks of custom, family and religion, to 'negative communities', in which individuals create meaning in terms of their own personal experience. In premodern societies, when people were in pain or distress, they sought meaning from the certainties of cultural tradition, habit and religion. Positive communities might thus be said to have created their own therapeutic order. Modernity, as a post-traditional order, offers no such guarantees as concerns personal doubts and anxieties. In conditions of modernity, self and society are in greater flux, and hence there is a turn inwards towards private, emotional experience. 'In the age of psychologizing,' Rieff writes, 'clarity about oneself supersedes devotion to an ideal as the model of right conduct.'[26]

Psychoanalysis becomes of crucial cultural significance, according to Rieff, because it forms a central connecting point between dislocating outer experience and the creation of inner meaning. In Rieff's terms, psychoanalysis emerges at a point of cultural 'deconversion', a time of breakdown in frameworks of meaning, of startling social transformations and dislocations. With this erosion of tradition, and most importantly religious authority, Freud's search for meaning in dreams, wishes, desires and fantasies was a radical counter-assertion of human possibility and hope. In a world of dislocation, uncertainty and change, psychoanalytic theory and therapy create an openness to the multiplicity of modern experience, offering the possibility of meaning and well-being. As Rieff puts it, psychoanalysis offers the individual a chance 'to keep going'.

The analysis set out by Rieff is of considerable critical power in terms of grasping the ways in which the cultivation of self-under-standing, and of intimacies of the self, emerge against the backdrop of the dislocations and uncertainties of the modern social order. Indeed, in recent formulations of this dynamic, it is often argued that, in the post-traditional order of modernity, self-revision or reflexivity is in-trinsic to the constitution of self-identity and intersubjective social relations.[27] In terms of the opening out of the personal sphere, psy-choanalytic theory and therapy can be said to offer individuals a radical purchase on the dilemmas of living in the modern epoch. From such a standpoint, it can be said that the subject is split, but crucially this is a splitting open to self-understanding. There is little in this account, however, to question the way an awareness of the more productive elements of imagination, and of unconscious imagination in particular, should have become open to cultural transmission at this historical point. Rieff's analysis seems to imply a causal connec-tion between the breakdown of tradition and the rise of psychoanaly-sis. But why psychoanalysis? Why was this conceptual map created to represent people's experience of subjectivity, sexuality and meaning? Is the turn inwards, of which Rieff speaks, merely a matter of the weakening of cultural tradition?

Unquestionably, reflexiveness relating to intimacies of the self is a highly personal matter, and there is an enormous variety of psycho-logical approaches and schools from which people might choose today. However, the core importance of therapy, psychoanalytic or otherwise, does not relate primarily to issues of personal choice. Rather, it relates to the self-awareness of human imagination, and the structuring role of fantasy in personal and social life. Rieff is led to obscure the decisive role of psychical imagination in the domain of culture by privileging social transformation, practice and ideology. Yet the actual practice of 'psychoanalysis' or 'psychoanalytic therapy' can surely be brought into existence only if the discoveries of Freud, as founding-father, hold up, and can withstand critical examination. All of which is to say that psychoanalysis comes to depend more and more on criteria that are internal to its own legitimation – that is, the recognition of the structuring role of fantasy.

In analysing the rise of psychoanalysis and therapy in modern societies, Rieff is undoubtedly correct to stress the central role of rapid social change in the fracturing of human experience. In the midst of an ever-expanding globalization of the social environment, tradition no longer supplies binding cultural prescriptions, and selfhood as such becomes intrinsically problematic. By means of psychoanalysis and therapy, people can find a new language for addressing, and thereby coming to terms with, private dilemmas. For Rieff, however, this correspondence between the loss of tradition and the rise of therapy appears as culturally structured and fixed: psychoanalysis functions essentially as a substitute for traditional moral, political and religious guidelines. Without severing its relation to social transformation, however, we should also see the emergence of psychoanalysis as part and parcel of the modernist attempt to embrace imagination, to uncover the contradiction and conflict of human passion. Understanding the development of the self in modern societies, and particularly its problematization, should focus on the imaginary capacities for self-representation and self-construction through which individuals express and transform themselves. In this view, psychoanalysis is not simply a social fabrication, but a creation of imagination and fantasy as well. We can thus supplement Rieff's account by highlighting that psychoanalysis plays a crucial role in the modern epoch in uncovering the presence of psychic processes hidden from awareness. The virtue of such an approach is that it underscores the point that it is the creative power of the unconscious imagination which underpins this searching of our innermost hopes and dreads.

In political terms, however, there is more at stake here than just personal and cultural self-understanding. Not only does modernity promote an uncovering of reflexiveness as concerns human subjectivity and the radical imagination, but this reflexiveness is itself embedded within a discourse of science and expert knowledge. That is to say, reflexiveness does not exist in a vacuum; it is situated rather in psychological, cultural and political networks. And it follows from this that such reflexiveness can also be drawn into, and indeed fuel, asymmetrical relations of power. This embedding of reflexiveness in asymmetrical relations of power is a central component of a discourse that I call the *psychologization of desire*. By the psychologization of desire, I refer to those institutionalized aspects of specialized knowledge in the sphere of human sexuality. Doctors, social workers, psychologists, psychiatrists and indeed many psychoanalysts (when analysis is practised reductively) trade in the isolation, classification and consolidation of a cohesive code of sexual rules. In ideological terms, the driving force here is the quest for sure knowledge: it is thanks to expert psychological insight that the 'right' or 'wrong' approach can be applied to troubled relationships in the home, schools, business, bureaucratic organizations and government agencies. Psychological expertise offers reassurance against the insecurities of living. Psychological know-how is also regularly used to keep at bay personal and cultural ambivalence, as the problems of daily life are recast within a fixed, technical vocabulary.

Surprisingly, Rieff has little to say about this rationalization of psychoanalytic knowledge. He does, as was stressed earlier, credit psychoanalytic therapy with supplying new personal and cultural guidelines in the late modern age. With the opening out of the personal sphere, psychoanalysis and psychotherapy become less centred around normative issues of a cure, and more and more a matter of self-actualization. Yet the prospects for self-actualization are deeply constrained, both from within and from without psychoanalysis. Rieff acknowledges that the professionalization and routinization of therapy have softened the critical edge of psychoanalysis, and have produced a 'boredom' within psychoanalytic societies. Yet Rieff fails to consider that the independence of psychoanalysis, at the levels of theory and of clinical practice, has often proved incompatible with the authority of specialized knowledge in the psychological professions. For this reason alone, much that is vital and alive in psychoanalysis has declined into dogmatism. These are issues which I now wish to consider in some detail.

To comprehend this psychologization of desire, we have to move away from an exclusive concentration on the sociology of modern societies, and look to the structuring of fantasy and power in the modern era. Consider, for example, the creation of psychoanalysis, and its embedding in modernity's institutional dynamics. Freud, as we have seen, uncovered the connections between self-identity and unconscious sexuality in a revolutionary way; revolutionary because it led men and women into a reflexive encounter with the condition of subjectivity as fractured, split and ambivalent. At the same time, Freud anchored psychoanalysis within a medical discourse of science – the design of which, I have suggested, sought to effect a subordination of inner nature to human control, order and mastery.

This preoccupation with desire as subordinate to the world of scientific knowledge and power has also taken place as regards the cultural, institutional development of psychoanalysis. Once more, it is fairly easy to trace out the interplay of anxiety and denial, insight and repression, which pervades the ideological function of psychoanalysis in modern societies. Against the backdrop of Freudian psychoanalysis, people seek to explore their deepest intrapsychic experiences and personal relationships – an exploration which is underwritten by the creativity of the unconscious imagination. The Freudian revolution is, in this sense, a revolution of the personal sphere; an opening out of the self to anxiety and ambivalence. This infiltration of Freudian psychoanalysis into the everyday social world, however, also brings it directly into contact with those institutional dimensions of specialized knowledge and power. In many instances, this contact has led to a deadening of psychoanalysis as an open-ended system of meaning; and also to a routinization in the application of its theoretical and conceptual resources. There has taken place a marked self-containment and fixation of Freudian concepts, as psychoanalysis has increasingly become a world unto itself. The reduction of psychoanalysis to a medical, mechanistic treatment of behaviour pathologies, seen as a method for adapting the individual to an objective, knowable reality, became widespread within the psychoanalytic movement, especially in the United States. Indeed, many psychoanalysts still understand the aims of clinical technique in such terms. On the other hand, and especially in France, psychoanalysis has been pulled in a highly abstract direction. In France, psychoanalysis became increasingly divorced from its founding concern with representation, fantasy and passion, and instead was projected into the academic discourse of philosophy, being read as a dislocation of theoretical knowledge itself. Sherry Turkle expresses the differences between these cultural, institutional appropriations of psychoanalysis well:

> In the story of what happened to psychoanalysis in the United States, the fact that the 'American Freud' was nearly monopolized by physicians, a social group under the greatest possible pressure to emphasize the useful, took the general American preference for the pragmatic and raised it to a higher power. In France, the psychiatric resistance to psychoanalysis allowed it a long period of incubation in the world of artists and writers before a significant breakthrough into medicine, a pattern which reinforced the French tendency to take ideas and invest them with philosophical and ideological significance instead of turning them outward toward problem solving.[28]

These cultural differences, between 'useful' and 'abstract' appropriations of psychoanalysis at the institutional level, have more in common than is often supposed – or, at least, this is the case as concerns the issue of expert knowledge. For both American and French appropriations of psychoanalysis, despite differences of content, express an overriding emphasis on control: in the case of American psychoanalysis, control over behavioural adaptation; in the case of French psychoanalysis, control over the metatheorization of the life of the mind.

The process of psychologization that I am describing here is but a variant of, in Michel Foucault's terms, the power systems of an 'apparatus of sexuality', one of the most unrelenting forms of domination and social control, as it transforms polymorphous sexualities into culturally routinized prohibitions and permissions pertaining to pleasure.[29] Foucault's provocative studies of the connections between discourse and sexuality capture well the sense of fixity prompted by the more normalizing forms of psychoanalysis detailed in the foregoing paragraphs. Pre-existing types of sensual pleasure, says Foucault, become 'sex' as the creation of discourses about it – such as medical texts, therapeutic books, self-help manuals and the like – bring about an ordering of 'normal' and 'pathological' sexual practices. The subject, according to Foucault, is not 'sexed' in any meaningful sense prior to its constitution within a discourse through which it becomes a carrier of a natural or essential sex. As Foucault puts this:

> the notion of 'sex' made it possible to group together, in an artificial unity, anatomical elements, biological functions, conducts, sensations, and pleasures, and it enabled one to make use of this fictitious unity as a causal principle, an omnipresent meaning: sex was thus able to function as a unique signifier and as a universal signified.[30]

As such, sexuality has as its focus the manipulation of the body, a manipulation that disguises and extends the power relations that connect domination directly with the individual subject.

For Foucault, sex infiltrates and controls everyday pleasure, since the self-awareness of the individual as a subject of sexuality is the result of a forgotten coercion and subordination to power–knowledge networks. The production of 'sex' as a category is the end result of the mystifying organization of power–knowledge relations. As Foucault writes of this intrinsic link between sexuality and expert knowledge:

> In the family, parents and relatives became the chief agents of a deployment of sexuality which drew its outside support from doctors, educators, and later psychiatrists, and which began by competing with the relations of alliance but soon 'psychologized' or 'psychiatrized' the latter. Then these new personages made their appearance: the nervous woman, the frigid wife, the indifferent mother – or worse, the mother beset by murderous obsessions – the impotent, sadistic, perverse husband, the hysterical or neurasthenic girl, the precocious and already exhausted child, and the young homosexual who rejects marriage or neglects his wife . . . [C]aught in the grip of this deployment of sexu-

ality which had invested it from without, contributing to its solidification into its modern form, the family broadcast the long complaint of its sexual suffering to doctors, educators, psychiatrists, priests, and pastors, to all the 'experts' that would listen.[31]

This process of psychologization, though, is in some ways even more alienating than Foucault's characterization suggests. For what is psychologized, and hence appropriated, by modern institutions is an awareness of the creative, dynamic realm of unconscious fantasy itself. The self-instituting force of imagination is translated and experienced as part of the iron grip of expert, psychological systems on knowledge. Desire has moved out of the domain of the self and into the institutional realm of laws and regulations; it is thus projected into something outside and other.

In Foucault's terms, the issue of a translation from fantasy to the institution as such is perpetually deferred, since the sexualized subject is always the product of subjection to power – a 'deployment of sexuality which had invested it from without'. Yet, what is it that frames this 'without'? What elements of fantasy, desire and affect are invested in systems of knowledge and power? How does the human subject experience expert systems as colonizing knowledge affecting personal relationships? How is psychoanalysis experienced as a delivery system of expert knowledge on sexuality, love and intimacy? These questions, so important to an adequate understanding of the relations between self and society, touch upon some of the core issues relating to the self-understanding of imagination in the contemporary era. Of crucial importance in this respect is the uncovering and denial of unconscious fantasy.

Modernity, fantasy, denial

Let us, then, rethink the relation between modernity and imagination, in a way that seeks to establish a psychopolitical link between the recognition and denial of fantasy. A driving concern with the fantasy life of the individual, with feelings, passions, wishes, fears and anxieties, as well as with the question of the delimitation of the psychic, emerges as intrinsic to modernity. This delimitation of the psychic is, in large part, an outcome of the transformation from premodern to modern cultures; a transition which, as seen by Rieff, emerges out of a loss of community and a softening of the boundaries between the private and public spheres. With the breakdown of tradition and the dissolution of meaning, the self turns inward. Yet there is more to this delimitation than sociology alone. The turn towards the 'inner life' of the subject, to psychic interiority, is itself attained through the activity of the unconscious imagination, and can be understood as a creative rewriting of the historical trajectory of modernity. It is a rewriting of the social-historical process in so far as it facilitates thinking, at once personal and social, of the *contingency of self and society*. Richard Rorty writes:

> Freud suggests that we need to return to the particular – to see particular present situations and options as similar to or different from particular past actions or events. He thinks that only if we catch hold of some crucial idiosyncratic contingencies in our past shall we be able to make something worthwhile of ourselves, to create present selves whom we can respect.

This uncovering of the particularity of unconscious fantasy and sexuality (analysed by Freud in terms of energy, pleasure, anxiety and repression) provides for self-knowledge of the constitutive role of human ambivalence, and promotes an engagement with psychic and sexual life.

The analysis in this chapter of Freud in the stream of modernity, however, has also shown that the instituting power of fantasy has been correspondingly neglected and repressed, in theoretical discourse and as part of modern social activity. As regards theory, it has been argued that there is a fundamental tension in Freud's thought between the creative power attributed to unconscious fantasy on the one hand, and a desubjectifying tendency which displaces imagination to the confines of rationalism, objectivity and scientificity on the other. Freud's thinking about the psyche takes place on these two distinct axes, which results in the radical power of unconscious imagination being at once discovered and expropriated, uncovered and denied. So too, the difficulties of ambivalence are side-stepped, or displaced, in whole sectors of contemporary culture. What I have called the *psychologization of desire* arises directly out of this repression of awareness of the profound fantasization of all personal and social life. In such instances, fantasy has lost its intrinsic connection with self-institution, as a central focus for 'experience', and instead is brought under the control of technical knowledge and rationalism. The connection to psychical imagination is lost in the sense that matters concerning fantasy, sexuality and intimacy are projected, and experienced, as part of the orderly, rationally structured domain of psychological and psychoanalytic expertise. The problem may lie within (at the level of the psychic), but it is a condition from which escape is sought from without (at the level of the social).

As regards the psychologization of desire, one can agree with Foucault that the pathologization of sexuality is constituted, and reproduced, by the expansion of power–knowledge systems. Discourses of science – especially psychological expertise – produce subjects by manufacturing the conditions and operation of sexuality, of normalization via the differentiation of sexual practices. This is achieved through the material inscription of discourses into social procedures and regulations which frame 'sex' and 'sexuality', and which constitute the way in which people forge self-awareness of their place in the sexual field. Yet this process of manufacturing sexual identity is much more of a psychical drama than Foucault recognizes. The self is both subject to power systems, such as discourses of the 'person' and 'sex', and engaged in responses to such classificatory operations through imagining, fantasy and in-depth reworkings of psychical organization. Unlike Foucault, then, I think that psychological repression is produced not only as the normalization of sexuality, but also as the sexualization of normalizing power. The trials of sexual prohibition are highly fantasized settings.

Paradoxically, this sexualization of normalization works to reinforce the principal dualisms of the modern era, such as the split between the psychological and the social, norm and anomaly, rationality and imagination, objectivity and fantasy. Certitude as a strategy of survival is central to the symptoms of modernity. Yet not only subjectivity is at stake here. The modernist aims of ordering and enframing, which destroy the alterity of self and society, penetrate theoretical knowledge and, crucially, psychoanalysis itself.

3

The Epic of Mastery

Modernist Edges of Fantasy

> But cleverness becomes meaningless as soon as power ceases to obey
> the rules and chooses direct appropriation instead. The medium of the
> traditional bourgeois intelligence – that is discussion – then breaks
> down. Individuals can no longer talk to each other and know it: they
> therefore make the game into a serious and responsible institution
> which requires the application of all available strength to ensure
> that there is no proper conversation and at the same time no
> silence.
>
> Max Horkheimer and Theodor Adorno

The modernization and postmodernization of social and political
processes is characterized by widespread cynicism about knowledge
and rationality. Today, in a globalizing, culturally cosmopolitan society, knowledge brought about by expert decision-making and institutions (knowledge that is largely dominated by technoscientific
rationalization) is no longer equated with increasing mastery and
control of the social order. In fact, to the contrary, the advance of
technoeconomic modernization is increasingly equated with the production of risks, hazards and insecurities on an unprecedented global
scale. Put more accurately, technological knowledge and control of
the social world today are as much about managing socially produced
risks and dangers which are worldwide in their consequences as
about unbounded mastery in the service of political domination. The
awesome destructive power of nuclear weapons, global warming, the
pollution of the earth's ecosystems, the rise of totalitarian nation-
states, overpopulation: these are some of the broad contours of risk
and uncertainty in the late modern age.

Recognizing this, some have recently suggested that reflective
awareness of the problematic consequences of technical knowledge

actually enters into, and profoundly shapes, our attempts to control and master processes of social change. This awareness is that of the emergence of 'reflexivity', and it is connected in an essential way to the development of modernity. The purpose of this chapter is to analyse such reflexivity. The chapter will critically examine two influential accounts of this increased reflexivity in contemporary societies – that of Ulrich Beck and Anthony Giddens. My argument is that, while the notion of reflexivity as elaborated by Beck and Giddens captures some of the basic dilemmas now faced in personal and cultural life everywhere, it fails to account for the new dialectics of fantasy and globalization, repression and power, in the late modern age. Accordingly, I propose a different interpretation of reflexivity – one that provides a detailed treatment of the place of fantasy in linking reflexivity and power relations. Since I want to situate my discussion of reflexivity in the context of changing relations between fantasy as a political factor on the one hand and the expert-systems of science and technology on the other, I have selected to discuss at some length Western responses to the Bosnian war. The aim of this discussion is to elucidate some of the affective, fantasmatic significations that framed the social conditions of the West's institutional reflexivity or discourse on Bosnia. In the concluding section of the chapter, I consider some of the general issues raised by the issue of reflexivity in relation to autonomy as regards the modernization and post-modernization of politics and society.

Modernity as risk and reflexivity

In his *Risk Society: Towards a new modernity* (1992), Ulrich Beck argues that contemporary social life creates new parameters of risk and danger which we must face as individuals and collectives. According to Beck, we are today witnessing not the final breakdown of the Enlightenment, or a transition to some postmodern social universe, but instead modernity coming to terms with itself – its *radicalization*. Beck argues that the technoscientific development of contemporary societies in the West has now developed to the point where humankind is released from traditional constraints of the natural and social worlds. The development, says Beck, opens the social landscape in the widest possible sense to a systematic questioning and critique of modernization. History is today being rewritten, as it were, backwards: problems resulting from technoeconomic development are increasingly subject to reflexively infused systems of action aimed at preventing, minimizing or reordering the unintended, destructive effects of industrial modernization.

What are the contours of risk in advanced modernity? Beck acknowledges that the notion of risk can be applied to all forms of social organization. Yet risk in the late modern age, he says, becomes fundamental to the reflexive ordering of social life itself. Of central importance in this respect is the impact of globalization. The globalization of social institutions radically intensifies risk, transforming local happenings into contexts of global danger. Thus the panic selling of shares on the New York stock exchange has implications for the entire global economy, from local retail trade to the international division of labour. The risks of modernization, says Beck:

> possess an inherent tendency towards globalization. A universalization of hazards accompanies industrial production, independent of the place where they are produced: food chains connect practically everyone on earth to everyone else. They dip under borders. The acid content of the air is not only nibbling at sculptures and artistic treasures, it also long ago brought about the disintegration of modern customs barriers. Even in Canada the lakes have become acified, and forests are dying even in the northern reaches of Scandinavia.[1]

Globalization thus creates risks which transcend boundaries of space and time. The distribution of risk, from the destruction of rain forests to nuclear calamities like Chernobyl, dislocates national, temporal and spatial boundaries.

Significantly, Beck contends that the opening out of risk to every niche of society is deeply interwoven with the restructuring of politics, and in particular the management of *political consequences*. In industrial societies, risk calculation operated through the logic of the 'insurance principle'. The insurance principle, says Beck, was an effective means of legitimizing the immensely productive, yet nevertheless very destructive, forces of modernization. The welfare state and company insurance were prime instances of risk institutions aimed at reducing, in some sense, the catastrophic consequences of industrialization. In contemporary societies, however, the advent of globalized risk changes all this. The insurance principle collapses, as globalized risk threatens irreparable and incalculable damage which cannot in principle be limited. 'Along with the growing capacity of technical options', writes Beck, 'grows the incalculability of their consequences.'[2]

It is against this backdrop of a diminishing protection in the realm of social organization that modernity becomes reflexive. In a post-traditional order, Beck argues, existing modes of thought and action are pushed into the open: justifications have to be given, and compromises have to be reached, in negotiating the boundary between self and society. The key principle of the risk society, says Beck, is reflexivity: the emergence of institutionalized scepticism as regards new information or knowledge, which itself radically undermines the certainty of knowledge. Such reflexive scepticism, produced by modernization, is increasingly evident in science, technology and bureaucracy, as well as in the sphere of politics. Thanks to science and technology, in particular, new risks and hazards can be discovered, confronted and coped with – especially as concerns those risks which are 'invisible' to the naked eye, such as AIDS and technoepidemic illnesses produced through the pollution of water and food. For on a personal and social, as well as a global level, the statistical calculation of risk – governed by the logic of reflexivity – is constitutive. The condition and outcome of reflexive modernization is an increasing awareness about the social landscape of risk, which in turn helps to define and reshape the nature of risk and the ways in which it is reacted to in advanced modernity.

In the late twentieth century, a world of intensified reflexivity is a world of people reflecting upon the consequences of their action, in both the personal and social domains. The spread of reflexivity, says Beck, is grounded in the development of *individualization*: sources of meaning derived from tradition become increasingly open to interrogation or discourse, and are reformed in such a way that the individual has to live with a broad variety of personal and social risks *as* an individual. This opening out of individual identities to choices, opportunities, dangers and ambivalences occurs as a more or less continuous reflection on the conditions of social activity. Such a situation depends upon the information-processing abilities of individuals and collectivities, a phenomenon that Beck links to the increasing focus on knowledge and education characteristic of our lives today. 'The more societies are modernized,' Beck writes, 'the more agents (subjects) acquire the ability to reflect on the social conditions of their existence and to change them in that way.'[3] In other words, the more modernity reflects on itself, the more agency breaks from traditional structures. In Beck's account of reflexive modernization, then, the status of the subject is conceived of as in some sense autonomous, as personal and social identities are actively discovered, constructed and refashioned through a reflexive engagement with the outside world.

The recent work of Anthony Giddens also underscores the reflexive ordering of the social institutions of modernity, and of the vital role that risk assessment plays in the contemporary era. In *The Consequences of Modernity* (1990) and *Modernity and Self-Identity* (1991), Giddens develops a comprehensive analysis of the relations between self and society in the late modern age, in all its fullness of opportunities and dangers. 'The reflexivity of modern social life', writes Giddens, 'consists in the fact that social practices are constantly examined and reformed in the light of incoming information about those very practices, thus constitutively altering their character.'[4] Reflexivity, according to Giddens, should be conceived as a continuous flow of individual and collective 'self-monitoring', a monitoring in which due recognition is given to the contingency and ambivalence of social life today. As Giddens puts this:

> To live in the 'world' produced by high modernity has the feeling of riding a juggernaut. It is not just that more or less continuous and profound processes of change occur; rather, change does not consistently conform either to human expectation or to human control. The anticipation that the social and natural environments would increasingly be subject to rational ordering has not proved to be valid. The reflexivity of modernity is bound up in an immediate way with this phenomenon. The chronic entry of knowledge into the circumstances of action it analyses or describes creates a set of uncertainties to add to the circular and fallible character of post-traditional claims to knowledge.[5]

The experiential character of contemporary daily life is well grasped by two of Giddens's key concepts: *trust and risk* as interwoven with *abstract systems*. For Giddens, the relation between individual subjectivity and social contexts of action is a highly mobile one; and it is something that we make sense of and utilize through 'abstract systems'. Abstract systems are institutional domains of technical and social knowledge: they include systems of expertise of all kinds, from local forms of knowledge to science, technology and mass communications. It is important to note here that Giddens is underscoring much more than simply the impact of expertise on people's lives, far-reaching though that is. Rather, Giddens extends the notion of expertise to cover 'trust relations' – the personal and collective investment of active trust into social life. The psychological investment of trust underlies specialized, expert knowledge, and it also plays a key role in the forging of a sense of security in day-to-day social life.

Trust and security are thus both a condition and an outcome of social reflexivity. Giddens sees the reflexive appropriation of expert knowledge as fundamental in a globalizing, culturally cosmopolitan society. While a key aim may be the regularization of stability and order in our identities and in society, reflexive modernity is, however, radically experimental, and is constantly producing new types of incalculable risk and insecurity. This means that, whether we like it or not, we must recognize the ambivalence of a social universe of expanded reflexivity: there are no clear paths of individual or social development in the late modern age. On the contrary, human attempts at control of the social world are undertaken against a reflexive backdrop of a variety of other ways of doing things. Consider the example Giddens offers in relation to global warming:

> Many experts consider that global warming is occurring and they may be right. The hypothesis is disputed by some, however, and it has even been suggested that the real trend, if there is one at all, is in the opposite direction, towards the cooling of the global climate. Probably the most that can be said with some surety is that we cannot be certain that global warming is *not* occurring. Yet such a conditional conclusion will yield not a precise calculation of risks but rather an array of 'scenarios' – whose plausibility will be influenced, among other things, by how many people become convinced of the thesis of global warming and take action on that basis. In the social world, where institutional reflexivity has become a central constituent, the complexity of 'scenarios' is even more marked.[6]

The complexity of 'scenarios' is thus central to our engagement with the wider social world. And it is reflexivity, according to Giddens, that influences the way in which these scenarios are perceived.

The split subject of reflexivity

The theory of reflexive modernity, outlined in different ways by Beck and Giddens, involves a radical reconceptualization of the relations between self and society. The theory breaks from orthodox sociological versions of subjectivity and agency, where a self-identical subject unproblematically confronts a stable object-world; yet it also rejects the post-structuralist critique of the 'decentred subject', of a subject thoroughly fragmented in and through language. Instead, the theory of reflexive modernity proposes that self and society interconnect in a global context of manufactured, institutionalized *uncertainty* – uncertainties that are confronted and coped with through a reflexive tracking of knowledge and information. The reflexivity of contemporary social life consists in a complex interplay between human action and systems reproduction, such that the links between self and society are reordered as a continuous process. Late modernity – with its technoscientific rationality, its restructuring of tradition and history, its mass media, its separation of time and space – introduces into the very heart of social life the means by which social frames of action are constantly monitored and reconstructed in the light of the instantaneous global communication of information and knowledge. Beck and Giddens thus emphasize, rightly in my view, that reflexively organized ways of doing things – in matters of sexual relationships, health, diet, work and the like – are open, in turn, to ongoing reconstruction. The contingency of our reflexive involvement in social life is such that there can be no 'expert of experts' as concerns personal choice; rather, the filtering of reflexivity into social life means that individuals more or less have to recognize other possible forms of life in the course of their everyday actions. This is the case even in those 'private' domains of personal life, including therapy and counselling of all kinds, where emotions count strongly. In this connection, therapy is a kind of internal expert-system utilized and drawn on in the refashioning of the self. Therapy is a form of 'life-planning', deployed for the reflexive reordering of personal decision-making.

However, what is not so clear is that this interweaving of self, society and reflexivity breaks with certain assumptions of high, Enlightenment modernity. Beck and Giddens may offer a path towards thinking personal and social reflexivity as a process of 'detraditionalization', but the thread of this approach remains caught within a modernist prism that grants metaphysical privilege to rationality, unified selfhood and emancipation. In this respect, Scott Lash and John Urry have argued that the work of Beck and Giddens is profoundly constrained in its particular concentration on the cognitive dimension of reflexivity.[7] By this criticism Lash and Urry mean to focus on the attributions of cognitive capability and agency in the theory of reflexive modernity; an attribution which they believe implicates human agency in an almost cybernetic-like functioning, and further results in a neglect of the affective–aesthetic sources of the self.

Let us consider this point about reflexivity in its subjective dimension in more detail.

For Beck, the driving expansionism of reflexivity is connected to the steering of rationality in line with contemporary risks. This process forces men and women to take control over aspects of their lives that previously were left to traditional conventions or the institutionalized forms of simple modernity. Advanced modernity spells the end of such external anchoring, however, and necessitates personal decision-making of a radical kind. Arenas of life – such as gender and the family – are opened up to reflexivity in the sense that decisions are subject to 'assessments of risk', calculations concerning the flattening or deepening of personal life and life-style options. The development of reflexive rationality is thus tied to a heightening of individualization, theorized as the increasing capacity to think about and make deliberative choices as regards risk.

Yet Beck, in typical sociological fashion, is little interested in the psychical processes which frame the links between the cognitive and the affective, rationality and desire. This, however, does not mean that Beck has no time for rethinking the state of the subject in reflexive modernization. What it means, rather, is that he attempts to reconfigure the relations between self and society in strictly sociological terms, locating the inner depths of subjectivity as fully structured by wider institutional transformations. As Beck observes: 'Who is the subject of reflexive modernization? The answers here vary: individual and collective agents are the primary subject of reflexive modernization or scientists and ordinary people, institutions and organizations, all the way to structures.'[8] Yet the key difficulty here, especially as regards the individual and the private sphere, is that no adequate account can be given of how the human subject comes to make sense of the social transformations being described. That is to say, there is little room accorded to the transformative power of subjectivity – of fantasy, drive and affect – in the signifying stakes of reflexive modernization.

Giddens, by contrast, offers a more complex picture of the subjective capacities that underpin reflexivity. Processes of reflexivity, says Giddens, imply the attainment of 'ontological security', a formed sense of continuity which is essential for any self-monitoring of risks and opportunities. Drawing upon the object-relational psychoanalysis of Erik Erikson and D.W. Winnicott, Giddens argues that ontological security is grounded in trust relations – relations constituted at the level of unconscious communications which relate infant and prime caretaker. From the early days of life, the forging of core emotional connections with parental routines, and especially routine modes of handling absence, are vital to the formation of a framework of self-experience and ontological security. Giddens views Winnicott's notion of 'transitional objects' as of key importance for understanding the psychical shift from omnipotent fantasy to the recognition of other persons; yet he gives this notion an idiosyncratic inflection by tying it to routinization as the basis for an ordered and consistent sense of self-identity. 'These first "not-me" objects', writes Giddens, 'like the routines with which they are virtually always connected, are both defences against anxiety and simultaneously links with an emerging experience of a stabilized world of objects and persons.'[9] An early involvement with routine activities is itself held to constitute a sense of basic trust and ontological security; and such trust in the continuity of objects and persons functions to screen out anxieties and fears which erupt at the level of the unconscious. Trust, then, brackets unconscious dislocation; it provides a kind of 'emotional inoculation' against anxiety. Significantly, this reworking of the object-relational view of trust and self-continuity is pivotal to Giddens's account of the links among trust, reflexivity and modernity. For trust, according to Giddens, is not only invested in interpersonal relationships – that is, in the realm of face-to-face interaction. Trust is also invested into the abstract systems of modernity: abstract-systems such as money, and expert-systems which produce technical knowledge.

There are, however, important limitations in Giddens's interpretation of object-relational psychoanalysis and, more generally, the psychic relations which link self to other. To begin with, Giddens uses object-relations theory as a conceptual resource for explicating reflexive self-continuity and self-mastery. While such a focus on the formation of the ego is fundamental to the object-relational revision of Freudian theory, what is not so clear is that the realm of the unconscious – of anxiety and repression in particular – can be done away with so conveniently. Giddens speaks of transitional routines as 'bracketing' or 'screening off' unconscious anxiety. Yet, as I have argued elsewhere, Winnicott's work (upon which Giddens relies) actually underlines the split and divided nature of self-experience – itself an outcrop of unconscious sexuality.[10] Whereas Giddens sees transitional space as a kind of learning process that results in familiar and predictable routines, Winnicott views it as a lifelong dialectical exploration of inner and outer worlds, of the tensions of self/other, sameness/difference, anxiety/play, and the like. Moreover, having obliterated the subjective weight of unconscious desire, Giddens's contention that trust provides protection from anxiety is open to the charge that it is a conceptual translation of an imaginary wish for continuity and sameness. That is, although ego identity might appear as a development away from the unconscious, it is in fact always implicated in the functioning of the 'primordially repressed', the self emerging as a distortion of unconscious fantasy itself.

This last point returns us to a different understanding of object-relational psychoanalysis, one that was discussed in some detail in chapter 1. The internal world of fantasy, the heterogeneous passions and anxieties of the unconscious, at once structures and dislocates the self–other boundary. Unconscious fantasy, whilst framing the contours of self-experience, continually transgresses the boundaries and distinctions of self and other: through projective identification, fantasy is inserted into the other as a means for both exploring difference and maintaining the self. Such an interpretation of fantasy and the unconscious also has something in common with the Lacanian understanding of the unconscious as the 'discourse of the Other', as well as commonalities with French psychoanalytic feminism. What all these perspectives share, in contrast to Giddens's recasting of the self as ego-mastery, is a strong emphasis on the split and dislocated nature of self-experience.

These conceptual limitations in Giddens's approach also carry important consequences for understanding the nature of social reflexivity. Giddens's conceptualization of social reflexivity, as previously noted, concerns the 'filtering' or 'monitoring' of information about the conditions of activity as a means of continuously restructuring what that activity is. Yet, when viewed in the light of the foregoing psychoanalytic ideas, a range of difficulties inevitably arises. In the first place, if reflexivity is constituted only through 'monitoring', then how might human beings come to understand the complex, contradictory affective sources that also influence and shape their social activity? What, exactly, are the links between the cognitive ordering of reflexive rationality and the frames of desire and passion which underpin contemporary cultural forms? What of the connections between the unconscious, reflexivity and collective autonomy? And if it is recognized that repressed desire is, in certain respects, built into reflexive social practices, then how might this affect our understanding of personal and social autonomy?

When it is claimed that there has been a dramatic increase in the scope of reflexivity in social life, this implies that: (1) social systems and social contexts of action have come under the sway of reflective decision-making and agency, and (2) social-historical change is produced in and through self-monitoring and self-interpretation. But it might be just as well to ask something about the kind of knowledge and social practice that is placed under the microscope of contemporary reflexivity. Who, for example, could make an analysis – even according to the logic of resource maximization and cost–benefit modes of thinking – between money spent on fashion design in the West and the financial amount needed to reverse the dramatic climatic changes associated with global warming that threatens our survival? Who could devise a reflexive option between the money that anonymous bureaucracies spend on surveillance technologies and the amount that might be needed to reverse the proliferation of nuclear and chemical weapons? At this point, the notion of reflexivity as the monitoring of information reaches its limit. This, however, is not to say that processes of reflexive rationality do not pose serious challenges to scientific authority and political forms of hierarchical domination. Rather the problem of power and ideology comes to the fore in addressing issues of risk in contemporary societies, and the implications of these issues need to be traced out. Reflexive rationality, as Michael Rustin has argued, is connected to power in ways that social theory cannot afford to ignore. As Rustin puts this, 'an alternative possibility is that "knowledge" is becoming more exclusively the property of the particular interests it serves'; reflexive knowledge that is deployed 'in a world which is dominated by intense concentrations of power'.[11]

Fantasy and reflexive turbulence: an alternative view

In the light of the foregoing criticisms, I want to propose a different interpretation of reflexivity – an interpretation that provides a more differentiated account of the subjective dimensions of reflexivity in both the personal and political domains. Reflexivity, in my view, should be conceptualized in terms of the structuring and dislocation of the self–other boundary that I sketched in chapter 1. In this respect, reflexivity is conceived of as the outcome of a dialectical interplay between paranoid-schizoid and depressive modes of subjectivity and intersubjectivity, an interplay that underlies attendant transformations of social, cultural and political life.

Recalling Kleinian and post-Kleinian conceptualizations of psychical organization that I discussed in chapter 1, the depressive mode is the principal medium through which reflective subjectivity is attained and the richness of reflexive rationality is generated. The depressive mode of subjectivity is the world of whole object relations: experience of self and other develops in relation to loving and hating feeling-states, an ambivalence of emotion that forms the basis for a creative engagement with the outside world. This reflexive awareness of emotional ambivalence brings with it the capacity to feel concern and guilt about the fate of other persons. For Kleinians, the origins of depressive anxiety and depression are tied to such an awareness of envy, hate and guilt; an awareness which gives rise to an affective process termed 'reparation'. In this view, the capacity to feel guilt and pain is interwoven with a fear that envy and rage have, to a large degree, damaged or destroyed another person about whom one cares. In response to such fear, fantasies of reparation represent an unconscious attempt to recapture the imagined goodness of the other person, to bring the relationship back to life, and to protect self and other from further unacceptable aggressive and destructive wishes. The depressive mode of generating interpersonal experience is therefore one that operates in the service of containment: the 'holding' or 'containing' of intolerable fantasy and anxiety coupled with efforts at managing ambivalence as regards the discontinuities of interpersonal experience.

Otherness, as constituted within the structure of subjectivity, is of key importance in this respect. The depressive process – and all its operations that bear upon reflexivity – can be thought of as involving the eruption of an otherness at the heart of the self and of its internal objects. In attempting to struggle against the pressure to destroy this otherness, as well as the noxious affects generated by it, the depressive process opens the self to a relational world in which unacceptable feelings and thoughts can be confronted, thought about and reconstructed. Reflexive knowledge is thus generated not only through a monitoring of subjective awareness (as implied by Beck and Giddens), but as an encounter with the anxiety of managing ambivalence in both personal and relational terms.

Yet we need also to look at that mode of psychical organization which depression reconstructs: the paranoid-schizoid mode. A useful starting point can be found if it is recalled that the paranoid-schizoid mode of generating personal and interpersonal experience is considered more primitive in the Kleinian approach than the depressive mode. It is more primitive in the sense that it is highly defensive as regards the management of psychic pain. In the paranoid-schizoid mode, the psyche is a battleground of love and hatred, a constellation of such powerful affects that it is as if the subject can manage such feelings only by splitting and isolating them into either good or bad.

Splitting defensively translates a disappointing experience into a 'bad object', such that loving and hating aspects of the self are experienced at the removed distance of 'good' or 'bad' objects.

In the paranoid-schizoid mode, personal and interpersonal experience is generated through the defensive use of omnipotent thinking, idealization, denial and, crucially, projective identification. In this way, a powerful affective state of self-sufficiency is reached, but only at the cost of rigid and alienating internal object relations. It must be stressed, however, that this realm of tyrannizing paranoid-schizoid experience is not sealed off from processes of reflexivity. On the contrary, here lies a central domain of generative cultural experience, and a key defensive component in the social reproduction of knowledge and of reflexivity.

In sum, then, reflexivity can be grasped as an interplay of paranoid-schizoid and depressive modes of symbolizing and processing human experience. The depressive mode, as a symbolically elaborate and complex form of processing, operates primarily in the service of containment, of the exploration of difference and otherness. The influence of the depressive mode on intersubjective and social relations lies in the holding of a psychological space between reality and fantasy, the capacity to generate and recognize transitional space. The paranoid-schizoid mode, by contrast, is symbolically more primitive, and primarily operates through splitting as a means of generating experience. Subjective and intersubjective experience in a paranoid-schizoid mode is predominantly fragmented and discontinuous; the splitting of self and objects presses for, and in some part represents, the evacuation of psychological pain into something outside and other. Yet such changes from depressive to paranoid-schizoid modes of generating experience, and also from paranoid-schizoid to depressive states, are vital to creative living in the personal and social domains. This is a crucial theme of this book. The paranoid-schizoid mode and the depressive mode fuse to produce a dialectic of experience: paranoid-schizoid turbulence breaks up the closures of thought and affect reached in the depressive mode, just as depression serves to negate the psychic dislocations of pure loving and pure hating.

Reflexivity, however, is seriously impaired, in the viewpoint I am proposing, when depressive modes of generating experience and managing psychological pain fully collapse into paranoid-schizoid defences of excessive splitting, omnipotent thinking, and denial. The unleashing of omnipotent fantasy, when operationalized through projective identification, permits an imagined 'control of the other'.

Object relatedness in this mode is brittle and thin. Through splitting and denial, other people can be ruthlessly treated as objects, devoid of feeling and subjectivity. In attempting to control the other through the omnipotent use of fantasy, which involves an evacuative method of dealing with psychological strain, self and object are increasingly split and disconnected. Paranoid-schizoid splitting thus functions in and through fantasies that distort self–other boundaries: the projection of fears and anxieties into the other permits the expression of unmanageable feelings, an expression directed towards an imaginary 'outside'. Here lies the domain of distorted intersubjective communication, or of the influence of the paranoid-schizoid mode of generating experience upon reflexivity, and it is now necessary to relate such reflexive turbulence to a wider appraisal of social and political processes.

Technoscience, power, mastery

In the institutional arena, the expert knowledges of large organizations – with their bureaucratic hierarchies – are constituted, according to Weber's portrayal, through social rationalization. Bureaucracy for Weber harnesses scientific rationalism to modern organizational demands for mastery; and indeed it is this theorem of 'rationalization' that informs Weber's analysis of the problem of 'world disenchantment'.

The rationalization view of bureaucracy advanced by Weber grasps some core aspects of contemporary 'instrumental' relations between social institutions and discourses on the one hand, and the internal beliefs and values of human subjects on the other. We need today, however, also to consider the fetishizing of the formal organizational arena; or of what might be termed the autonomization of science and technology. For the constant rationalization of technological resources gains much of its impetus from the impersonal and mostly purpose-orientated imperatives of expert, scientific knowledge. The application of technological know-how to social problems, according to Jacques Ellul, is done because it is done. That is to say, the legitimation of technology has become self-propagating: social and political priorities are increasingly determined by expert-systems reporting on the feasibility of technological capacities, from DNA and the genetic code to cyberspace and the information superhighway. As Ellul comments:

Technology never advances towards anything because it is pushed from behind. The technician does not know why he is working, and generally he does not much care. He works because he has instruments allowing him to perform a certain task, to succeed in a new operation ... There is no call towards a goal; there is constraint by an engine placed in the back and tolerating any halt from the machine ... The interdependence of technological elements makes possible a very large number of 'solutions' for which there are no problems ...[12]

Expert skills and resources are considered expert in this conception only when subjective and psychological variables have been reduced to a minimum.

The debilitating, rigid fantasmatic structures of contemporary technoscience have been analysed with great lucidity by Cornelius Castoriadis. Technoscience for Castoriadis embodies a fantasmatic illusion of omnipotence – the illusion of mastery. 'With technoscience,' writes Castoriadis, 'modern man believes he has been granted mastery.'[13] Yet this mastery, as illusion, is no more than *pseudorational* in character. The one-dimensional, goal-orientated purposes of technological know-how are informed by 'social imaginary significations' of power, control and mastery. A very precise speculative proposition follows from this – namely, the *supraindividual process of technoscience*, as something that happens and makes things happen. The pursuit of technological mastery is a journey into the fantasmatic realm of control and power, where vulnerability and pain are magically sidestepped.

Significantly, it is precisely such fetishism for 'rational mastery' which grants science, technology and administration its own legitimation. The destination of technoscience is a declaration beyond the political and ethical realms; in practical terms, a realm which it colonizes so forcefully, technoscience pushes towards a brutal and ruthless celebration of the 'can do', the so-called technological fix. As Castoriadis observes:

Who among the proponents of technoscience today really knows where they want to go – not from the standpoint of 'pure knowledge' but with regard both to the kind of society they would wish to live in and to the paths that will take them there? ... This path – quite paradoxically, considering the amount of money and effort being expended – is less and less that of the *desirable* in any sense, and more and more that of simply the *doable*. We do not try to do what 'would be necessary' or what we judge 'desirable'. More and more, we do what we can, we work on what is deemed doable in the approximate short term.[14]

The doable thus becomes equated with the rational, and that in turn is equated with the goal-effective.

Expert organizational knowledge, as Ellul and Castoriadis powerfully disclose, is to some considerable degree a closed system of fantasmatic illusion. This illusory realm of the technological fix is characterized by fantasies of power, control, mastery and omnipotence. Defined in such a way, expert-organizational knowledge poses significant problems for personal and social autonomy.

Situated in the context of reflexivity, technoscience and expert systems (when operating as closed systems) encourage a shift away from the dialectical interplay of depressive and paranoid-schizoid modes of generating experience in favour of psychically defensive forms of splitting, denial and omnipotent thinking. At this level of distorted intersubjective communication, technological resources are sliced away from communal ends, and the prime imperative is simply 'to do something'. That 'something' which must be done, and which is experienced culturally as a kind of drive to action, serves to wipe out anxiety – of ambivalence, of alternative social possibilities, of the fragility of knowledge. In Freudian terms, such a translation into action occurs as a traumatic injunction, indifferent to personal and social fears, anxieties and tensions. The domain of the superego, we have entered the Law of modernity.

Excursus: on Bosnia and the otherness of fantasy

In August 1992, the mass media relayed a series of images around the world of the deathly, inhuman conditions in which Muslim prisoners were being held in Serb detention camps in Bosnia-Herzegovina, images which disturbed and outraged the Western world. Despite evidence that the Bosnian Serbs had for months been pursuing a policy of 'ethnic cleansing', these haunting images of barbed wire and bare ribs galvanized Western nations and international organizations into strenuous debate as to how best to save the Bosnians from institutionalized political terror. As Yugoslavia disintegrated, and against the backdrop of policy assessments that the defence of Bosnia was not a major security or geo-economic interest, Western policy makers sought to apply diplomatic pressure against the warring ethnic communities – the Serbs, Croats and Muslims. Yet such attempts to negotiate and compromise with the warring parties in Bosnia did amount to 'direct intervention' from the international community. As Marko Prelec has observed:

> The West, of course, did intervene, but not in the manner the Bosnians hoped for. The international community did nothing to protect them from the genocidal warfare waged by the Serbs, now known as 'ethnic cleansing'. Instead, led by the UN, the West launched a two-pronged effort, aimed at providing humanitarian relief and brokering a negotiated solution.[15]

In what follows I want to discuss some of the psycho-political dimensions relevant to this 'two-pronged' Western institutional response to the Bosnian war. My discussion will directly draw on ideas discussed in earlier parts of this book, especially the relation between fantasy and reflexive rationality. There are a number of key issues that will be addressed in this respect. What were the inherent contradictions in Western policy responses to the Bosnian war? What shaped the Western fascination with the disintegration of Bosnia, and what led to the psychic fantasies that framed responses to the horrific images of terror in Bosnia? Among the multiple points of cultural reference, how were these images related to a wider appraisal of global politics? It seems that they certainly led to an eruption of feelings of intense discomfort as to our political, moral and historical identity, but did they not also pertain to a deeper, repressed truth of the contemporary social order?

Psychoanalysis and the issue of violence: identification, guilt, death

One of the most astonishing aspects of Western institutional responses to the war in Bosnia was the sheer speed with which political apathy was reversed, denial switched to moral condemnation. In the first few months of the war, Western governments had given the crisis relatively little attention. For example, it had been reported by the United Nations that seventy-five people had been killed on average each day in Bosnia during the first four months of the war – a total of nine thousand human beings.[16] Yet this horrific statistic attracted little media, or public, attention. Conversely, within twenty minutes of the television reports of the atrocities in Serbian detention camps, President Bush publicly stated that the USA would urge for a United Nations resolution authorizing the use of force to end the conflict. Meanwhile, the popular press began reports about 'murder camps'

and 'factories of mass death' in Bosnia, thus redrawing events as a
historical rerun of the Nazi period. Such media discourse on mass
death underlined the point that the Serbs' policy of 'ethnic cleansing'
had turned Bosnia into a state of terror. Against this backdrop of
public outrage and a media discourse of 'totalitarian genocide', Western governments attempted to frame their institutional responses,
largely through the United Nations and NATO.

How did this media focus on 'death camps' serve as the basis for a
wider collective perspective on the war in Bosnia? It would seem that
the media, in focusing on the brutalities of the detention camps,
reawoke certain collective horrors, or what Christopher Lasch has
called our 'public obsession' with mass death, and with the Holocaust
in particular.[17] Psychoanalytic theory can be used to provide a theoretical and political context here. By condensing the war in Bosnia into
a discourse of totalitarian genocide, the mass media evoked a structuring point of identification. What this means, essentially, is that
people were given something – an image – with which to forge an
identification; an image which was invoked for the constitution of a
collective identity (the West) that is outraged at the sufferings of
people in Bosnia. (The fashioning of this identification around images
of totalitarian genocide was not, of course, without its limitations –
and I shall discuss shortly the complex ways in which these disturbing
images framed, and indeed constrained, modes of reflecting upon the
political implications of the war in Bosnia.) At this point, however,
what must be underlined is that the media images of terror in the Serb
detention camps condensed the crisis in such a manner as to engage
collective sympathies and affective concerns, the prime movers of
identification. For as Julia Kristeva has argued, identification is a
central psychical mechanism for constituting cultural and political
relations in a cosmopolitan globalizing order: 'It is not simply –
humanistically – a matter of our being able to accept the other, but
of being in his place, and this means to image and make oneself other
for oneself.'[18] The distressing images of maltreatment in Bosnia, I
suggest, permitted the West to put itself in the place of what was
other.

However, identification involves more than sympathy. In psychoanalytic theory, identification is understood – and this is fundamental
– as a complex *structure of ambivalence* which constitutes human
subjectivity; an ambivalence with respect to the object itself. But
what, then, is the nature of this ambivalence? For the late Freud, the
one of *Beyond the Pleasure Principle*, this ambivalence connects to a
profound sense of guilt, an inner guilt which springs from the conflict

between the life and death drives (of *Eros* and *Thanatos*) and which then fuels the acting out, or projection on to others, of aggression and hate. Like the shaping of ambivalence in the Oedipus complex, the intense feelings of love and hatred towards parental figures, identification is itself part of a complex interplay of life and death forces. The death drive, or primary aggressivity, leaves mutative effects on psychical structure. As that which cannot be represented, Freud's erotic, deathly repetitious unconscious cuts deeply into human relationships, leaving guilt in its wake. The hateful feeling-states generated by the death drive – destructive, fearful, guilty, empty – are so painful and discomforting that they are, in turn, subject to denial.

To move from the death drive back to Western responses to the war in Bosnia might appear a somewhat tenuous link. Yet there are important connections here. How, for example, might the unconscious dynamics of ambivalence, guilt and repression have shaped the West's identifications with the political and cultural destruction of Bosnia? If identification is always deeply coloured by affects of hate, then what was the ultimate condition of the West's sympathy with the others of Bosnia? And, crucially, if the concept of the death drive bears directly on this issue, how did such fears and anxieties influence institutional responses to ethnic conflicts in ex-Yugoslavia?

In a social frame, Freud argued that modernity destabilizes the dialectic of the life and death drives, of *Eros* and *Thanatos*, turning the latter back upon itself through repression. On one level, then – and this aspect of Freud's thought is more commonly known – culture works to repress our violent feelings of hatred and aggression. On another level – and, I think, a deeper one – Freud suggests that our erotic, death-bearing unconscious is disseminated within the technical framework of modern institutions. In this connection, Freud suggests that the death drive is subject to distortion and displacement, returning in the form of nameless dread. Freud ties this nameless dread to social and political relations time and again when considering the nature of death, war and aggression. In his 1915 essay 'Thoughts for the times on war and death', Freud traces the psychical forces which led to the eruption of hatred and conflict in the First World War. His conclusion is that modern culture extracts a devastating repression from human beings, leading women and men to 'live psychologically beyond their means'. Significantly, Freud claims that modernity squeezes to the sidelines our psychological relation to death. This displacement, he suggests, is ramified by the unconscious, which disowns recognition of death due to the absence of contradiction in the primary processes. Thus, our relation to death is denied at a psychical level and, in turn, is shunted away from general view in the social-historical world. From this angle, Freud focuses upon war as recovering a repressed truth of modern culture; a truth that forces subjects to confront their prime fears and anxieties concerning mortality. For Freud, the recovery of a reflective relation to death is of prime importance in the refashioning of the individual and of society and culture.

The persistent problem in this respect, however, is that culture weakens and disarms our capacity for self-knowledge. Our unconscious sense of guilt, rooted in the repressive, political structuring of the life and death drives, tends to outstrip our capacity for self-reflection. Thus the dreaded, destructive powers of war, which force a confrontation with the social and technical frameworks that negate mortality, are regularly defused through a denial of guilt in the mind. As Freud writes in *Civilization and its Discontents*: 'It is very conceivable that the sense of guilt produced by civilization is not perceived as such . . . and remains to a large extent unconscious, or appears as a sort of malaise, a dissatisfaction, for which people seek other motivations.'[19]

So too in object-relational and Kleinian versions of psychoanalysis, the status of cultural dehumanization is linked to guilt projection: the denial of an inner guilt which is then projected on to the other. In the language of interpersonal psychoanalysis, however, guilt projection is linked more centrally to the emergence of an unmanageable reality – to the issue of knowledge of ambivalence, conflict and fluidity. The basic question here is not so much whether individuals and collectives are able to undertake the difficult work of mourning in response to destructive unleashings of the death drive, as whether they are able to accept a relational world in which both they and others are conflicted over interests and desires, as well as the cultural context in which emotional attachments are regulated. Seen in a negative way, the danger is that a manic attachment to an idealized object will degenerate into an ideological commitment to absolute truth and knowledge. In this context, the absolute (State, God or Cause) filters out awareness of ambivalence in human relationships and cultural association.

On the psychopathology of reflexive expert-systems

'Since Auschwitz,' writes Theodor Adorno, 'fearing death means fearing worse than death.'[20] Western responses to the crisis in Bosnia certainly indicate that a fear 'worse than death' had been tapped. Against an emotional backdrop of nameless dread, the overwhelming Western response to the crisis took the form of denial, in the Freudian sense. Hence the broad reaction: 'The crisis in Bosnia is terrifying and horrible, but nonetheless it does not really affect our everyday life here.' Or, more personally: 'Bosnia is a war of ancient ethnic hatreds, and so I will not let it disrupt my own interpersonal world.'

As regards international policy, the application of reflexive knowledge to the war in Bosnia best typifies key elements of the West's obsessional, persecutory response. Expert-systems monitoring the war, such as the European Community and the United Nations, fashioned reflexively infused knowledge systems concerning ethnic tensions in Bosnia, the unleashing of nationalisms and religious identities, as well as the economic and territorial ambitions of the warring parties – in particular, the carving up and annexing of Bosnia to 'Greater Serbia' and 'Greater Croatia'. Such reflexive knowledge was not merely incidental to Western diplomatic action; rather, Western policy was filtered in and through this reflexive knowledge, and Western diplomatic engagement in Bosnia was, in part, a product of reflexive mediation. Yet the internal form of these reflexive mappings suggests something rather different about the nature of contemporary rationalism. It suggests a ruthless splitting between Western identity and Bosnia as Other, between modernity and the premodern, between rationality and desire, between civilization and primitivism. The international policy debate on Bosnia – staged between the European Community, the United States and the United Nations – was, above all, a discourse of many political and cultural differentiations. These differentiations were played out along the multiple axes of ethnicity, nationalism and democracy. As regards ethnicity, for example, the horrors of Bosnia were continually portrayed as the product of senseless, primeval ethnic passions; a premodern, tribal blood-feud that was refractory to the Western civilized world. Commenting on Western policy debate, Rabia Ali and Lawrence Lifschultz note: 'In the Balkans "ancient hatreds" became the central motif of every cliché. "Their" wars were irrational, insensate, primeval bloodletting; "our" wars were fought for principles – democracy, freedom, God and Free Trade.'[21] Such dichotomy, itself a symptom of paranoid-schizoid splitting, was also expressed by Western policy makers in their labelling of the Balkans tragedy a 'civil war'. Consequently, the issue of responsibility for violence began to dissolve. Approached as participants in a civil war, all three warring parties were equally responsible for the explosion of political terror in Bosnia. Failing to see that Bosnia was a state under attack from Serbian military forces, the Western focus on 'primitive ethnic passions' and 'warring national- isms' served to displace attention from the more generalized disinte- gration of this multinational, cosmopolitan, pluralistic society.

These were exactly the pre-understandings which American foreign policy – under the reflexive, geopolitical discourse of eco- nomic calculation – used to assess the possibilities of Western military intervention in Bosnia. In the USA, the State Department ran cost– benefit analyses of the military options open to the West to stop the Bosnian war. In the face of a military estimate that ran to tens of billions of dollars, and with the collective memory of the foreign policy disaster of Vietnam, the Secretary of State, Warren Christopher, declared in February 1993 that Bosnia was not of 'vital interest' to American foreign policy.[22] Yet in this rendering of reflex- ive foreign policy calculation, the ideological perversion by expert- systems of exactly *what* was at stake is all too clear. The implications of this cost–benefit analysis involved a major displacement of the Bosnian crisis – social, historical and ethical – as impersonal and inhuman. The very horizon of meaning raised by the disintegration of Bosnia – deathly, social destruction – was denied and disowned, thus raising 'dehumanization' to the second power. The moral horror of 'ethnic cleansing' had been neutralized at one stroke through a bu- reaucratic, fetishistic disavowal.

Significantly, such denial reproduced itself in a sort of destructive spiral, ranging from the issue of military intervention to the problem of the arms embargo against Bosnia:

> The debate was remarkable for its narcissism. From afar Bosnians listened in exasperated disbelief. Much of the American intelligentsia, its press, its military, and its politicians were living in a peculiar world all their own. They argued, wrung their hands, and expressed great angst over the question of massive intervention and what it might cost the United States. The last superpower could only conceive of itself being involved on some extraordinary grand scale or not at all. No one took note of the fact that the Bosnians had not asked for massive intervention. Sefer Halilovic, at the time the Commander of the Bosnian Army, repeatedly stated that Bosnia did not want the United States or any other power to deploy its ground forces in the Balkans. The Bosnian request was straightforward. If the United States or Europe would not assist Bosnia in defending its integrity as an integral state or believed they were under no obligation to forcefully deter acts of genocide, then at the very least these Great Powers should cease to

deliberately obstruct the ability of Bosnia to act in its own self-defence. The simple, yet fundamental, maxim of the Bosnians was: If you cannot or will not help, then have the moral decency to cause us no harm.[23]

A good deal of harm was done, however, and it was primarily inflicted by Western policy attempts to regulate, control and administer its peace plan in Bosnia. It is possible to see in Western policy responses, in so far as the guiding ethos was one of 'controlling the other', an extension of political violence into areas imagined as 'external'. Perhaps the single most important factor here was the West's attempt to be an 'impartial mediator' of the peace negotiations, and thus to avoid the ideologically contaminated realm of ethnic and nationalist politics. This fantasy-image of Western 'impartiality' played a key role in the maintenance of the arms embargo against Bosnia, and was at the centre of the division between the deliberations of the UN General Assembly, which voted to lift the embargo in support of Bosnia's territorial integrity, and the UN Security Council, which refused to do so on the grounds that impartiality needed to be maintained.[24] The position of the Security Council was supported strongly by British and French officials, who sought to prevent the USA from taking sides in Bosnia and hence developing a more active policy to support the Bosnian Muslims. (In fact, the British Prime Minister, John Major, warned in 1994 of a 'massacre' if the UN embargo on arms to Bosnia was lifted.) Without pursuing here the difficult question of political support for maintaining this so-called neutrality within the UN foreign ministries, there can be little doubt that this stance was a concrete means of displacing problems relating to Bosnian sovereignty, and of reframing the crisis as that of an internal, fanatical, ethnic conflict.

It should, of course, be noted that Western institutional responses to the war in Bosnia were neither uniform nor homogeneous. At the London Conference in August 1992, for example, the German Foreign Minister, Dr Klaus Kinkel, won support for the establishment of a UN tribunal to investigate Bosnian war crimes. At the conference, Kinkel directly accused the Bosnian Serbs of 'genocide' and 'crimes against humanity'. Shifting the focus from the issue of Western military intervention in Bosnia, Kinkel's proposals sought to encourage the warring parties, and observers worldwide, to reflect on the terrible nature of a whole community saturated in atrocity and grief. Perhaps most importantly, the London Conference explicitly recognized Bosnia's territorial sovereignty. The European Community called for a negotiated solution between the warring parties on the basis of the agreements reached at the Conference; yet the effect of this brokered solution was actually the orchestration of the partition of Bosnia along ethnic divisions. The ethnic partition of Bosnia was carried out under the Vance–Owen plan, which in principle sought to maintain the ethnic and nationalist unity of the Bosnian state by demanding that the Serbs renounce their aspirations for secession and accept Bosnian sovereignty. At the same time, however, a central component of the plan was the division of Bosnia-Herzegovina on the basis of 'ethnic dominance', the international legitimization of assigning a given territory to the largest ethnic community. Seen against the barbaric events of ethnic cleansing, the practical consequence of this blueprint was a settlement that placed the Bosnian Serbs overwhelmingly in control.

It has been said of the Vance–Owen peace plan that it was 'an unworkable attempt to divide the indivisible.'[25] Yet the divisions effected by the Vance–Owen plan, however politically maladroit and morally deplorable, serve to highlight the extent of Western institutional involvement in the Balkans tragedy, and raise the much neglected issue of the underlying fantasy structure of this involvement. For what can be seen here is not only the enforced division of what was previously a multiethnic country, but the carving up of global political space itself, operationalized through a mechanical splitting of identity and difference, of the inside and the outside. The rampant insecurity that pervaded Western policy attempts to control the excessive brutalities of multicultural Bosnia produced such high levels of anxiety, it seems to me, that they could no longer be contained, in the sense of working with the parties to the conflict and thus formulating a coherent international policy for peace in ex-Yugoslavia. Instead, the reflexive encounter with pathological politics, or the re-emergence of fascism, seems to have produced a radical escalation in denial in Western institutional politics and international agencies; denial relating, above all, to the West's involvement and implication in the tragedy of Bosnia. Hence, despite the actual geographic proximity of the Balkans conflict to Europe, a ruthless splitting organized the perception of ex-Yugoslavia as the Other of the West. This was a splitting in so far as it operated to freeze political space, thus opening out to an ideological fantasy that the eruption of 'primeval ethnic passions' was essentially domestic in character, that it was neatly confined within a distant, 'foreign' territory, and that it was indeed alien to the principles of the advanced modern order.

From this angle, the reflexive dimension of the Western response to

Bosnia can also be seen as a modernist enframing of political communication within the logic of mastery and domination. I am speaking of the notion, discussed in the previous section of this chapter, of
the omnipotence of fantasy; and in this particular instance of the
powerful role of fantasy in bending the other (Bosnia) in the
direction of dominant Western geopolitical narratives. One place in
which this can be detected is in the antagonism between Western
representations of 'three warring factions' in the Balkans and the
local understandings of these divisions in Bosnia and Herzegovina.
For it is precisely within this antagonism that Western preoccupations
with warring nationalisms and fanatical passions are revealed as a
symptom in which the deeper issues raised by the Balkans tragedy are
masked. As Renata Selecl has argued:

> it is significant that in [Bosnia] we do not have the usual fantasy
> construction regarding the nation. At the beginning of the war,
> Muslims still organized their fantasy scenario of the homeland around
> the idea of Yugoslavia: they were the only ones who took literally the
> transnationality of the Yugoslav federation and believed in the notion
> of 'brotherhood and unity'. The whole existence of Bosnia and
> Herzegovina was, in a way, a realization of the socialist aim to erase
> the element of the nation from social organization. The Muslims
> persisted in this transnational attitude even after their towns had been
> bombed; they did not want to give him [the Serbs] a national conno-
> tation. Thus at the beginning of the war, the aggressors were referred
> to as 'criminals, hooligans', and only much later were they named
> Chetniks or Serbian nationalists.[26]

But not so Western international politics: the erupting tragedy of
barbaric slaughter and mass rape in Bosnia was framed against the
master narratives of ethnic and nationalist histories. This political
discourse, it should be noted, is not so much wrong as pathologically
particularist: it enlarges the axes of ethnicity and nationalism to a
level of such fixity that the ideological realm is divorced from its
social and cultural context. In doing so, it also brackets issues of
political domination and aggression in Bosnia from the actual impact
of the disintegration of Yugoslavia, as well as associated factors
such as globalization, universal commodification and economic
polarization – matters which, psychically and ideologically, had to
be bracketed from awareness if the crisis was to be successfully
'localized'.

But localized and reshaped it was, with the world's attention
shifting from the underlying causes, as well as the far-reaching conse-

quences, of the Bosnian war to the more 'practical' issues of humanitarian relief and international protection. Hence the tendency of
expert-systems monitoring the war to focus policy around humanitarian issues: air-drop operations, supervising aid distribution, patrol-
ling the convoy routes, and the like. Against such a backdrop of
reflexively shaped international action, the tragedy of Bosnia was
recast as a kind of 'natural disaster'. And once naturalized, knowledge of the political dimensions of the Bosnian war could be refused,
indeed foreclosed. Compassion and sympathy for the victims of
Bosnia became a central organizing position in Western representations and policy.[27] At this point, however, there was a dramatic return
of the repressed, of the anxiety of political violence, as Western
attempts to negotiate peace in Bosnia became hostage to the Serbs. As
Prelec summarizes these obstructions:

> The massive humanitarian relief operation was an object lesson in the
> dilemmas of Western engagement in Bosnia. The UN chose to operate
> only with Serbian consent, giving besieging forces and paramilitary
> units a veto over any particular activity. The Serbs blocked deliveries
> to outlying towns, far from the view of Western media coverage,
> and confiscated about a quarter of everything the UN brought
> into Bosnia ... The Serbs threatened to massacre huge numbers of
> refugees, thus forcing the UN to remove them from Bosnia, com-
> pleting the process of 'ethnic cleansing'. At every step, the Serbs
> extorted compliance with their wishes from the UN by threat-
> ening violence.[28]

Eventually, via many twists and turns, the Western attempt to translate the war in Bosnia into an abstract language of victimization, one
that demanded the international provision of humanitarian relief,
broke down. Significantly, this fracturing of Western mastery brought
with it an unleashing of intolerable anxiety, enunciated at the
policy level in demands for a 'Desert Storm' style rampage into
Bosnia. Military action of this kind was undertaken at several points
in 1994. NATO air strikes, for example, were launched against the
Serbs on their airfields in Croatia in response to Serbian attacks on
the Muslim safe area of Bihac and the threatening of United Nations
forces.

We are now in a position to summarize some of the key features
of Western institutional responses to the conflict engulfing Bosnia-
Herzegovina. The provisional response of Western governments to
the tragedy of Bosnia, in the face of public dismay and moral outrage,
was one of assessing security interests within a tight-meshed bureau-

cratic discourse – that is, the cost–benefit analyses of the military defence of Bosnia's territorial sovereignty. Notwithstanding the conclusions reached by Western governments that Bosnia was not a vital geopolitical or security interest, the connection of expert-systems with the fantasy of mastery and control is quite central. For the omnipotent fantasy of control of the other was integral to the Western splitting of political space (insiders/outsiders, democracy/barbarism, principles/passions), and to the foreclosure of ethical and humanitarian considerations. Indeed, omnipotent thinking and splitting characterize the emotional vocabulary of these preliminary political assessments in that the Other (Bosnia) appears as a force which *impinges* on the West, rather than as a threatened nation-state of the international democratic system. Bosnia, in this sense, quite clearly became a 'bad object'.

It has been noted that splitting, omnipotent thinking and projective identification all form part of an evacuative method of managing psychological strain. Looked at from this angle, Bosnia, in being ejected to the 'outside' of Western political space, was cast as Other, but an otherness that could still be controlled from within. Hence the drama of the demand to find a 'solution' to the Bosnian war, first at the level of a negotiated peace solution, and second at the level of providing humanitarian aid. As a result, the link between symbol (Bosnia) and symbolized (endangering object) operated in a persecutory manner, at once underwriting the ideological fiction of Western impartiality, the anxious insistence that the West was free from the turmoil of the Bosnian war, and informing a translation into action of unbearable fantasy, the NATO airstrikes and military retribution. Such translation of fantasy into action erupted at those points at which Western expert-systems could no longer tolerate the intrusiveness of Bosnia as an object of political danger. Yet the escape into action served only to confound Western attempts at mastery and control, since it served to reinscribe Western international agencies within the moral and ethical issues which had previously been sidestepped.

Mastery, control, omnipotence, translation into action: these modes of paranoid-schizoid processing that informed both institutional reflexivity and international politics had the effect of recasting perceptions of the conflict in ex-Yugoslavia within the same imaginary networks of meaning of which the brutalities of Bosnia are actually a part.[29] This statement may seem excessive; but it is, perhaps, less so when one considers the interconnections between fantasies of mastery and omnipotence and the destruction of freedom, as the denial of cultural multiplicity and difference. Political domination institutes multiplex pathological symptoms, certainly. But it is surely not too fanciful to detect similarities in the fantasy scenarios of a fascist politics which believes it can destroy a whole population (i.e. the mind-breaking brutalities of Serbian detention camps) and a modern bureaucracy which conceals its own functioning under an illusion of omnipotence.

Reflexivity and critical self-reflection

In the preceding sections I have raised a number of critical remarks concerning the theory of reflexive modernity, tracing specific distortions or pathologies in contemporary rationalism. The theory of reflexive modernity, as we have seen, posits a radicalized rationality in social action, interpersonal relations and systems domains. Contemporary experience is intensively reflexive; it is self-transgressive in that it is continually open to internal monitoring, revision and restructuring. Yet it is at this point, in effect, that the theory of reflexive rationality falters, discovering a grave split between the circular and fallible character of knowledge in the late modern age, and the concrete issue of critical reflectiveness and the imaginative capacities of human subjects for creative activity. Critical social theory, I suggest, needs to retrace this split in contemporary rationalism, in the hope of pressing through the calculating reflexivity of self-monitoring to somewhere on the other side. From such an angle, reflectiveness will still be of capital importance, but at a 'higher' level: reflectiveness *as* imaginative, critical activity. It is at this point, I want to argue, that social and cultural theory must undertake a more systematic analysis of the notions of reflexivity and social transformation, of rationality, self-reflection and the imagination.

To what extent is a social and political reconstruction of reflexivity possible? How might it be possible to place modes of reflexive rationality under individual and collective self-determination? For contemporary critical theorists like Jürgen Habermas, the utopian outlines of a social condition beyond the calculating self-reference of technological knowledge and expert-systems is to be found in the intersubjective structures of communicative rationality.[30] Such a communicative dialogue is at the basis of our personal and social interest in the reflexive, discursive ordering of truth and knowledge. Communicative rationality thus bears an internal relation to the critique of ideological and political domination. Yet the question of the possibility of reflectiveness, I want to argue, goes much deeper than this. It is not a matter of undoing the internal dross of communicative dialogues; or, as Habermas is fond of saying, of making the unconscious conscious. For one of the fundamental conditions of critical self-reflection lies precisely in those points of impasse or indeterminacy of desire and the unconscious imagination. Reflectiveness, then, is not only a realm of cognitive, discursive intersubjectivity. Reflectiveness presupposes – and this is crucial – the creative dimensions of imagination, passion and desire.

A different conception of the relation between reflectiveness, knowledge and autonomy is required in order to assess critically the potential pathways of late (or post-) modernity. A conception is required which enables us to break with theoretical standpoints which idealize abstract rationalities and technical, expert discourses. As John Dunn expresses this:

> The claim to know better is flourished menacingly at identities, personal, cultural, and political, from the outside as much as it has ever been before in human history. But today – more clearly than ever before – we know that it can be vindicated only within identities, that the only authority which it can possess is a human authority, an authority for human beings not an external domination over them.[31]

There are several points that follow from this. To begin with, reflectiveness is not something that can come about through mere institutional self-reference. It requires, instead, an openness to our ethical and moral capacity to tolerate difference and otherness; which in turn implicates the imagination, the bringing in of the human element. To this extent, reflexivity as reflectiveness requires a shift beyond self-monitoring to the point where knowledge is turned back upon itself to examine its presuppositions, thus allowing room to unearth the contradictions of the established social order. Following from this, reflectiveness also requires consideration of the self-interpretation and self-framing of ideological discourse by human subjects. This demands a full taking in, holding and containing of what Theodor Adorno calls the 'torn halves' of the social field – individual and culture, theory and practice, universal and particular, sameness and difference. In post-Kleinian terms, such taking in and holding of such contradictions and antagonisms can be characterized as the dialectical interplay of paranoid-schizoid and depressive positions, an interactive psychical process which is essential for the symbolization of things other than that which are. For no creation occurs where imagination is inhibited or repressed.

Yet, as radical thought, we are talking about modes of reflexivity which can engage with more than simply contradiction and conflict. Creative reflexivity means the capability to think, feel and act innovatively in relation to representations imagined beyond the instituted realm of society and culture. This is the principle of what I call *critical self-reflection*, which is connected in an essential way with personal and social autonomy. Such reflexive activity involves an engagement with the deep structures of subjectivity, of unconscious sexuality, otherness, difference, needs, wishes, passions and desires. As Cornelius Castoriadis argues:

> It is because the human being is imagination (non-functional imagination) that it can posit as an 'entity' something that is not so: its own process of thought. It is because its imagination is unbridled that it can reflect; otherwise, it would be limited to calculating, to 'reasoning'. Reflectiveness presupposes that it is possible for the imagination to posit as existing that which is not, to see Y in X and specifically, to see double, to see oneself double, to see oneself while seeing oneself as other.[32]

Instituted reflexivity, as Western institutional reactions to the war in Bosnia highlight, displaces the possibility for this type of reflectiveness. No one knows if reflectiveness will become further disfigured with the impact of globalization upon social institutions, marked by viciously regressive forms of nationalism and racism, or further colonized by the one-dimensional logic of bureaucratic systemization. For the resurgence of critical self-reflection, however, new prospects, objectives and imaginations are urgently required.

4

Postmodern Contexts, Plural Worlds

The Possibilities and Pressures of Social Change

A self does not amount to much, but no self is an island; each exists in a fabric of relations that is now more complex and mobile than ever before. Young or old, man or woman, rich or poor, a person is always located at 'nodal points' of specific communication circuits, however tiny these may be.

Jean-François Lyotard

If modernity is about the production of order and mastery, then postmodernity is about disorientation and chaos; or, at least, so it would seem from the wave of dichotomy that has swept over social theory of late. It is this impression that, more than anything else, is conveyed by the general characterization of postmodernity as a culture of endless fragmentation, dislocation and simulation. Significantly, this dispersal which characterizes postmodern culture is nowhere more obvious than at the level of human subjectivity itself – in the split, surface-obsessed, narcissistic forms of contemporary self-experience. The demolition of any possible inner experience, and indeed the impossibility of thinking itself, according to the thesis put forward in French post-structuralism, is one precise consequence of the 'death of the subject'. The French post-structuralist conception of the postmodern is one of pleasure and plurality, of the exuberant and discontinuous, a dispersed network of language-games in which discourse (following Lacan) speaks the subject.

One might, however, argue exactly the opposite. If the postmodern proliferation of signs and images of the world entails a radical transmutation of the deep structures of human subjectivity, perhaps this marks a positive point between identity and politics, the creation of a reflective, discursive space for the mapping of individual and collective autonomy. It would thus be possible to see postmodernity as the expression of identities and cultures coming to terms with inner hopes and dreads, discarding the modern desire for an ideal fit of map and experience. From such an angle, it is not hard to see the multiplication of identity as revealing a novel cultural concern with the rich textures of psychic experience.

Some time ago Marike Finlay coined the duality *post-modernizing psychoanalysis/psychoanalysing postmodernity* for thinking anew the relationships between self and society, identity and politics, in the current era.[1] In Finlay's view, the status of the subject in postmodern conditions is rendered politically and historically contingent. Contingency is discovered in postmodernity as the psychic location where fragmentary identities link and intertangle. Or, rather, people become self-consciously concerned with the mapping of experience because of the oscillation and plurality of postmodern social conditions. In this connection, Finlay poses a series of critical questions that concern the odds – the chances and limits – of psychically negotiating the postmodern political condition. 'Does postmodernity', writes Finlay, 'post-modernize psychoanalysis out of existence? Or, perhaps, is there still a place for an *evolved* psychoanalytic discourse which would account for the post-modern destruction of the subject?' And, later: 'can psychoanalysis psychoanalyse the post-modern attack on a subject of interiority, intuition, and significance?'[2] The political stakes here are certainly high. Either these discourses intersect (in which case, one renders the other 'transparent'?), or one or another must opt out of existence.

This may or may not be so; I will not pursue the implications of this theoretical dichotomy here. But the issue of the development of postmodernity, and with it that of the state of the human subject, is central to the concerns of this chapter. For the human subject in postmodernity, I shall argue, should not be identified exclusively with fragmentation as such, as it has been in many discussions of psychoanalysis and postmodernity. By contrast, I shall propose a psychoanalytic framework within which to conceptualize a complex interplay of deintegration and restructuration of self-constitution and intersubjective relations in the postmodern age. Moreover, I shall examine some of the ways in which postmodernity contributes to, and strains against, the psychic processing and thinking of fantasy.

Postmodernity, space-time transformations, floating identities

Previous chapters examining the contradictions of subjectivity in modernity have suggested that there are both positive and negative senses in which self-constitution can be understood. On the one hand, modern institutions prise selfhood and social relations free from the hold of tradition and custom, rendering identity inherently problematic and indeterminate. With modernization and the decline of cultural tradition, the individual subject becomes a 'project' that has to be defined and managed against the backdrop of institutional risks and opportunities. Selfhood in this context becomes 'open-ended' – elaborated not through pre-given social roles, but through the indeterminacy of desire-driven personal and social relationships. Modernity is the uncovering of imagination, the revelation that selfhood and otherness are constructed categories; categories which, the discussion of Freudian psychoanalysis in chapter 2 has underscored, are fabricated through the specific operations of fantasy. On the other hand, we have seen that the material presence of fantasy is regularly displaced within the control-systems of modernity: namely science, bureaucracy and technology. The expert-systems of modernity squeeze to the sidelines the profoundly imaginative engagements of people with one another, thus displacing core problems concerning the subject's relation to sexuality, nature and death. Within a rationalistic system of causes and effects, all experiences are measured, manipulated, dominated and controlled, including, ultimately, the interiority of the individual subject. Put differently, the modern conception of desire provides no adequate defence against the world of expert knowledge and institutionalized power, with its rigorous codings and scientistic determinism. These and similar instabilities help adduce the contradictory status accorded to the imagination in the modern era, and also some of the dislocating pressures at work within the institutionalized world of modernity itself.

Modernity, then, is at once radical and conservative; and this is especially evident, I have suggested, in the modern conception and practice of the transformative power of human imagination. Put simply, modernity uncovers the profound connections between imagination and being, and yet, in a tragic irony, refuses to want to know anything about it. The irony is that this state of not-knowing or, better, denial is construed as essential for a principled commitment to freedom and rationality.

97

Things go differently with postmodernity. The central message of the past few decades in social theory and philosophy, and a core tenet of the postmodern revision of modernity as a historical paradigm, is the impossibility of fashioning ourselves and the world within the grand narratives of reason, progress, emancipation. The contemporary postmodern landscape, having eroded former cultural and ideological horizons and transfigured the old geopolitical world order, is marked by a view of the world as irreducibly multidimensional and pluralistic. Postmodernity – with its proliferation of media simulations, its global restructuring of social activity, its radicalization of technologism, its self-reflexive deconstruction of ideological closure – unleashes a multiplicity of local identities and cultures without any 'central' or 'authoritative' co-ordination.

This decomposition of the normative force of a unilinear view of the world and history into a flow of episodes is itself the upshot of a social-historical restructuring of space and time. All social life is plotted and woven across intersections of space and time. Where modernity has been concerned with establishing a continuity of social life and social institutions across space-time contexts, postmodernity, on the contrary, is about disconnectedness and equivalence in space-time. Postmodernity, says Jean-François Lyotard, increasingly separates time from space, recombining intersections of presence and absence as *open space-time*.[3] What is at issue is not just a different means of constituting psychological reality within space-time paths of daily life, but irreducibly and irrevocably pluralistic forms of experience and meaning as multiplied by the spatial and temporal contextuality of postmodern social life. In open space-time, action and experience are constituted and reconstituted in different configurations in relation to the structure of communication that is engendered. The quintessential awareness here is of immersion within experience, an experience of the moment, the particular. An identity without guarantees. Individuals in postmodern social conditions do not bind space-time from the point of view of one placed at the centre (whether this be the coming of a 'universal class' or the realization of 'sexual emancipation'), but move through space-time configurations in order to discover the possibilities of what one might become.

In this new cultural experience, generalized media communications and information technologies are of core importance in the restructuring of symbolic exchange.[4] The electronic mediation of information, such as television, video, facsimile, compact discs and computer conferencing, radically alters the space-time parameters of interpersonal interactions. The advent of postmodern communications increasingly cancels the presence of space-time contexts, such as those rooted in face-to-face interaction, creating new modes of symbolic exchange between 'absent' interlocutors, spatially and temporally distant from each other. The fantasmagoria of the mass media, for instance, negates the limitations of space and time distances, making possible new 'gatherings' of heterogeneous cultures.[5] Sitcoms like *Roseanne* and soaps like *Baywatch* transgress social and cultural boundaries, mixing diverse life-forms together. So too, the presentation of news increasingly concentrates on global events, or on what Brooker-Gross calls 'geographic bundling'.[6] In this connection, news is represented in ways unrelated to the pressures of space-time differences, as place is divorced from context.

The political implications of this transmutation in spatial and temporal coordinates is nowhere more obvious than in the attention that postmodern culture lavishes on identity. Just as the shift from tradition to modernity could be seen as undermining the purportedly neutral and universal self-identical subject of Western reason, so the transfiguration from modernity to postmodernity marks a delegitimization of the deep structures of experience and subjectivity of the self. This delegitimization has been informed or, better, constituted by the heterogeneity of space-time configurations that circulate in postmodern society. Ousted from the secure terrain of theoretical and practical reason, identity and subjectivity in the postmodern age are positioned within contingent, politically and culturally variable social, linguistic and discursive practices which are co-ordinated by space-time zonings. As such, it can now be said that there are just as many identity-profiles as there are discourses and messages proffered by informational simulations.

We have now entered that realm of the postmodern 'dismantling of the human subject' in which identity is fragmented, dislocated and multiplied in ever-increasing fields of instability. In social and political theory, such analyses of the state of the subject have been promoted in post-structuralist circles. At the centre of these standpoints lies an unrelenting conviction of the irrelevance of selfhood, ego, intentionality and agency. In its place, the logic of contemporary social processes is seen as one of multiple and dispersed discourses, of which the individual subject is little more than a flesh-and-blood passing function. This dissolution of identity into language as such further suggests that any critical space for reflection between the subject and the chain of significations in which it is embedded (whether these be moral, political, sexual or cultural discourses) is eroded. 'The subject', says Jacques Lacan, 'is separated from the

Others, the true Others, by the wall of language.'[7] From this angle, the self-identical subject capable of critical reflection is rendered little more than a modernist fiction, an illusion that masks the painful lack of human subjectivity itself. Rather, the situated and contingent subject of postmodernity experiences cultural diversity in relation to open space-time configurations of discourse.

If the dislocation and dispersal of identity has loomed so large in contemporary theory, it is because it has been so powerfully to the fore in postmodern political conditions. The expansion of identity as a discursive phenomenon has been fundamental to the reopening of cultural issues of language, experience, value, rights and justice. In recent decades, political struggle has focused in particular on the ways in which gender, race and class intersect and circulate in discourse and power relations, privileging certain images of identity and marginalizing others. The enabling and troubling effects concerning relationships of sexuality and power have been explored in terms of the construction and deconstruction of identity. From this angle, it is perhaps no accident that the domain of sexuality, and the imbalances of gender power, become highest on the global political agenda at that historical point at which the principle of identity is radically displaced by the women's movement within the male–female asymmetric binary. The ideal of identity, in these postmodernist days, is reconfigured in terms of the circuits of fantasy and as a regulatory effect of power. In postmodernity, the subject is without clear boundaries, and has no fixed place. This disorientation of the subject, however, is not to be lamented; or, at least, not according to many post-structuralist thinkers. The deconstruction of identity in post-structuralist theory is said to be all for the political good. The key focus here is on questioning the foundational assumptions of modernity, and of working against a premature closure of political problems in the face of anxiety. What is the subject? And how, and with what political consequences, does it differ from the 'I'? These are core postmodern political concerns, and they are imposing significant changes in personal and social life.

There is, however, a less positive sense in which identity has figured so prominently in postmodern cultural conditions. Although the multiplication of identity has served as a basis from which to open previously repressed social and political issues, this very dispersion introduces a feedback effect on postmodernity, further dividing and atomizing human subjects. In other words, the postmodern dismantling of the human subject rebounds upon itself with a vengeance, splitting and fragmenting the relationship between cultural meanings and politics. What is so startling about postmodernity is not the multiplication of psychic states arising from technology-induced meetings of self and other, but the way in which experience is condensed in such a manner as to deny distance and awareness. Postmodernity multiplies experience, and especially mediated experience, through its growing expansion of self and other linkages in space and time. In the postmodern world reflexively mapped by computational systems, an opening out to alien experiences grows in line with the global construction of local orders. Yet immersion in experience is quickly dislocated by other images of the world. Things get cut up and denuded of meaning. It is as if involvement with the self and others takes place in random bits and pieces, one at a time, with little in the way for the making of connections. As Bauman notes of this fragmentation of self and world:

> On no occasion does the subject confront the totality – of the world, or of the other human. Life is a sequence of many disparate approaches, each one being partial and hence, like the techniques themselves, entitled and prone to claim moral innocence. Fragmentarity of the subject and fragmentarity of the world beckon to each other and lavish mutual assurances upon each other.[8]

To summarize the foregoing discussion: in conditions of post-modernity, subjects *float*, suspended in open space-time, being constituted and reconstituted in relation to different configurations of experience. Such floating involves various tensions and pressures as regards self-experience, the contours of which I shall discuss more fully in the following pages. In this chapter I shall (1) review contemporary psychoanalytic dialogues on the multiplication of self-experience and fantasy; (2) provide a characterization of both enabling and troubling modes of psychic processing which come to the fore in postmodern conditions; and (3) discuss several kinds of response to the possibilities and pressures of living in a world characterized by ambiguity and flux. I shall explore both the way psychoanalysis permits an understanding of the creation and dislocation of desire, and the way postmodern social conditions open questions about the structure and limits of psychic processing.

Contemporary psychoanalytic dialogues

The development of postmodern discourses concerning shifting and fluid identities parallels, in many ways, recent psychoanalytic dialogues. In contemporary psychoanalysis, in the work of its most radical contributors, psychic reality is located in a state of continuous non-linear movement, within an interpersonal field of interactions which frame personal meaning and authenticity, in close connection with fantasy and the imagination. It is beyond the scope of this chapter to discuss in any detail the multitude of psychoanalytic contributions that place emphasis on the links between psychic creativity and authentic experience. In the following pages, however, I shall briefly discuss some concepts developed in contemporary psychoanalytic thought that have particular relevance to the connections discussed in this chapter between psychic processing and postmodern social conditions.

Cornelius Castoriadis, an important contributor to French psychoanalytic dialogue, has discussed subjectivity in terms of the creative indetermination of unconscious representation. Indeed the capacity to represent one's life, as an articulation and organization of conscious and unconscious contents, is seen by Castoriadis as evidence of a radical imagination or primary meaning for the subject. He understands the creative flux of the unconscious as a primal architecture of representations, drives and passions in and through which the human subject creates a world for itself. The precondition for this state of being, says Castoriadis, is originary fantasmatization, the psyche's capacity to posit an image *ex nihilo*. 'The original narcissistic cathexis or investment', writes Castoriadis, 'is necessarily *representation* . . . (otherwise it would not be psychical) and it can then be nothing other than a "representation" (unimaginable and unrepresentable for us) of the *Self*.'[9] For Castoriadis, such self-representation is profoundly imaginary in character; yet this imaginary dimension of self-experience is radically different from the Lacanian imaginary of mirror self-distortion. The 'radical imagination' of which Castoriadis speaks is not constituted by the reflecting surface of a mirror. Instead the imaginary constitutes, via representation and figuration, the conditions of possibility for both mirroring and otherness. The unconscious, as radical imagination, is thus a kind of representational flux, which underlies all configurations of self-organization and intersubjective settings.

This ceaseless mirroring of self and object is therefore underwritten by the profoundly imaginary dimensions of unconscious representation and affect. But what actually knits intersubjectivity together, I have previously argued, is a *representational wrapping of self and other*, which can be thought of as a preliminary ordering of pre-self experience, otherness and difference.[10] Such wrapping lies at the core of shared, intersubjective space – indeed it is the libidinal investment in the shapes, textures, surfaces, and objects which comprise psychic space itself – and it functions as a kind of perpetual self-constitution. Identification, and especially what I call 'rolling identification', plays a key role in this inmixing of subjectivity and intersubjectivity; it is precisely that libidinal assimilation of all the fragmentary identifications of the pre-Oedipal phase of development.

The work of the French psychoanalyst Didier Anzieu has also afforded psychoanalytic theory a way of conceptualizing the earliest organization of self-experience in an interpersonal matrix. Anzieu portrays the psyche as constituted through a complex interweaving of fantasy and interpersonal experience. He argues that the link between imaginary and interpersonal orders frames a 'skin ego', a fantasy image of maternal holding, 'a system of double feedback as an envelope of mother–child'.[11] 'The skin ego', writes Anzieu, 'is the original parchment which preserves, like a palimpsest, the erased, scratched-out, written-over first outlines, of an "original" preverbal writing made up of traces upon the skin.'[12] These skin traces function as a narcissistic envelope and container, comprising affects, drives, representations and memories. Influenced by the work of Klein and Winnicott, Anzieu argues that the skin ego, and its containment function, derives from the sensual dimensions of maternal holding, which he relates to the Kleinian theory of introjective and projective mechanisms. The skin ego is built upon sensations of maternal bodily experiences, registered through a fantasized contact with the object, a contact from which the beginning separation of inner and outer worlds takes place through introjective and projective identification. Anzieu argues that the subject has need of a skin ego, a containing envelope for the holding of emotional states, from which experience can become known, recognized and more fully developed.

Such a conception of the importance of contained images and affective states as organizers of psychic development is also powerfully developed in the writings of British psychoanalyst Christopher Bollas, one of the most interesting theorists in contemporary psychoanalysis. Bollas emphasizes both the creativity of subjectivity itself and the key place of experience in the formation of psychical constructions and fantasy. He underlines the relational aspect of very early experience in the infant's encounter with the mothering environment. This represents the core grounding of the self, or what he terms the 'idiom', by which he means a psychical grid through which experience is generated and meaning created. We do not move past, or grow out of, this psychological grid according to Bollas. The idiom of psychic organization is not a developmental phase; rather, it is an unconscious space between experience and fantasy. As Bollas puts this:

> The self does not evolve unconsciously; rather, the self *is* unconsciousness, a particular inner presence, reliably vectored by the forms 'it' uses to find expression ... [E]ach of us at birth is equipped with a unique idiom of psychic organization that constitutes the core of our self, and then in the subsequent years of our life we become our parents' child, instructed by the implicate logic of their unconscious relational intelligence in the family's way of being: we become a complex theory for being a self that the toddler does not think about but acquires operationally.[13]

Subjectivity is theorized by Bollas as a kind of dream-work: over-determined, displaced, condensed, symbolic. Each of us, as human subjects, integrates daily experience into the inner texture of our psychic worlds. We abandon ourselves to the dreaming of life; we immerse ourselves in others and in the object-world; a dissolution essential to the inner complexity of psychical life. We dream ourselves into being, says Bollas, 'as we dissolve consciousness, disseminate parts of the self in units of experience' and, by turning the self back upon its immersion in experience, 'use objects as lexical elements in the elaboration of idiom'.[14]

In contemporary psychoanalysis, then, psychical life is portrayed as a stream of fantasies, representational wrappings, bodily sensations, idioms, envelopes, containers, introjects and memories. Yet although the internal world is understood as comprising such multivalent psychical forms, it is also said to be patterned through an interpersonal field of interactions with significant other persons. The individual, as representational flux, is embedded in both intrasubjective and intersubjective relations. This focus on fluid, multiple subjectivities in contemporary psychoanalysis overlaps in many respects with the postmodern stress on the dialectics of identity and difference, on the irreducible multiplicities of experience and world.

Experience, thinking, containment

The question arises as to how it is possible for the human subject to move from immersion in experience to a capacity to think objects as independent of the self. Indeed, how does the subject disseminate parts of the self in sectors of experience, and subsequently retrieve such abandonments to experience through consciousness and reflection? What creates the bridge between such fragmentations of unconscious life and the reclaiming of self in symbolic forms of thinking? Trust in the anchorings between lived experience and intersubjective relations provides, to a significant degree, the emotional structure from which imagination, symbol formation and personal meaning develop. What D.W. Winnicott calls the 'transitional object' forms the original nexus from which reality enters into a mutually defining and creative relationship with fantasy. The child's relationship to a transitional object, such as a blanket, teddy bear or doll, allows for a recognition of the external world as something separate from, yet connected to, the self. The child, says Winnicott, 'creates an object but the object would not have been created as such if it had not already been there'. The transitional object is thus discovered and created; it is at once reality and fantasy. Most importantly, the transitional object gives rise to an experience which is *transformational* in nature. The transitional object allows the subject-to-be an intersubjective space to release fantasy into lived experience, to abandon itself to the dialectics of imagination and being.

Even in these transitional spaces, however, the individual subject will not know the meaning and significance of the lived experience in which it is free-floating. Feelings, and especially anxiety, are poured into transitionally constituted objects, whether the object itself be music, literature or investment banking. Yet subjective awareness of feelings always falls behind the object's impact on the self, the subject having surrendered itself to the pleasures or tensions of the moment. In this respect, then, there is a *time-lag* between feelings and the objects into which they are poured on the one side, and reflective awareness of experience on the other. Awareness, or non-awareness, of this time-lag is crucial to the subject's management of anxiety.

All individuals create a framework for the generation of psychological meaning, a framework which develops through the attachment of meaning to experience. The analysis of psychological thinking elaborated by the British psychoanalyst Wilfred Bion is especially relevant here, and requires detailed consideration, given that I use much of his work in the arguments I develop concerning the links between postmodernity and the personal sphere. Like Klein and Winnicott, Bion stresses that a containing and responsive emotional environment in the earliest years of life is crucial to the creation and recognition of authentic self-experience. The capacity to register personal and interpersonal experience comes from infancy, from the love and containment offered to the child by its mother. This is what Bion calls 'reverie', the mother's receptivity to her infant's presymbolic experience, her 'holding' of the infant in a state of mind which is open to the reception of good and bad feelings. In this intersubjective context, thinking is approached by Bion as a kind of *processing of emotions*. If the mother can hold the infant's projective identifications of distressing affects (such as greed, envy or hate), if she can think about them and pass them back in a more understandable form, the inner world of the infant opens to psychic experiencing and thinking. If this process of reverie cannot be undertaken by the mother (either because her own mental capacity for processing emotion is underdeveloped or impaired, or because the infant's projections of envy and hate are excessive), emotional experiences are cut off from thinking and psychic elaboration, the upshot being that the subject lives in a state of psychological deadness in relation to its internal objects. But this is jumping ahead, without really identifying the core elements in Bion's account of psychic processing and thinking. It is necessary, therefore, to return to the issue of self-experience, paying special attention to Bion's arguments about thinking and the psychic mechanisms that have to be elaborated to process thoughts.

In *Learning from Experience* (1962), Bion proposes that, in order to reach knowledge of self-experience, the psyche has to make a series of transformations of the raw emotional material impinging on it. These transformations concern the turning of sense impressions into materials for awareness, and Bion terms this the 'alpha-function' of psychic processing. Alpha-function operates on the emotions, and is essential to the processing of raw experiences into thoughts. All emotional experience, says Bion, has to be worked on, or processed, by alpha-function. As Bion writes:

> Alpha-function operates on the sense impressions, whatever they are, and the emotions, whatever they are, of which the patient is aware. In so far as alpha-function is successful alpha elements are produced and these elements are suited to storage and the requirements of dream thoughts. If alpha-function is disturbed, and therefore inoperative, the sense impressions of which the patient is aware and the emotions which he is experiencing remain unchanged. I shall call them beta-elements. In contrast with the alpha-elements the beta-elements are not felt to be phenomena, but things in themselves.[15]

We shall return to consider beta-elements in more detail shortly; at this point, it is necessary to focus on alpha-function and alpha elements. Alpha-function operates to transform raw experience into psychical significance, alpha-elements of conscious and unconscious thought, a transmutation of affect into the inner elaboration of thinking and the creative dreaming of daily life. Bion draws an analogy between psychic processing and dreaming, the transformation of inner experience into differing modes of potential thought and being:

> If the patient cannot transform his emotional experience into alpha-elements, he cannot dream. Alpha-function transforms sense impressions into alpha-elements which resemble, and may be identical with, the visual images with which we are familiar in dreams . . . Freud showed that one of the functions of a dream is to preserve sleep. Failure of alpha-function means the patient cannot dream and therefore cannot sleep. As alpha-function makes the sense impressions of the emotional experience available for conscious and dream-thought the patient who cannot dream cannot go to sleep and cannot wake up.[16]

Waking life mirrors dream life for Bion, in that both psychic states require a profoundly unconscious processing of raw experience into the self. Without such processing, the subject is cut off from unconscious thinking, barred from dreaming. Without alpha-function one is psychologically dead, a subject that cannot sleep, or enter experience and meaning.

The prospects for arresting raw blocks of experience and transforming them for conscious thinking and reasoning depend upon the emotional capacity of the subject to tolerate the more frustrating and painful elements of reflective awareness. According to Bion, there are two basic psychic modes that operate here. The impinging of thought, he says, 'can be got rid of either by evasion or modification. The problem is solved by evacuation if the personality is dominated by the impulse to evade frustration and by thinking the objects if the personality is dominated by the impulse to modify the frustration.'[17] Thought, in this account, precedes thinking. Thoughts chase or hunt for a thinker to 'think things through'. Thought requires an emotional container for the realization of its inner conceptualizations. Significantly, however, the creation of reflective psychic space for the processing of thought is rooted in the dynamics of intersubjectivity, originally in maternal reverie and later in interpersonal containment. As such, internal psychological space and the capacity for thinking is interwoven in the intersubjective recognition of meaning and desire. An intersubjective intolerance to pain and frustration, however, can mean that the capacity for thinking is never properly established.

> If a patient cannot 'think' with his thoughts, that is to say that he has thoughts but lacks the apparatus of 'thinking' which enables him to use his thoughts, to think them as it were, the first result is an intensification of frustration . . . The steps taken by the patient to rid himself of the objects, the proto-thoughts or thoughts which to him are inseparable from frustration, have then led him to precisely the pass that he wished to avoid, namely to tension and frustration unalleviated by the capacity for thought.[18]

However, it is not only an inability to register thoughts that follows from the inability to process human experience. Rather, there is a loss of parts of the mental apparatus itself, projected out into external objects through multiple splittings. This is mental space dominated by beta-elements, undigested blocks of experience which are psychically lodged as concrete facts and forces, of 'remnants, debris or fragments floating in space without limits'.[19] It is a destroyed mental space of infinite dimensions, with no boundaries, and which therefore fails to function as a container for conscious and unconscious thought. Bion contrasts alpha-elements as inner conceptualizations, digested by alpha-function and thus made available for thought, with beta-elements as phenomenological things-in-themselves, undigested objects that frighten and alienate. Beta-elements, if not emotionally processed, are alienating precisely since they cannot be thought about; they are experienced as external forces or physical objects bombarding the self. The frightened subject, says Bion, 'splits his objects, and contemporaneously all that part of his personality, which would make him aware of the reality he hates, into minute fragments'.[20] Experience becomes dangerously concrete; self and objects minutely fragmented and endangering. The collapsing self, brittle and fragmented in the face of such persecution, seeks an evacuative method for managing such a meaningless and scattered internal object-world.

Such emptying out of the psyche of undigested facts and intolerable material is referred to by Bion as 'anti-thought' or 'attacks on linking'. Bion describes anti-thought as an attack on alpha-function which smashes the distinction between self and object, as well as the space between symbol and symbolized, ejecting destructive and unmanageable aspects of the self on to external objects. In this paranoid-schizoid mode of functioning, anti-thought is predominantly in the form of projective identification, the evacuation and fragmentation of mental contents.[21] Bion emphasizes that at the root of such excessive projection is envy and hate, an uncontained destructiveness that attacks all meaning, all comprehension and knowledge, all learning from human experience. According to Bion, this facet of the destructiveness of projective identification involves not only a freezing of beta-elements as things-in-themselves, but an evacuation of whatever meaning had already been forged at the level of psychological experience. There is therefore a kind of psychotic splitting of oneself and one's experience into tiny bits and pieces, a dissolution of the self into many particles, accompanied by the projection of such fragments into what Bion calls 'bizarre objects'. As Bion observes:

> Each particle is felt to consist of a real object which is encapsulated in a piece of personality that has engulfed it. The nature of the complete particle will depend partly on the character of the real object, say a gramophone, and partly on the character of the particle of personality that engulfs it. If the piece of personality is concerned with sight, the gramophone when played is felt to be watching the patient; if with hearing, then the gramophone when played is felt to be listening to the patient. The object, angered at being engulfed, swells up, so to speak, and suffuses and controls the piece of personality that engulfs it: to that extent the particle of personality has become a thing.[22]

Bizarre objects are therefore particles of residual internal meaning, shot through with a destructiveness and hate which leaves the self drained and lifeless. Engulfing the self, bizarre objects are experienced not as subjective creations but as things that simply exist. Thus, bizarre objects represent a projective identification which severs the subject from reality through psychotic attacks on meaning, on thought, and on all links with other people.

The prime importance that Bion attributes to thinking can be said to connect directly to different modes of generating experience, and it is important to distinguish the form of symbolization characteristic of each of these modes of psychological organization. Bion emphasizes that a certain level of containment of aggression and hatred is the precondition for reflective thinking, as a processing of unconscious affect. Psychic space acts as a container for constituting human experience, processing affect and fantasizing thoughts and feelings, and their inner conceptualizations. The intersubjective process which underlies such containment, says Bion, is built out of an emotional receptivity to the experience of otherness, a state of mind of reverie, an openness to being without fictitious dreams of certitude, as well as a tolerance for ambiguity and confusion. This capacity for ambivalence allows the individual to experience itself as a subject that creates its own thoughts and feelings, to develop a sense of responsibility for its actions, to engage with others as subjects, and properly to own loving and hating feeling-states in interpersonal relations. In short, this is the Kleinian notion of the depressive position, now modified by Bion to underscore the point that the capacity for thinking is essential to this development of reflective subjectivity. In this psychological state, in which the pain of loss and guilt is made bearable through mourning, it is the capacity for thinking which permits the desiring subject to mediate a space between symbol and symbolized. This type of symbol formation in the depressive mode is what Hanna Segal calls 'symbol formation proper',[23] a formation in which the symbol, a creation of the ego, represents the object – a recognition, or thinking through, of the independent existence of the object.

As we have seen, however, psychic processing and thinking can go awry, either because of the mother's incapacity for reverie in the original developmental situation or because excessive envy and hatred arises in the subject-to-be. Without such a container to transform negative feelings into a tolerable form, the individual increasingly resorts to projection and splitting as a defence and as a way of organizing experience. In this mode, there is little mediated space between symbol and symbolized; thoughts and feelings are not creatively experienced as existing in relationship with others, but are experienced as facts, pure and simple. This type of symbol formation in the paranoid-schizoid mode is what Segal calls 'symbolic equation', a form of experience without creative dreaming or reverie. It is a world in which things simply are what they are; a dangerously concrete and alienating world made of raw blocks of experience, of bizarre objects, in which thinking is attacked, and emotional connection with others is eaten away from within.

Thinking and denial, postmodern

What has happened with the advent of postmodernity, it might be argued, is precisely the creative rewriting – premised upon a new cultural awareness – of this duality which underpins thinking and reflectiveness: the dialectic between thought and thought-mechanism, emotion and conceptualization, beta- and alpha-elements. The play-ful, reflexive bent of some postmodern culture emerges as a radical rejection of the modernist demarcation between fact and fiction, reality and imagination, identity and non-identity. As a reaction against modernity, the distinctions between nostalgia, memory and time begin to blur. Thinking in postmodernity is reflexively deployed as a *sensitivity to difference*: involvement without classification, het-erogeneity without hierarchy. Instead, reasoning becomes equated with the principle of equivalence; thinking is shifted from the idea of a central rationality of knowledge to a local processing of 'difference', with the experience of oscillation and disorientation to the fore. In this new cultural setting, experience is marked by plurality and multiplicity; the holding together of complex, contradictory images and signifiers, without the pressure or demand for a closure of horizons.

To put it in a different way, the postmodern world-view entails a radical dissection of the notion of normativity. The attempt to pre-scribe ideal norms as an objective ground for truth or meaning is deconstructed as a conservative, modernist desire for the universaliz-ation of order and hierarchy. The main objection here concerns the profoundly anti-democratic tendency of thinking society as unilinear; a centralization of power which ruthlessly excludes any difference or opposition of local rationalities and identities in the name of progress (as can be gleaned from even the most cursory glance at the history of colonialism and imperialism in the twentieth century). The post-modern sensibility, by contrast, refuses to engage in any such ration-alistic foreclosure of conflict and contradiction in the contemporary political world. On the contrary, postmodernity marks an opening up of sites of contestation, all the way from the divisions of gender and sexuality to issues of democracy and citizenship rights. The wave of 'particularism' that has swept over social theory and philosophy of late is wedded to precisely such a political understanding of demo-cratic contestation.

'Long live heterogeneity!': this might well be the rallying cry of politics in the postmodern. There is, however, a deeper political irony in this underwriting of difference and otherness. On the one hand, postmodernity enters into an egalitarian compact with politics, marked as it is by an ability to reflect back difference and multiplicity, and thus to destabilize the ordered, hierarchical domains of expert knowledge in the contemporary world. On the other hand, however, this valorization of difference is often achieved only at the expense of *value*, of the disconnection between meaning and human social relationships. The irony, then, is that postmodern culture comes to have less and less time for the differences it fosters. The emotional processing of experience, this would suggest, cannot be adequately performed. In Bion's terms, this amounts to saying that postmodernity is a culture which notices the sheer amount of experience, or information, available; but, crucially, subjects are unable to think about it long enough to be socially useful. A volatile containing situation might thus be said to haunt the field of the postmodern, and it is perhaps for this reason that much of postmodernist culture is firmly discarding. Such forms of anti-thought can be given powerful connotations at the level of contemporary theory: the end of history, the death of the subject, the reductive conflation of reasoning and logic with totalization, and the demise of the ethical accompanied by the fashionable imperative of 'anything goes'. Viewed as a kind of postmodern dreaming state, such pessimism can be said to encode powerful feelings of hatred and despair. As Paul Hoggett comments on the negativity of this vision of the postmodern: 'It is the fantasy of an exhausted breast with nothing left to give and, at this deeper level, the abandonment of hope.'[24]

Earlier I mentioned a complex, contradictory interplay between thinking and denial, reflexive mapping and the refusal of experience. We need to examine how this interplay is manifested in conditions of postmodernity. However, before doing so, it is necessary to consider the manner in which these features have been approached in current social theory.

Social theory and postmodernity: Jameson and Baudrillard

Fragmentation of the psychic subject, or the rhetoric of schizo-fragmentation, is probably one of the major themes which have been developed by social theorists who have written on postmodernity. For Fredric Jameson, this disintegration of the postmodern human subject is the cultural correlate of advanced consumer or multinational capitalism. Jameson discusses how the extentionality and intensification of media messages, computational information and technological codes in postmodern society are initiated by, and indeed are deeply interwoven with, the commodifying abstractions of late capitalism. The random pluralism of the contemporary social world – with its multiple subject-positions, fractured discourses, compartmentalization of events which are all of equal value, and hallucinogenic cultural planes – is for Jameson a radical extension of capitalist exchange-value itself. This time, however, it is a kind of technological caricature of the intrinsic contradictions of bourgeois society, a cultural mutation of the commodity as pure fetish to accompany the more general dehumanization of need. Another way of putting this point is to say that Jameson sees postmodernity as a lifting of the technology of global capitalism into the operations of the human psyche itself. Advanced capitalism is so saturated with goods, services, information, codes and messages that it is as if we all now live in some communicational network of random signifiers, a network which produces fascination and stupefication in equal measure. The postmodern individual subject, in this reading, lives life moment by moment, with an attitude of 'anything goes' – and consequently, nothing has any special value. For Jameson, contemporary fractured and multiple subject-positions replicate slices of capitalist rationalization, the cultural subsystems of postmodernity – which are 'subsystems' only to the extent that such differentiations and boundaries of the cultural sphere are self-reflexive, mutable and open-ended.

Jameson suggests that postmodernity, in the very act of fashioning itself, subverts all features of previous historical development, especially universal standards of representation, spawning instead a 'semi-autonimization' of the linguistic and communicational realm. This semi-autonomization, he suggests, involves an endless proliferation of social forms and adaptations, an unstoppable breeding of the signifying chain which profoundly dislocates any imagined Saussurean equilibrium between sign and referent. In postmodernity, every sign simply refers itself to another, and that to another, in an infinite regress. As Gordon Gekko, the stock-exchange villain in Oliver Stone's movie *Wall Street*, ironically comments: 'Money isn't lost or made, it's simply transferred from one perception to another.' All of this can be redramatized, in Bion's terms, as a kind of *de-differentiation* of alpha-function and beta-elements, an attack on thinking which leaves the mind disconnected from self and world, immersed in the perception of bizarre objects. Just as money breeds money, so too the persecution and hate invested in bizarre objects produces more psychotic thought. But there are surely problems with the view that social meanings are completely destroyed in postmodernity, since (as Jameson points out) it is exceedingly difficult to switch off from the communicational setting of 'current events' in and through which postmodern culture is reproduced. For, more than ever before, we are tuned into the 'image of the other' as refracted through mass media, from the small screen compartmentalization of reality to new information technologies. Rather, media simulations continually surpass themselves in postmodernity, and as such must be mapped at the psychic, perceptual and cultural levels.

But what consequences does this carry for human subjectivity, especially as regards creativity, imagination and knowledge? Jameson thinks that if we understand the logics of postmodernism critically, then we can see that subjectivity (and, by implication, thinking) is recast as a kind of pseudo-processing of information at best. In conditions of postmodernity, Jameson writes, there

> is a new way of defusing information, making representations improbable, discrediting political positions and their organic 'discourses', and, in short, effectively separating 'the facts' from 'the truth', as Adorno put it. The superiority of the new method lies in its capacity to coexist perfectly adequately with information and full knowledge, something already implicit in the separation of subsystems and topics in various unrelated parts of the mind, which can only be activated locally or contextually ('nominalistically') in distinct moments of time and by various unrelated subject positions.[25]

Indeed, in the face of the sheer heterogeneity and profound discontinuities of postmodernity, the subject appears to Jameson as so disjointed that thought-processing is rendered little more than just random forms and libidinal impulses of all kinds. In particular, there is a breakdown in the intricate connections between received social meanings, subjective feelings and the capacity for thinking historically. In the postmodern context, the unleashing of pure experience, without the codifications of modernist hierarchy and ordering, reconstitutes the subject as a *disconnected self*. This is a self that confronts the 'signifier in isolation', understood in Lacanian terms as a snapping of the signifying chain, a 'schizophrenia in the form of a rubble of distinct and unrelated signifiers'. Yet, oddly enough, the subject's engagement with the 'signifier in isolation' produces not fragmentation as such, but a euphoric intensification of libidinal intensities as refracted through the fetishism of style and surface of contemporary culture. Reflexive appropriation of such personal and cultural de-differentiation, Jameson argues, will take the form of a 'cognitive mapping' of the multinational world-system, a kind of utopian reimagination and respatialization of the relation between self and society as regards institutional structures. For such mapping to be successful, says Jameson, it must occur through political reflection upon the intertwining of the local and global, identity and non-identity, the present and the past. Cognitive mapping is projected by Jameson as an emancipatory principle of individual and collective autonomy in the postmodern age, a countertrend to fragmentation, dislocation and dispersal.

The ambivalence of this description of postmodernity, which sits uneasily between the despair of fragmentation as an outcrop of late capitalism and the utopian possibility of new cognitive mappings, can be contrasted to that more catastrophic understanding of the contemporary epoch in the writings of the French sociologist Jean Baudrillard. Postmodernity is seen by Baudrillard as reframing the subject within the simulatory dimensions of hyperrealism, of locking perception into an aesthetic hallucination of culture, and of inscribing desire within the seductiveness of consumer objects in contemporary society. In contrast to the cultural scene of modernity, Baudrillard speaks of the cultural *ob-scene* of postmodernity: a world of excess and non-determinancy, of seduction and fascination, a commodity-object world that continually outstrips all assigned representations, boundaries and limits. As Baudrillard says of the commodity-object in the postmodern hyperreal:

> Things have found a way to elude the dialectic of meaning which bored them: it is to proliferate to infinity, to fully realize their potentialities, to surpass their essence in going to extremes, in an obscenity which henceforth takes the place for them of an immanent finality and of an insane rationality.[26]

The hyperreality described by Baudrillard is that of simulational excess, devoid of logic or direction, complicated by proliferation and acceleration – a mesmerizing non-representational communications mode that continually turns back upon itself. The real as more real than real in TV, the beautiful as more beautiful than beautiful in supermodel fashion, the political as more political than political in terrorism: these are the contours of Baudrillard's hyperreal postmodern.

This is clearly an incorporating social logic indeed, one in which a multiplicity of objects triumphs over human subjects, rendering human subjectivity defeated, outmoded and redundant. Moreover, Baudrillard says that there is but little point in deploring such cultural and ideological incorporation, since the human mind in the postmodern age is so immersed and seduced by the world of things that any attempt to distinguish between inside and outside, or surface and depth, will always be reabsorbed or, better, always-already caught, within the ecstatic and hyperreal. Put simply, there

115

is nothing beyond the cult of surface and style. There is nothing going on behind the scenes. The political message then offered by Baudrillard is that postmodernity can be fully equated with the *supremacy of the object,* and that, like it or not, every mode of thought is at once found and lost in simulations. All of which suggests that any return to the specific figure of the subject, even if pushed up a conceptual level to some global type of cognitive mapping, is simply untenable.

Again, this raises the question of political resistance and emancipation. Can anything be done, in terms of political strategy, to confront a world that continually outstrips existing boundaries and rules? In this connection, Baudrillard argues for a 'fatal strategy', by which he means 'to pass to the side of the object, to take sides with the object'.[27] In a world which cancels self-constitution and self-differentiation, it seems that the only way out is to succumb to the logic of the object itself, in all its seductive transparency and hyperreality.

These two positions on postmodernity – those of Jameson and Baudrillard – carry important implications for the critique of identity, and it is worth distinguishing them here, even though I wish to suggest that neither view is entirely satisfactory. On the one hand, the fractured and multiple subject-positions of postmodernity are viewed as the result of capitalism in its most advanced and global stage. Seen in this light, the decentred subject of post-structuralist perception is fully penetrated and constructed by the economic imperatives of global markets of production and appropriation, with the personal sphere recast within a standardization and mechanization of the autonomous logic of the commodity form itself. Postmodern selfhood is thus fractured and fragmented – a self-divided subjectivity to the nth degree. Moreover, from Jameson's perspective, only some future 'cognitive mapping' of postmodern space, culture and identity can reconcile human subjects to the unwelcome meaninglessness of their fragmented lives. On the other hand, this ever-expanding production and consumption of goods, services, information, messages and codes in postmodernity can be said now to totally outflank the human subject's capacities for self-differentiation and self-reproduction. Here it is recognized that postmodernity does more than merely colonize the personal sphere, and signifies more than a painful breakdown of the conceptual limits of the human mind itself. Rather, the self becomes decentred, dispersed and multiplied within the spectacular excesses of postmodern cultural forms; an excess in which subject-positions overflow into the spiral of continuous instabilities of the object itself. And, according to Baudrillard, the best possible political strategy, within the hyperreality of postmodern simulations, is simply to submit to the mysterious rule of objects and events.

But these logics of the postmodern surely represent a false opposition, about which it would be just as accurate to say that reflective cognitive mapping is already implicated in multiperspectival fatal strategies. By this I mean that postmodernity, as a self-reflexive mode of transmuting binary oppositions, opens out on to an agonizingly confused, contradictory realm of social practices, processes and possibilities. There is therefore little point in attempting to sort out the 'identities' or 'life strategies' which the postmodern world inaugurates, if by such conceptual classification is intended a once-and-for-all assessment of the alternatives of mapping vs. fatality, agency vs. structure, imagination vs. determinism. For it seems to me that cognitive mapping is not merely some utopian moment to be contrasted to the fragmentation of human experience, meaning and interpersonal communication. Rather, and in a somewhat analogous manner to Winnicott's thesis that 'fear of a breakdown' is a fear of something that has already happened,[28] we might say that cognitive mapping is a representation of social forms that already relates, in a complex way, unconscious thought and fantasy with the interpersonal, communicational structure.[29] So too, it should be understood that the option of 'fatal strategies' is an option only to the extent that human subjects imaginatively engage with social and cultural forms, irrespective of whether such engagements result in a challenging or reinforcement of the political order.

Having described some of the principal limitations of the foregoing accounts of postmodernity, let me now modify and recast the relations between the psychic subject and postmodern social and cultural forms. So far as fragmentation of the self is concerned, we can say that, in conditions of postmodernity, subjects are constituted in different configurations in relation to interpersonal structures of communication which promote the defensive use of denial in general and anti-thought in particular. The simulational hyperreality of the media, the communicational explosion of computational networks, the global spread of capitalist consumption and production, state and corporate surveillance: these and other dimensions of contemporary political life can indeed generate profound anxiety and terror. In such a frightening mode of experience, technology confronts the individual as impersonal, the market renders objects meaningless through its commodity abstractions of equivalence, and the ongoing psychological dilemma of discriminating between the real and the superficial, the inside and the outside, the authentic and the inauthentic, is broken down into random signifiers and codes. The connections between postmodern cultural consumption and the internal world of the self is, therefore, one of deintegration as regards the containment of psychic experience. Since social and cultural forms offer little emotional containment or personal anchoring, psychological anxiety and despair inevitably increase and our inner resources for managing psychic pain weaken. When the world loses its reality in this manner, the evacuation of pain becomes essential for the emotional survival of the individual. Excessive projective identification occurs, bizarre objects predominate, meaning is attacked, and thinking is refused.

But if we understand that such paranoid-schizoid discontinuity of experience exists in a dialectical relation to reflective thinking, and if we see that postmodernity generates complex, contradictory patterns of object relatedness, then a different picture emerges of the possibilities for the containment and integration of the self. Once again, it is necessary to underscore the profound importance of representational contingency for grasping this dialectical interplay between deintegration and restructuration of subjectivity in the contemporary epoch. In conditions of postmodernity, ego and self are displaced as pre-given entities and the representational, intersubjective fashioning of subjecthood becomes central. Underpinning this self-fashioning there lies a novel awareness of the creative characteristics of imagination and desire. The deconstruction of meaning – as an unpacking of signification and a tracing of the displacement of desire in its shifts from one signifying chain to another – breaks the hegemony of modernist codes and blueprints as regards personhood. It highlights that personal and interpersonal experience is embedded in sociocultural and political contexts as filtered through representational wrappings, fantasies, passions – in short the 'social imaginary', to borrow Castoriadis's term. This social imagination is, of course, constant throughout history; but, in the postmodern age, a new kind of reflexive scanning· of imagination and desire presents itself in processes of self-constitution and intersubjective relations.

These reflexive scannings run in various directions in postmodernity, and are created and sustained through the filtering of new experiences into conscious and unconscious representational space. In the disparate worlds of postmodernity – of the computational superhighway and CD-ROM, of AIDS and the resurgence of religious fundamentalism, of postcontemporary musical configurations (such as rap, techno and ambient), of the emergence of globalized political orders and new social movements (such as human rights, ecological and peace movements), of 'life-style' options and reproductive tech-nologies – the achievement of reflexive awareness and thinking allows an affective processing of diffuse cultural experience. It is this kind of experience of the discontinuity of self which opens subjectivity to the indivisible difference of the other, a kind of deintegration of the rootedness of the socialized self and deconstruction of the familiar range of one's thoughts, ideas and feelings. This opening up of the mind marks a shift into the bewildering stages of the otherness of the other, and is experienced as bewildering or startling precisely since it involves a splitting of self and object. But, as with so much of postmodernist culture, the creative core of this opening to otherness lies not in some newly established claim to know the other better (though that may sometimes be the case), but in the processing of experience itself. Deintegration of self provides the necessary representational basis for fresh thoughts and feelings, and, crucially, for an unravelling of the representational limits of the human imagination.

Postmodern dimensions of processing and misrecognition: some implications

Postmodern knowledge and wisdom are not built of necessities; they are generated through the reflexive constitution and recognition of desire. Postmodern subjectivity, rooted in a reflexive awareness of representational contingency, is a state of mind receptive to the other, without the need for certitude and with remarkable tolerance for ambiguity and confusion. Postmodern receptivity, or that state of mind that Bion calls reverie, is the antithesis of the modern romance with order and uniformity.

Postmodern receptivity is reflexive and other-centred; receptivity to differing areas of potential being and otherness. It is not, however, without its risks and fears. Indeed, the contemporary cultural setting offers an endless array of substitute formations to ward off feelings of ambiguity, ambivalence and confusion. In this section, I offer some clinical illustrations which focus on the psychic pressures and possi-bilities of postmodernity, tracing the dialectic of thinking and misrecognition in the current era.

The Primitive Edge of Experience, by Thomas Ogden, investigates the psychodynamic life histories of a number of American men and women, examining their deepest hopes and fears in the cultural context of the late 1980s.[30] Consider the case of Dr L, a clinical illustration selected rather arbitrarily from Ogden's research. Dr L was forty-six when he began analysis with Ogden. His life history was presented to Ogden as a narrative of driving ambition and determination, of wealth and success. Dr L was internationally recognized for his innovative contributions in the area of computer technology, work from which he had generated a considerable fortune by the time he was forty. He had invested this money conservatively. Success, however, was not what it seemed. In analysis, it transpired that Dr L was extremely nervous about his financial position, and similarly anxious about his professional standing. Such anxiety manifested itself in an inability to relax and to sleep. This inability to discover enjoyment in his lived experience, to 'let go' of dominating thoughts and ideas, was reacted to by Dr L with an ever-increasing attention and devotion to his work. The filling of time with work, often feverish work, did not keep anxiety at bay, however. Dr L complained of feeling anxious in various situations, such as while making business phone calls or while waiting to get a table in a restaurant, yet he had little idea of what was really distressing him in such situations.

Mirroring his wealth and career success, Dr L also displayed a certain self-confidence. But this personal confidence and assurance was also rather brittle in nature. Dr L was a person adept at giving the appearance of being self-assured and in control; and yet this appearance masked a profound anxiety about personal experience and meaning. Ogden writes:

> It had taken me most of the first year of the analysis to become aware of the way Dr L unconsciously attempted to lure me into misrecognitions of his internal state by repeatedly mislabeling them, giving me misleading pictures of himself and of his relationships, leaving out important details, leading me to believe he understood what was going on in an interpersonal situation when he did not.

Dr L is described by Ogden as a person who does not know what he feels, and therefore as a self out of touch with personal meaning and authenticity. Overwhelmed by the flux and intensity of experience, Dr L seeks to escape the negativity of such feelings through illusions about his place in the world, through narratives of misrecognition, and the misnaming of his internal feeling states. For example, although Dr L seemed not to know what motivated him to undertake therapy, he regularly offers Ogden explanations about his anxiety and confusion, which are described by Ogden as 'formulae extracted almost verbatim from his extensive reading of popular self-help books'. According to Ogden, this frantic search for meaning, for meaning authorized from pop-psychology handbooks, is a defence against the 'unconscious fear of not knowing'. It represents an inability to feel at a loss about what one wants, or to tolerate confusion and ambivalence as regards personal thoughts and feelings. As such, the construction of 'bits of meaning' gleaned from these various handbooks was a way of filling potential space, a filling designed to keep feelings of 'not knowing' at bay. Significantly, through such covering over of contingency the capacity for reflective thinking is also limited, with meaning expelled from the self into objects, returning only as alarm or intense anxiety. 'The defensive internal misrecognitions', says Ogden, 'had made it impossible for him to feel that he had understood anything of what he felt toward other people and what they felt toward him.' On the surface, then, confident and self-assured; yet deep within, disconnected and dislocated.

Disconnected though his personal history is, there is some attempt by Dr L to tolerate feelings of ambivalence, emptiness and despair. For it is Dr L's very misnaming of his feeling-states and sense of self that alerts Ogden to the repressed emotions being aroused; and it is in tracing these self-deceptions that Ogden attempts to prise open a space between lived experience and symbolic possibility.

Analysis in the second year, notes Ogden, became tensional, because confusion and distortion developed as core reflective themes in Dr L's self-exploration. As Ogden writes:

> Dr L became increasingly able to understand why he had come to see me in the first place and why he was continuing in analysis. Although he had been unaware of it at the time, the anxiety that he had experienced in going into restaurants and before making business phone calls had in part reflected an anticipation of the painful confusion and loneliness that he would feel in talking to people.

This confusion and loneliness connects directly to the surface-centredness of contemporary life, to postmodernity – with its fragments of mediated experience, its communicational and computational dislocation of human social relationships, its narcissistic consumption patterns, in which both persons and objects are rendered interchangeable and equivalent. This fluid, dislocating cultural experience is full of contradiction, particularly as regards self-experience. Postmodern culture inaugurates a multidimensional set of radically discontinuous social contexts, in which the fragmented and dispersed subject is wedged uneasily between reflexive self-actualization and capitalist pressures that promote narcissistic, materialistic self-enclosure. In terms of capitalist hierarchical domination, there lies real terror and despair: the inner core of the self is depleted, experience and meaning are torn apart, and desire is rendered an imaginary construct of the commodity form itself. Despite variations in self-experience, the danger here is that disconnection will slide into complete withdrawal – a refusal of experience, a foreclosure on thinking. In this instance, what is vital to interpersonal relationships is eaten away, desire and creativity having been replaced by ravaging confusion and fragmentation. Such confusion can be defended against, however, through an immersion in mirrors: that is, the appearance of integration constructed by a consumption-based culture which creates within the subject a mirror-image of its own inner logic. This state of affairs, it seems, is what Ogden is seeking to deconstruct, and refashion, in Dr L's self-awareness: a reflective scanning of his severing of emotional connection between self and other. As Ogden writes of Dr L's loneliness in conducting business transactions: 'He unconsciously expected that once again there would be only the illusion of two people talking to one another.'[31]

It is beyond the scope of the concerns of this chapter to document the psychological changes that Dr L underwent during his analysis with Ogden. However, it is worth emphasizing that in uncovering a space for reflective awareness as regards his more immediate, lived experience, Dr L gradually came to confront this fear of 'not knowing'. That is to say, he was increasingly able to tolerate feelings of ambivalence, confusion, emptiness and despair, and to reflectively scan such feelings and thoughts as a constitutive part of his self-identity.

Compare Dr L's experience with that of a more extreme case of self-misrecognition. 'A romance with pain: a telephone perversion in a woman?', by Arlene Kramer Richards, is a psychoanalytic investigation of a woman with a sado-masochistic telephone perversion.[32] The article describes the psychodynamic experiences of a twenty-year-old woman who compulsively engaged in telephoning in order to enact a fantasy of phallic intrusion into the space of the other. This compulsive telephoning, the author points out, was not of an obscene type, but rather was an intrusion into the field of the other which allowed access to repressed sexual experience. The woman, for example, one evening telephoned her room-mate (who was over at her boyfriend's apartment), seemingly unaware that the actual purpose of her call was to intrude into her friend's sexual relationship. As this is reported:

> The patient got [the boyfriend's] phone number, called, asked to speak to her friend, and began her usual litany: 'You don't know how much it hurts inside'. The friend snapped: 'What are you, some kind of pervert? You want to get in the bed with us, or what?' She hung up. The question opened a new phase of the analysis; the patient went into detail about her feelings when she made such calls. She would become more and more tense until she achieved relaxation. The pain inside referred to her retention of urine until the bladder became painfully full and an orgastic shudder ended the tension and the content of the calls was a reflection of their content.

Denial of experience, the pouring of sexual desire and affect into the telephone call, and a genital sensation derived from the urinary stream: these are the core elements of this elaborate fantasy scenario. In order to access her sexual experience, this woman had to involve the listener, through the electronic mediation of the telephone, in her inner bodily pain – a drivenness of which she had but dim awareness.

The person whom this young woman telephoned most frequently was her mother; she 'soothed herself' by contacting her mother 'at all hours of the day'. This self-soothing, says Richards, was experienced by the woman as essential to combat the increasing difficulties and tensions of her daily life, especially her inability to get along with the people she lived with in a college dormitory. By telephoning her mother, the woman was able to transcend these personal difficulties, at least momentarily. The telephone offered a means of escape, an electronic diversion elsewhere and other, beyond the realm of immediate experience, a transcendence of the here-and-now. 'With the telephone in her mind', writes Richards, 'she felt powerful.' The telephone, Richards argues, was used to filter out awareness of the missing phallus in this woman's psychical economy. It offered the fantasized illusion of narcissistic self-unity. It allowed her to imagine, and thus experience, her voice as a phallus. Here Richards draws a parallel between her subject and the female singer in the French film *Diva*, who refused to allow her voice to be recorded because she did not want the audience to enjoy her singing away from her. In *Diva*, recording of the singer's voice was perceived as a kind of rape or female castration.

The woman's personal narrative demonstrates a highly conflicted sense of sexual identification, brought about partly by stereotypical gender roles within her family, and partly by fantasies of voyeurism and exhibitionism experienced at different points of her life. Richards suggests that the woman was plagued by envy, especially penis envy, which she documents by noting a key childhood memory of watching her four older brothers engage in 'pissing contests'. The urinary stream, she argues, may have been imbued with special importance as a result of this identification. Significantly, memories of having been displaced by her father in the winning of maternal love are also prevalent. During her childhood, the woman's father was often absent from the family home. To compensate, her mother would take her along on shopping outings, leaving her four brothers at home; and as such she became 'her mother's escort'. But when her father was at home, he would accompany his wife, and she would be left at home with her brothers. As a consequence, she would stage temper-tantrums when her parents were about to go out, pleading to be taken along. It is at this point that the telephone enters the narrative. 'Mother would telephone her to make sure she was all right. The telephone came to her rescue, gave her powers over her brothers, symbolizing the fantasy penis.'

The other key component leading to the woman's perversion, says Richards, stems back to her complaints of genito-urinary pain, which was so severe that she underwent several operations, from the age of eight. In particular, she had a mechanical stretching of her urethra. The bodily pain she experienced, coupled with the anguish and humiliation suffered during the interviews and examinations for the operations, fused to produce agonizing memories of this period that had been repressed into her unconscious.

For our purposes, what is especially significant is that Richards makes the degree of awareness of the erotic nature of the woman's excitement and satisfaction crucial throughout the article. As she comments:

> Her telephone calls condensed her fantasy of her father's phallic intrusion on her mother with the patient's auditory intrusion on her . . . At the same time, she was dependent for her sexual pleasure on the use of the telephone and on the power and narcissistic enhancement of the urinary stream. Genital sensation was available only through this deviant scenario which had to be acted out in reality, compulsively, frequently, and with a sense of being driven that prevented her from experiencing actions of her own.[33]

It is interesting to note that it is the electronic mediation of the telephone which has absorbed the woman's outpouring of fantasy.

For the telephone is a medium, an electronic trace, which links self and other through the restructuring of space (and time as well, in the case of international calls where there is a temporal lag between caller and called), a restructuring that brings absent speakers together. This restructuring of space between self and other achieved through use of the telephone is compatible with the preservation of the fantasy scenario under consideration here – that is, a fantasy of phallic intrusion on the other. From this angle, the memory of telephone rescue – the telephone symbolizing the fantasy penis which links child and mother – can perhaps be regarded as a screen memory. It was information, or more accurately an unconscious representation, that the woman was unable to process emotionally as a child; but the critical point is that it was a thought that was retained in fantasy due to its affective significance. It was 'stored' for later thinking: emotional processing that was to be activated in psychoanalysis because of the harnessing of this fantasy to reality, the acting out of phallic intrusion on the other via the telephone. Significantly, in the course of the analysis, Richards reports, the woman attained some reflexive awareness of the pain and anger being displaced in the fantasy scenario, and was gradually able to reorganize her psychical relation to self, others and objects in a more autonomous manner.

A man out of touch with his inner needs and desires, a woman overwhelmed by anxiety in the face of daily life: common enough case-studies, each of them, and there are many more like them in the contemporary psychoanalytic literature. But the significant feature of each case-study for our purposes is the place of postmodern technical and cultural forms in the binding and holding of unconscious representation and affect. The process of binding and holding is registered in differing ways in each case-study: one through an immersion in the computerized world of multinational capitalism, the other through electronic mediation. In the context of not being able to process one's internal state emotionally, these socio-institutional formations are used to ward off anxiety, and to hold or freeze unconscious fear until it is capable of being addressed and thought about. Both examples demonstrate the use of substitute formations to enact obsessional practices (the displacement of anxiety in feverish work and compulsive telephoning), and both contain elements of a refusal of experience in the fashioning of a false self.

But notwithstanding the use of postmodernist technical and cultural forms in defending against awareness of anxiety, these examples also show their subjects to be capable of exploring other psychical paths – to tolerate the beginnings of feelings of emptiness confusion, ambivalence and despair. We do not see here a totalized disintegration of the self (despite the existence of traits which indicate imprisonment in a frightening world in which feelings and thoughts are experienced as things); but nor is there a failure to make use of the raw material of experience in thinking and reflecting on unmapped territory of the self. These subjects demonstrate, on the contrary, that the emergence of thinking and the processing of affect are deeply interwoven with the ability to use objects in fantasy, not as foundations or groundings, but as contingent indicators of the representational activity of the self. Both subjects, through thinking and reasoning, which are tied to the toleration of ambivalence and ambiguity, shift away from their rigid defences against anxiety and towards a higher level of self-reflexivity, based on an appreciation of difference and multiplicity.

5

Postmodernity, or Modernity in Reverse

Reflexive Scanning, Strangeness, Imagination

As we move through the object world, breathing life into the impersonal, we gather and organize our personal effects. As we collide with other subjectivities, we exchange differing syntheses, and leave the other with his or her inner senses of our self, just as we carry the spirit of the other's idiom within our unconscious. We can conjure these spirits within us as we evoke the name of the other, although what we deeply know is only ever partly thought, and strangely defies the codes of thought we have valued so highly in Western culture.

Christopher Bollas

Unlike the post-structuralist vision, the question of subjectivity cannot be limited to a schizo-fragmentation of experience, but should instead be understood within an intersubjective realm of multiple, reflexive fashionings. Reflexivity today is not only a core means for the generation of experience, but is central to the interplay of identity and culture. This reflexiveness of self intersects in novel and unexpected ways with postmodernity, the world of globalized social institutions, mass media, information technology and computational networks.

Let me briefly contrast recent understandings about the contemporary culture of postmodernity with the arguments I have sought to develop in the preceding chapters. The era of postmodernity – with its globalized market pluralism and hallucinogenic surfaces, its media populism and fetishism of information and codes, its unexpected institutionalized violence and reifying of high-tech, its unrelenting deconstruction of totalization and ideological closure – has been identified by many commentators with a deep anxiety, and accompanying disavowal, of social meanings and political involvement. The contemporary mode of the social and political as such witnesses the transition to an atomized landscape of the self-same, a new era of 'anything goes'. So too, the collapse of the centred, self-identical subject of modernity has been viewed by many as signalling the end of the line for subjectivity, meaning, truth and ethics. The inauguration of the postmodern spells the death of the subject, its displacement to fractured and multiple identity positions, theoretically bundled in contemporary discourse or rhetoric under the register of *fragmentation*.

The ideas I have developed in this book challenge such presuppositions. Postmodernity dislocates – that is certainly true. The postmodern condition is fraught with dislocations which arise as an outcrop of cultural standardization and capitalist commodification. But if we understand psychic dislocation and fragmentation principally as *reaction* to the cultural multiplicity and institutional dynamism of postmodernity, as something like a knee-jerk response to the new and the unfamiliar, and if we see that such reactions are in turn open to reflective thinking and scanning, then a more complex picture emerges. This is a picture of the self-reflexive subversions of postmodernity being shifted up a gear into a fully blown processing and mapping of the psychic, social and cultural levels. By this I mean that experiences of dispersal and fragmentation, or more commonly of shock, are regrooved into the textures of everyday life, and thus become available for thinking and processing precisely *as* reactions, responses, feelings, moods, dispositions. What is perceived, in short, is the role of anxiety in the shaping of thought-systems and discourses. The chance of imagination lies here in an opening out of the self to difference and otherness. The anxiety of fragmentation is discovered as fear, as interwoven with memory, and thus as *not* prophetic of the future.

'Postmodernity', writes Zygmunt Bauman, 'means a resolute emancipation from the characteristically modern urge to overcome ambivalence and promote the monosemic clarity of the sameness.'[1] This postmodern practice can also be thought of as a psychic capacity to become immersed in experience without the need for codes and explanations, and with tolerance for confusion and ambiguity. Such tolerance, and the mode of thinking in which it is implicated, signals a revision of modernity, a reflexive engagement with the modern urge to control, order and enframe the other. Indeed, following Bauman's critique, 'postmodernity reverses the signs of the values central to modernity'. This reversal primarily involves a rejection of the quest for control and certitude, and a deintegration of personal and cultural experience within a plurality of differences – indeed to the otherness of the Other. This deintegration is not, however, to be thought of as necessarily involving self-disintegration. On the contrary, an openness to experience, and especially experience of other persons and forms of life, is essential to the enrichment of imagination, symbolization, reverie – in short, to *reflective subjectivity*. As distinguished from modernity, then, postmodernity replaces the codification of experience (the enframing procedures of rational ordering and hierarchy) with multiple modes of communication and discourse, of 'open systems' (to transpose Kristeva's psychic topology) connected and engaged with individual particularities and differences. The psychic and personal effects of postmodernity are the emergence of new forms of thinking, mapping and scanning as regards relations between selfhood and otherness, identity and non-identity, and sexuality and gender.

In the previous chapter, the interconnections between postmodernity and the reflexive mapping of subjectivity were explored, primarily through an application of contemporary psychoanalytic theory to issues of self and fantasy. In this concluding chapter, I shall explore further the nature of self-experience in the postmodern, especially as regards the reflexive scanning of identity, difference and otherness. In exploring postmodernity in this way, I want to trace and rethink some ideas articulated by the British psychoanalyst Christopher Bollas concerning the psychic mechanisms which underpin the transformation of subjectivity into the object-world. Furthermore, I shall suggest that it is through strangeness and shock that self-experience opens out to difference and otherness in the postmodern. This interplay of strangeness and containment will be drawn upon to show some of the ways in which postmodernity radicalizes the political dimensions of fantasy and personal life.

Reflexivity, scanning and postmodernity

Postmodernity presumes a certain advanced degree of reflexivity and scanning of the affective contradictions of subjectivity in relation to cultural reproduction. The interpretation of postmodernity I have sought to develop in this book focuses on what happens once the psychic subject becomes dissociated from the normative force of

129

modernist codes and blueprints, as well as from modern conditions of hierarchical domination. The postmodern rejection of unified subject-selves, along with its refusal to frame the problem of desire in terms of a normative discourse of Law or the Name-of-the-Father, asserts an emancipatory development in which subjectivity reaches new and second-degree levels of reflexive scanning of the intricate connections between the internal world and cultural forms. Another way of putting this point is to say that, in breaking from the normative enclosure of modernist rules, foundations and laws, postmodernity inaugurates a reflexive world of self-constitution – a world in which our innermost hopes and dreads are mapped against an awareness of the multidimensional forms of self-experience. Postmodernity thus gives rise to a reflexive mapping of *ourselves*, a mapping of selves multiple, other and decentred.

The reflexive mapping of self-experience – the modes in which we endow objects with psychic representation – has been one of the principal themes of this book and I shall attempt to elaborate upon the connections between such reflexive mapping and postmodernity in some detail in what follows. Reflexive awareness of the unconscious instantiation of the self into the object-world, I have suggested in earlier chapters, can be traced to the emergence of modernity itself – that is, to post-traditional social contexts in which meaning is constituted in and through desire-driven self-actualization and interpersonal relationships. Yet although reflexive mapping can be traced within the culture of modernity, it is only with the advent of postmodernity that such scanning of our psychic states emerges as a fully distinctive set of possibilities and pressures as regards personal and social development.

Such postmodern mapping and scanning connects directly with a radical shift in the whole status of subjectivity itself – a shift which, I have suggested, involves Wilfred Bion, Cornelius Castoriadis and Julia Kristeva as much as Freud and Klein, as well as Jean-François Lyotard and Jean Baudrillard. For it is not just that the globally colonialist media of random images and jumbled signs in the postmodern profoundly dislocate those representational spaces that were once the private domain of the liberal autonomous subject or ego, for such speeding-up of the disintegration of the illusion of unified subjectivity has been greeted mostly with a sigh of relief everywhere. Rather the contemporary subject, in full postmodernity, now appears more and more aware of an unconscious realm of representational contingency which, if appropriately reinterpreted or turned back upon itself, can be put to a multiplicity of uses in the fabrication of significance and meaning. As for dispersal and fragmentation, meanwhile, these remain dominant aspects of the chaotic surfaces of postmodern society. But the critical point here is that such cultural fragmentation can be plucked from the realm of imaginary fictive appearances, whose compulsive repetitions should certainly not be underestimated, and redeemed as nonetheless a self-defining experience within a cluster of broad affective states. From this angle, postmodern society and culture can now be understood as that dispersal of objects and experiences that release a polyvalence of meaning into elaborating subjectivities, where 'representational wrappings' of self and world are grasped in the unfolding of sexual desire, memories, feelings, dreams, projections and introjects.

At the same time, there is a profound dislocation of those universal maps which offered modes of measurement for action and experience, and which claimed direct access to a social reality presumed unproblematic and given in advance. It is precisely this dislocation of centralized perspectives and world-views which inaugurates post-modern subjectivity and constitutes the reflexivity of representational contingency specific to it. What qualifies for this specifically postmodern mode of reflexivity, to repeat, is an enlarged cultural and technical space for the interplay of psychic simplification or de-differentiation on the one hand, and new forms of psychic scanning and registration on the other. Put simply, this expansion in subjectivity refers to an enlarged awareness of those objects and experiences that betoken an unleashing of the complexity of self, an immersion in the experience of complex, contradictory worlds. The central subjective tension, then, is precisely that of a relationship between unconscious dissemination and reflective subjectivity, of the representational wrapping which underpins psychic signification (the conversion of beta-element into alpha-element in Bion's terms) and elaborated thinking. In the words of Christopher Bollas:

> The concept of self experiencing is ironic, as its referential ambiguity (does it mean the self that experiences or the experiencing of our self?) is strangely true to the complexity of being human. All self experiencing involves this split, which can be described as a division between ourself as simple selves (when we are immersed in desired or evoked experience) and ourself as complex selves (when we think about experience). Naturally such distinctive states may overlie one another, so that I may be reflecting upon an experience in the immediate past while another part of me is already within a disseminating experience.[2]

The central tension or contradiction in self-experiencing is therefore reinscribed in every process of object selection: an unconscious immersion in units of experience which are only partly thinkable (since that immersion is itself a dense condensation of self and object-world), and a reflective lifting of such unconscious experience into thinking and articulation.

The account of self-experience and reflection offered by Bollas strikes me as largely right, save that in conditions of postmodernity there is a multiplication in the linkages – or a kind of criss-crossing – of this interpenetration of the personal and social spheres. In the globalizing society in which we now live, it is not the reflexive awareness of inner experiencings as such that somehow leads us into other possible worlds; rather, alternative futures (that is, possibilities of existence different from those previously imagined) are opened up by the endless cross-referencing of experience and reflexivity from inside of the social realm itself. Against a backdrop of high technology and computational information, postmodernity is a culture of all-embracing self-referentiality. This self-referentiality is perhaps most apparent in those forms of media popularism that promote the dispersal and multiplication of sectors of experience that were previously subject to modernist modes of classification and compartmentalization. Postmodern styles appropriate and recycle mass culture in all forms of contemporary media and image production, from the playful mixing of past pop classics with rap and techno music, through to contemporary blendings of street and punk fashion with *haute couture*. A playfulness of form, the key signature of which is pastiche (according to Jameson), explodes established differences between 'high' and 'low' culture, that realm of the aesthetic which in various modernist modes ruthlessly divided all cultural production into either the 'popular' or the 'elite'. What, after all, is the aesthetic location of, say, Prince – who renounces his stage name in order to reinvent his identity and releases a range of new musical productions that soar to the top of the pop charts, and whose back catalogue is used as the score for a world tour by the Joffrey Ballet Company? Or Dennis Leary, who in his solo performance, *No Cure For Cancer*, firmly situates comedy within the cultural sublime, as a turning back of modernist American prejudices upon themselves to produce an uncanny laughter effect?

But the problematic of postmodernity can also be approached in another way, investigating it not only for its dislocation of modernist modes of classification and critique, but also for its mixing of experience and reflectiveness in various social and cultural phenomena.

With the intensification of our media-dominated world, and the speeding-up of electronic communication, there is an effort to reconstruct psychic mechanisms for new identifications and cultural expressions. That is to say, there is a certain parallel between the self-referentiality of postmodern cultural and technical forms on the one hand, and experience within and reflection upon these forms at the psychic and personal levels on the other. This possibility of thinking the liberation of differences in the postmodern might be approached through reference to the representational instability of media information in the late twentieth century; the 'instantaneity of communication', as Baudrillard conceptualizes the simulatory dimensions of contemporary culture. New technologies of communication – VCRs, satellites, cable TV, the information superhighway – are seen as exemplary of a world fragmentary and chaotic on its surfaces, yet one that also offers an opportunity for the recoupling of experience and significance. What, exactly, might such a recoupling of multidimensional experience and polyvalent meaning mean for human subjectivity and psychic processing? Recoupling, here, consists in *the making of affective contact between identity and non-identity* in productive ways, whether this takes the form of reimagining self-identity, cultural products, social processes or political institutions.

Oddly enough, the relationship between identity boundaries, mass media images and consumerism has generally been theorized pessimistically within the dominant cultural and psychoanalytic treatments of the topic. We are told that, in the age of postmodernity, the multiplication of media perspectives on the world requires increasing projective identifications from the subject; identifications that, once invested in chaotic social and cultural forms, lead to a loss of those parts of the self regarded as essential for inner-directed subjectivity and personal agency. It is as if the multiplication of electronic communication (and the symbolic transmission it encodes) leads to a 'wearing out' of significance and meaning, all of which is translated at the psychical (or psychoanalytic) level as a deadening of human subjectivity, as a kind of non-subject – the fragmented or schizophrenic self – reduced to little more than random TV channel changing or the libidinal excesses of consumerism. Yet the other, psychical and political side of postmodernity – I have argued – is an opening out of subjectivity to an immersion within experience, worlds which invite us to emphasize the more positive aspects of this reconfiguration of identity and non-identity, selfhood and otherness. For the projection of self into objects, through the reflexive framing

133

and intersubjective recognition of fantasy, marks a psychical signification of affective states, an unconscious communication of the mental interplay of desire and death, sexual excitement and rage, anxiety
and guilt.

Bion's work, discussed in detail in chapter 4, is especially important here, since it helps us to see the transformative aspects of experience in the projection of affective states into persons, objects and
events. Bion highlights that, in order to psychically signify, the subject
must become immersed in sectors of experience, a type of surrender to
the here-and-now of the moment which underpins the attachment of
meaning to experience. Indeed, this transfer of unconscious affective
states into units of experience is the precondition for thinking as well
as the storing of thought as memory, of which more will be said
shortly. At this point, the crucial aspect to note of this interplay of
experience and thinking is that it underpins the subject's capacity to
engage with other people in elaborating, and reflecting upon, the
affective and representational realm of their unconscious world.
Viewed this way, projective and introjective identification are key
mechanisms in the constitution and transformation of self-experience
and intersubjective relations, as well as society and culture more
generally.

However, the thorny question still remains as to the impact of
postmodernity upon psychic experience, especially as regards projective identification and the interplay of lived immediacy and reflective thinking. So far I have underscored the various unconscious
oscillations between self and object, oscillations located in the
intersubjective realm of postmodern culture. But what has been said
about the social and technological dynamics of postmodernity in
previous chapters suggests that transformations in self-experience are
not limited to the regulation of interpersonal relationships alone.
Rather, there are also new and profound transformations at the
intersection of postmodernity (as an institutional globalized system)
and human subjectivity (as the reflexive mapping of the creativity and
indeterminacy of fantasy and imagination). What I shall endeavour
to show here is that personal and cultural experience is shaped by, yet
also shapes, *postmodern containing environments*. By postmodern
containing environments I refer to institutional settings which function to secure and structure boundaries in the translation or
transcoding of unconscious affective states into polyvalent significance and meaning.

Postmodernity places a question mark against the unconscious
psychic investment of persons, objects and events. The age of the

postmodern extends and radicalizes the reflexive instantiation of the self into the object world. Produced by the end of modernist codes and traditions, the processing of affective experience runs up against its limits as governed purely by external norms. All of which is to say that fantasy, as the psychical structuring of personal and social life, has become a category which can now be filled – or, better, reflexively fabricated – according to emotional character and intersubjective regulation. To put it in this way is to say that men and women, in conditions of postmodernity, are increasingly finding ways of think-ing about, or more typically of thinking less defensively about, their own affective and representational experience, as well as the role of fantasy in their own lives. Anxiety, guilt, rage, sexual excitement and memory are put under a microscope in both personal life and cultural production in the postmodern. This process is registered, say, in explorations of private terrors and anxieties in psychotherapy or psychoanalysis, in cultural debates and historical interpretations of the role of testimony and memory in relation to the Holocaust, in institutional mappings of multiple consumer markets, in the zoning of the politics of identity – and especially marginalized identities – in the popular and academic culture of the West, and so forth. Implicit in all this is an attempt to take in, scan and think about something other, something beyond the realm of conscious knowledge and experience. Moreover, such mental activity implies a reflexive awareness of fan-tasy as a constellation of representations and feelings in which the form of object relatedness, the degree of ambivalence and the intersec-tion of projections and introjections are subject to the flux of ongoing development.

In a passage in *Being a Character*, Bollas makes the following point about the process of object engagement:

> the processional integrity of any object – that which is inherent to any object when brought to life by an engaging subject – is used by the individual according to the laws of the dream work. When we use an object it is as if we know the terms of engagement; we know we shall 'enter into' an intermediate space, and at this point of entry we change the nature of perception, as we are now released to dream work, in which subjectivity is scattered and disseminated into the object world, transformed by that encounter, then returned to itself after the dialectic, changed in its inner contents by the history of that moment.[3]

This way of understanding the interweaving of self and object under-scores the multiplex contradictions of subjectivity itself, and so directs

our attention to the representational and affective forms in the production of meaning. In Bollas's hands, the Winnicottian theory of
transitional space becomes one not only of in-between experiencing,
but also of a holding of the trace of the object itself. The human
subject, for Bollas, inhabits highly condensed psychic textures of the
object world. Put simply, it is as if that unconscious communication
which arises between people in using everyday objects is somehow
deeply inscribed into these structures of interaction, preserved in the
object-world for self-experiencing and understanding in the future.
'As we encounter the object world,' writes Bollas, 'we are substantially metamorphosed by the structure of objects; internally transformed by objects that leave their trace within us.'

What exactly is this trace? From the perspective of post-Kleinian
theory and its object-relational offshoots, the trace of the object has
its roots in a web of affects, splittings, projective identifications, part-
object relatedness and omnipotent thinking, all of which marks a
structural boundary for the defensive self-holding of affective states.
The personal history of any object is that of an unconscious oscillation between love and hate, excitement and guilt; a kind of holding of
both libidinal *jouissance* and tormenting frustration. This is in part
what Bollas is getting at when he says that certain objects are like
'psychic keys' for particular individuals, in that they enable an opening out of unconscious experience, a symbolic context for the elaboration of selves. Hence, Bollas speaks of the *transformational*
aspects of the object, as something which releases and preserves the
erotics of individual subjectivity.

Provocatively, Bollas claims that the preservation of affective states
is based on modalities of *conservative or mnemic objects*; the *storing*
of affects within the object-world of places, events and things.[4] This
investment of affect in conservative objects can remain 'stored' until
such time as the subject is able to reclaim such self-defining experience
in and through symbolic elaboration. In so doing, the human subject
might be said to be engaged in an act of 'emotional banking', de-
positing affects, moods and dispositions into the object-world and
storing such aspects of self-experience until they are withdrawn for
future forms of symbolization and of thinking. As an example of such
affect-storage, the self-psychological analysts Atwood and Stolorow
discuss the case of a man who regularly used a tape recorder to
deposit and monitor his feelings outside of therapy. 'This use of the
tape recorder as a transitional object', they comment, 'both
concretized the injured state of the self and reinvoked the empathic

136

bond with the therapist, thereby enabling the patient to regain a sense of being substantial and real.'⁵ Different objects, of course, have different levels of significance for each of us as subjects; and all of us, in the unconsciousness of day-to-day life, are investing objects both to contain and to elaborate our various selves. The investment of affect in objects is therefore something of an open-ended affair: such investment can help either to unlock or to imprison the creativity of the self. The imprisoning of the self within the object-world – in which thoughts and feelings are experienced not as symbolic elaborations, but as things-in-themselves – is theorized by Bollas as a point of affective closure. Further, the mind is emptied of pain through the defensive use of omnipotent thinking and denial, and the self is fixed through an ideological framing (familial, religious, nationalistic and so forth) of what the world is really like. The unlocking of the self through the storing of affects in the object-world, however, permits a multiplication of experience and a transformation in pleasure, creativity, fulfilment. The use of an object as transformational, whether we speak of an immersion in music, literature or horse racing, helps to open the self to the multiplicity and discontinuity of experience.

Pursuing the ideas developed by Bollas, let me now modify and contextualize this interpretation in terms of current social and cultural contexts. In contemporary societies, there is an increasing awareness of the multidimensional ways in which people use objects (both human and non-human) to elaborate and hold their affective states. This increasing awareness is that of postmodern reflexivity, and it marks the regulation of affective states off from other social-historical conditions precisely through this ceaseless 'self-monitoring' (to borrow a term from Anthony Giddens) of personal and social relationships. Such self-monitoring or reflectiveness exposes the self to intense ambivalence, that ambivalence which pervades self-constitution, intersubjective relations and cultural reproduction. Against this backdrop, the self-holding of affective states takes place not only in the domain of personal and sexual relationships, but also in institutional frameworks and generalized media communication. My argument is that postmodernity is a world in which the attachment of unconscious experience to polyvalent meaning is regulated in and through social, technological forms. That is to say, the technical and cultural forms of postmodernity play a central role in the *generation and containment of intersubjective affective states*, rather than simply being a realm on the 'outside' in which thoughts and fantasies play themselves out.

Strangeness, shock and the matrix of containment

We plunge, at this point, into the psychic modes of scanning affective states of ourselves and of the other, especially as concerns a toleration for the irreconcilable and the ambivalent at the level of desire. For what interpretative and affective capacities, we might ask, are called into play in registering the essential ambivalence of desire? How might the psychic process of holding affective states for self-reflection and thinking actually extend to new information about unconscious experience, and about the selves implicated in such experience?

One of the most interesting things about the problem of generating and renewing knowledge of self-experience is that a good deal of the intersubjective regulation of affect takes place outside of linear time. That is to say, the passing of affective states between people, back and forth in the post-Kleinian model of containment, is always overdetermined by personal histories, shot through with that 'compulsion to repeat' which locks the unconscious into a circular temporality. Such repetition forms the context for the transference and counter-transference (or, more commonly, of projective identification and counterprojective identification) in the analytic relationship. It is through unravelling the projections of transference – the repetitive modes of processing psychic activity relating to identity and otherness – that future selves and states of mind are brought to life. Significantly, the exploration of a person's internal, affective repertoire that transference makes possible is one of environmental and cultural as well as psychic history. As Betty Joseph puts this, 'By definition transference must include *everything* that the patient brings into the relationship. What he brings in can best be gauged by our focusing our attention on what is going on within the relationship, how he is using the analyst, alongside and beyond what he is saying.'[6] It is this stress on how the analyst, or other person providing containment in day-to-day life, is used in the regulation of affective states that is crucial to self-understanding: the complexity of mind is accessed through the interpersonal management of fantasy and affect, 'alongside and beyond' what is actually said. Further, the historical complexity of the construction of personal meanings at any given moment is also powerfully underlined in Winnicott's conception of the maternal holding environment. For the infant (says Winnicott) not only develops contact with the mother as an internal object, but creates a relationship with the mother as *general environment*, an environment in which familial and cultural life figure prominently. As such, transference, the intrinsic core of psychoanalysis, is itself traversed by codes of love, morality, ethics and community.

In conditions of postmodernity, what is it that enjoins the language of psychoanalysis with the languages of culture? How does the generation of experience, located within the cultural and technical frameworks of postmodernity, open on to strangeness of the other and of oneself? In this section, I shall briefly discuss some psychoanalytic accounts of otherness in the constitution of human experience. I shall then consider in more detail the relationship between the dynamics of strangeness and the restructuring of identity and difference.

In psychoanalysis, the boundaries of the self–other circuit are radically heterogeneous – both at the level of lived experience and at the level of theory; as something that at once makes our lives manageable and enjoyable on the one hand, and unacceptable and unbearable on the other. Freud, for example, locates this essential ambivalence of self – wishes, needs, desires, thoughts, histories – in that which is forgotten, in those parts of the self which are put beyond the reach of memory. In thinking about the interplay of desire, repression and memory, Freud began to raise such questions as why do people lose affective contact with that which was desirable for and about themselves? And why do such acts of forgetting always return to haunt the realm of psychic functioning – in dreams, in slips of the tongue, in free association and, perhaps most painfully, in symptoms? Freud's answer was that sexuality shatters the field of representation; he says that desire always outstrips the individual's capacity for representation of the self and other people. Desire, in other words, can become available to consciousness only through an exclusion or denial of its indeterminacy; through forgetting. A variety of disguises may be given to it, but the psychic construction of subjectivity, punctuated by sexual excitement and the death drive in Freud's view, depends upon repression and forgetting in order to make tolerable that which refuses to be contained.

If desire is always in excess of meaning, then the feeling of security or safety establishes itself only by getting rid of an awareness of anxiety – or so it often seems. That is to say, the human subject (or subject-to-be), overwhelmed by the force of desire, projects out of itself that which it experiences as dangerous and threatening. Freud writes of this fragile construction of the subject/object boundary in his paper 'Negation', commenting that the separation of self from the outside world is a first solution to difficulties – of desire, representation, otherness – which are intractable. The infantile, narcissistic self, writes Freud, creates an experience of itself through an act of judgement in which the inside and the outside are separated. Freud observes that:

> the judgement is, 'I should like to eat this', or 'I should like to spit it out'; and, put more generally: 'I should like to take this into myself and to keep that out.' That is to say, 'It shall be inside me' or 'it shall be outside me' . . . the original pleasure-ego wants to introject into itself everything that is good and to eject from itself everything that is bad. What is bad, what is alien to the ego and what is external are, to begin with, identical.[7]

In this way, the subject-to-be figures an 'inside' which is protected from the 'outside'; an 'outside' into which it has projected all that which it experiences as negative and frightening.

Yet that which is placed 'outside', beyond the realm of the familiar and the known, actually remains on the 'inside' – at the level of the unconscious – through repression and denial. In this respect, Freud takes up a very radical position as concerns the negativity and perversity of the human subject in its dealings with the object-world. For if it is the realm of desire and fantasy which brings an outside world into existence for the subject in the first place, then all experiences of that world as strange or other are indeed saturated with this originary imagination. This is not to say that human beings are not psychically equipped to register and deal with the outside world; on the contrary, making the unconscious conscious, remembering instead of repeating, creative engagement with the reality principle over domination by the pleasure principle – these were always Freud's aims. But the point is that there can be no return to purely rationalist concepts after Freud. His lasting contribution to social thought is that, from start to finish, subject and object are constituted through a mutually interpenetrating process. Someone or something is always inside us as much as we project and inhabit the space of the object landscape. As a result, the goal of psychoanalysis, and of critical social theory now recast in its shadow, lies in accessing those disowned parts of the self and of the other, parts which have been pushed to the furthest extremes of the 'outside' through repression.

How might these disowned parts of the self be reclaimed? Freud's intriguing response to this is given in his essay 'The uncanny' (1919). Tracing the semantic dynamism of the German adjective *heimlich* – 'homely', 'comfortable' – and its antonym *unheimlich* – 'unhomely', 'uncanny', or 'strange' – Freud suggests that the familiar is itself shot through with the unknown, the strange. The strange lies at the very heart of our identity, of the 'homely'; and strangeness is, so to speak, a way of holding unknown selves by projecting them into something elsewhere and other, through repression and defence. 'We can understand why linguistic usage', writes Freud, 'has extended *das Heimliche* into its opposite, *das Unheimliche*; for this uncanny is in reality nothing new or alien, but something which is familiar and old-established in the mind and which has become alienated from it only through the process of repression.'[8]

The issue of the deintegration and reconstruction of the self, fostered by experiences of uncanny strangeness, can be viewed from still another perspective that adds an important intersubjective dimension to our understanding of the process. In the context of Kleinian thinking on psychic development and change, the generation of experience is bound up with the logics of introjective and projective identification, of taking in and extruding, in the paranoid-schizoid and depressive positions. What emerges most powerfully from the Kleinian approach is that human subjects fashion their view of the world, in unconscious fantasy, through an interplay of projection and introjection of powerful affects – oral rage, paranoid anxiety, persecutory terror, omnipotence, guilt, despair, loss and depression. Affects, then, play a key role in the constitution of psychic meanings, entering into the creation and recreation of those unconscious fantasies that shape interpersonal relationships. Experience of persecutory and depressive affective states, in our contact with others, allows for an exploration and discovery of aspects of self-experiencing that have been previously denied or abandoned in favour of more familiar states of mind. In the Kleinian notion of projective identification, for example, it is possible to conceptualize the interpersonal exchange of persecutory anxiety and terror as containing information about dissociated experiences of mind. Reflective ways of thinking about previously unmanageable sets of fantasies, in the Kleinian view, help to promote an acceptance of the depressive position, as the individual develops an increased capacity for symbolization and thinking, as well as concern for other people.

In a very broad sense, anxiety is viewed through the Kleinian paradigm as containing both progressive and retrogressive functions. It is progressive in the sense that anxiety can be used for thinking about our experiences of pain and of the ways in which we attempt to rid ourselves of bad, persecutory feelings. It is retrogressive in that anxiety can also be used to bind unconscious fantasy and to generate excessive splitting and projective identification for the evacuation (and imagined destruction) of perceived sources of pain. In the contemporary post-Kleinian literature, however, there is a clear shift away from the valorization that Klein and some of her followers accorded to the depressive position over and above the paranoid-schizoid position in terms of psychic well-being. In this revised framework, it is the interplay of paranoid-schizoid and depressive positions which is seen as essential to possibilities for creative experiences and new states of mind. As Ogden observes:

> The paranoid-schizoid mode and the depressive mode serve as essential negating and preserving contexts for one another. The depressive mode is one of integration, resolution, and containment, and if unopposed, leads to certainty, stagnation, closure, arrogance, and deadness. The paranoid-schizoid mode provides the necessary splitting of linkages and opening up of the closures of the depressive position, thus reestablishing the possibility of fresh linkages and fresh thoughts. The integrative thrust of the depressive mode in turn provides the necessary antithesis for the paranoid-schizoid mode in limiting the chaos generated by the fragmentation of thought, the discontinuity of experience, and the splitting of self and object.[9]

Just as Freud suggests that uncanny strangeness functions to destabilize and reconstitute relations of identity and difference, so too the interplay of paranoid-schizoid and depressive positions functions to generate other ways of being and of human experience.

In trying to trace further the possible sites of subversion in subjective and intersubjective experience, it might be helpful at this point to recall Bion's account of the psychotic/non-psychotic aspects of personality. According to Bion, mental growth consists in the extension of thinking and of learning from emotional experience, both of which contribute to the enrichment of non-psychotic parts of the mind. Symbolic meaning is constituted by a subject mediating between the frustration implicit in thinking on the one hand, and contact with the affective roots in and through which thoughts arise on the other. Positing the coexistence of a psychotic aspect of mind, however, Bion argues that subjective experience is profoundly impeded by intolerance of frustration. Excessive envy and hate, when fused with projective identification, tend to denude thought of meanings. These attacks on thinking generate intense anxiety, which further contributes to the evacuation of pain (in projective identification) through omnipotent fantasy and denial.

In developing this outlook, Bion creates a vision of what thinking (as the processing of affective states) has to contribute to the generation of creative living and psychic change that is especially relevant to my argument about postmodernity and the reconstitution of personal and cultural experience. Let us briefly retrace this psychoanalytic construction. Thought, says Bion, precedes thinking. From the point of view of this model, thinking is at once a necessary and transformational process. It might be said that it is in the space between the thought and its elaboration – what Bion calls 'making the unthought thinkable' – that reflective subjectivity comes into being. In thinking, the subject discovers the multiplicity of the world of thought, abstraction and symbolization. The achievement of thinking and of symbol formation proper allows the subject affective contact with this ever-proliferating multiplicity of thought. This world of thought relates not only to internal states of mind (representations, feelings, desires), but also to the dialectical play between self and other of object relations in which identity is defined in terms of cultural, social and political contexts. Bion therefore does not propose a definition of subjectivity in which thinking is processed and experienced in terms of the internal world alone. On the contrary, the individual subject's capacity for processing the frustration implicit in thinking is extremely complex, involving the psychological actions of introjection and projection as well as the processing of self and other through interpersonal interaction. Such processing thus relates both intrapsychic representations and object relationships: the 'contact-barrier' between conscious and unconscious, the frustrations to be tolerated in loss and the absence of objects, the impossibility of absolute truth and certain knowledge, and the like.

It should be clear by this point that Bion regards thinking as an opening out to the complexity of mind, the multiplex processing of elusive experience. In this connection, experience can be viewed as something that always takes us by surprise. Persons, objects and events all have different levels of significance for us in day-to-day life, although the meaning that we attribute to the object landscape becomes known to us only in and through an affective processing known as 'thinking'. For Bion, therefore, the essential intrapsychic and interpersonal task is the 'thinking', or what I call 'scanning', of what has happened in experience in ways that promote personal significance, imagination and authenticity. Investing daily life, the subject creates a dialogue with the psychic dimensions of experiences of self and of others; and the more that complexity and ambivalence can be scanned and tolerated, the more subtle and rich self-constitution will tend to be.

Yet the profound irony of self-elaboration, says Bion, is that people often find it difficult to tolerate the ambivalence and frustration of imaginative and open-ended thinking. Shutting down on the complexity of differing states of mind, the human subject turns to that which is already known, which is perhaps part of a cultural preference for pre-existing patterns of thought and feeling over and above the discovery of new experience. Such flight from the complexity of mind into pre-existing narrative scenarios will tend to have its emotional roots in the unconscious sway of memory; the repetition of scripts or patterns of thought developed in childhood and in family life. In this way, the function of thinking in linking experience and meaning is derailed. Instead of attempting to modify frustration in and through thinking, experience is translated by the subject into the pre-packaged scripts of a reality that is treated as the self-same.

There are, therefore, two broad approaches to dealing with the complexities of mind. One is the intolerance of frustration, in which the subject translates events and experiences into old categories of thought, in order to maintain some level of self-protection in the face of the multiplicity of perspectives and world-views. The other, more taxing and creative approach is a kind of free-floating ambivalence, in which every aspect of the complexity of experience is potentially open to the scanning and enjoyment of the internal world. This latter solution, which Bion sometimes describes in Kleinian terms as a tolerance of the oscillation between paranoid-schizoid and depressive modes of generating experience, involves a working through of conflictive and coercive anxieties in order to set the scene for a transformation in the reflective dimensions of thinking. Since the subject presents itself as an expressive and interpretative being that is always divided in processing potential forms of the 'unthought', those aspects of sensations and perceptions that have not yet been subjected to 'alpha-function', its dissimulation involves a kind of scattering of subjectivity within heterogeneous sectors of experience. This is achieved, says Bion, through tolerated phases of 'catastrophic change'. By catastrophe Bion refers to the experience of dissolution, in which the relation between subject and world is pluralized and disarticulated, and then requires reinsertion into relations of identity and difference. An encounter with the unknown aspects of one's own reality, in Bion's terms, can break open the repetitions of the psychical realm, inscribing its own dislocation within the fixity of memory that persists in misapprehending the present and effecting distorted responses to the self and to others. In short, this is a working through of a misconceived reality. However, in Bion's hands such post-catastrophic working through carries with it the requirement to think about previously unthought aspects of experience, a thinking which is premised upon the creation of contact with wishes and fantasies, delusions and dreams, memories and affects.

The effect of catastrophe, then, is to release difference from the hold of repetition; and in psychoanalytic terms this can be grasped primarily in terms of the crumbling of imaginary fictions and the opening out of the psychical imagination to multiple meanings, to ambivalence and contradiction. Significantly, such a conception of personal and cultural transformation has certain affinities with the work of the German critic Walter Benjamin, especially his later doctrine of the shock-effects of mechanical reproduction. In his 1936 essay 'The work of art in the age of mechanical reproduction', Benjamin wrote of the 'shock effects' of contemporary technology and media, effects he regarded as promoting a 'heightened presence of mind.'[10] The shock-effect characteristic of technical reproduction which most interested Benjamin was that of cinema, that strange blending of montage and dream imagery which he believed derailed the sensory expectations and perceptual habits of the spectator's mind. Aware of the manipulations of capitalist mass media, and appreciative of the tendency of film to reinscribe standardized values at the heart of the narcissistic illusions of the ego, Benjamin nonetheless argued for the powers of technical and media reproduction to dislocate the 'natural' viewpoint cemented in social ideologies. The shock-effect of film and related media arises from its capacity to penetrate and segregate objects from familiar contexts of reality, and the recombining of relations of identity and difference in new and multiple forms.

The Benjaminian notion of shock is implicated in a theory of experience which privileges estrangement and disorientation as the means to recovering a sense of subjectivity which is vital and imaginative. It is a dialectical notion of experience, in which the concrete, intuitive responses of the subject link to broader conceptual, historical reflections.[11] In Benjamin's doctrine the human subject undergoes, as Terry Eagleton has argued, 'the shocking confrontation in which time is arrested to a compact monad, spatialized to a shimmering field of force, so that the political present may redeem an endangered moment of the past by wrenching it into illuminating correspondence with itself'.[12] Yet this registration of shock at the level of the 'monad' is, in my view, indicative of the central limitations of Benjamin's account of personal and cultural transformation. Negations may unfold through shock, certainly. But how, exactly, can shock itself be redeemed into a multiplicity of meanings in personal life? How are the subject's pre-reflexive responses to shock given elaboration, and actually contained, within interpersonal relationships?

A number of issues arise at this point. What changes are occurring in personal and cultural reflexivity in contemporary societies? In what ways are the complexities of mind modified by the development of, and developments in, postmodernity? What psychic meanings do these changes have?

Sketches of postmodern containment

The postmodern world of global institutional dynamism and media technologies does more than simply influence the shape of personal and cultural life; it interlaces in a direct way with psychic life and therefore transforms and reconstitutes the self and interpersonal relationships. My contention is that the world of MTV and widespread global transit, of facsimile and electronic mail, of telecommunications and the information superhighway, computer conferencing and database surveillance, of DIY psychological survival kits and self-help manuals, of burgeoning institutionalized reflexivity in a market-guided consumer society coupled with the technological convulsions of industrialization and modernization, can best be grasped as the achievements of a postmodern institutional system which structures and secures the containment and regulation of intersubjective affective states, rather than representing some of its ideological incarnations in which fantasy and desire simply play themselves out.

Central to the postmodern containment of personal and cultural life has been its radicalization of identity, informed by the multiplication of perspectives and points of view, and coupled with tolerance of ambivalence as concerns otherness and difference. The sketches that follow chart different aspects of postmodern containment – including affect storage, evocative and transformational objects, and post-catastrophic working through – and also the ways in which these institutional and technical forms are shaped by, yet also shape, our psychic and personal lives.

Scanning psychic space: the Walkman

Contemporary technological transformations – the advent of globalized communication systems and new information technologies –

transform our reflexive access to psychic life and affect the most personal aspects of experience. This relates not only to the speed of access to information, but most crucially to the emergence of new technological mechanisms that promote an engagement within imaginary worlds of self, desire, others and culture.

Consider in this regard the Walkman, that portable music system which many individuals increasingly use as they negotiate the time and space transformations of the postmodern age. Travelling through airspace, riding the tube, or perhaps simply wandering about urban shopping malls, the Walkman redramatizes experience between self and world through a condensation of social realities within the sphere of techno-auditory revolution. Superbly mobile and flexible, the Walkman is the perfect companion for those 'postmodern tourists' who move through social space in search of the novel and pleasurable. Perhaps it is also not surprising, therefore, that the Walkman has been targeted by social and cultural critics as that object which best demonstrates the capacity of technology to reconstruct human subjects as totally closed systems, cut off from social interaction and engagement. The Walkman user is a subject constituted through a defensive rejection of the social world in favour of private, aesthetic intensity.

Yet there is much evidence to suggest that such a view is substantially inadequate. A recent psychological survey carried out by Moebius and Michel-Annen suggests that Walkman users listen to music to increase their internal repertoire of affective states. In their view, the prime importance of the Walkman lies not in the direction of social escapism, but rather in a technology that promotes the intensification of inner life as filtered through music. As they write of the Walkman user:

> The music is perceived as consciousness-filling. The cognitive share of experience, intentional thinking goes on to the back burner. Emotions grow in importance, feelings are intensified, there is an increase of impressions. The Walkman brings about no ecstasy in a clinical sense because there is no intoxication, but the musical enjoyment mediated by it has an ecstatic appeal.[13]

Such ecstasy appears to have its emotional roots in the resuming of contact with disowned feelings that music, when heard in a mobile context, in some part promotes. Furthermore, it is in this sense that Moebius and Michel-Annen suggest that the Walkman functions as a transitional object, the creative bridging of inner and outer worlds, identity and difference. 'The Walkman', they conclude, 'recommends itself as an expedient against emotional emptiness.'

But in what ways does the Walkman, as a phenomenon of postmodernity, influence the scanning of psychic life? Julia Kristeva, in her book *Tales of Love*, offers a moving portrait of a young man, Matthew, who used a Walkman to store self-defining psycho-sexual experiences, and later as a sublimational device, through analysis, in the symbolic elaboration of new identifications and identities.

The Walkman functioned in Matthew's psychical economy, says Kristeva, as a defence against emptiness; a defence against that fading or disappearance that Kristeva ascribes to the 'abject' – a fantasized relationship to the archaic mother, a mother who threatens to devour and destroy the self. Without the mediation of an imaginary father, described by Kristeva as an object of the mother's desire, it is as though there is a crowding out of any psychic space into which the human infant can grow; the emerging sense of self being locked, through repetition, into its imaginary unity by the gaze of the mother. According to Kristeva, this was Matthew's predicament: as a child, he had been overwhelmed by the claustrophobic hold of his mother's desire. As Kristeva puts this, 'it seemed apparently inconceivable that she might have a desire other than her child'.[14] With nothing to disrupt it from within – the father failed to effectively intrude into their dual economy – the voracity of feelings of hate and rage directed toward the pre-Oedipal, phallic mother was projected on to the outside world, a world from which they returned to disrupt Matthew's fragile sense of self.

Against this psychical backdrop, the Walkman offered Matthew a preliminary method of searching for something else, some other landmark in the sorting of relations of identity and difference. Affects of both rage and excitement toward the absent father were projected, and stored, in the Walkman; a storage which allowed for the subsequent retrieval of these disowned parts of the self in the restructuring of Matthew's symbolic subject-positions. The Walkman, writes Kristeva,

> allowed Matthew to set up a mobile identity for himself and to reject out of it, as abject, whatever did not belong... Matthew was gleeful, ecstatic, and amorous but only as walkman. The headphones were a spot that included all other spots, an organized, differentiated infinity that filled him with consistency... Analysis made use of the walkman; identifying the shell that the headphones were destined to become; it turned it into a premise of autonomy, of demarcation.

In this account, then, the Walkman offered two kinds of solution to Matthew's personal turbulence. One was the pouring of his obsessional neurosis into the technology as a symbolic enactment. This functioned as a freezing of self-experience, an isolation that at once prevented symbolic elaboration and yet contained this experience of the self for future forms of thinking. The other, subsequent solution was that the Walkman allowed for an unlocking of Matthew's identity, being reflexively drawn into the space of analysis as an object of information about the self and its object relationships.

Stretching culture: the O.J. Simpson trial

Postmodern containing environments promote not only the storage and retrieval of affective states, but also the evocation and transformation of self-experience. 'To be a character', writes Bollas, 'is to enjoy the risk of being processed by the object – indeed, to seek objects, in part, in order to be metaphorphosed, as one "goes through" change by going through the processional moment provided by any object's integrity'.[15] Contemporary technological and media transformations affect the intricate connections between experience and meaning in two basic ways. One is a revolution in the technical frameworks that facilitate personal and social engagement with evocative and transformational objects, an engagement that is more far-reaching in terms of space and time than previously was possible. The second relates to cultural modalities of thinking, the dynamics of ideology. In conditions of postmodernity, there is a radical transmutation in information processing, the restructuring of how we make sense of cultural experience, and the subsequent enlargement or stretching of culture.

Consider the O.J. Simpson case in the United States, for example – where the football hero, media celebrity and sportscaster stood trial for the murder of his ex-wife, Nicole Brown Simpson, and her friend, Ronald Goldman. As with the Gulf War, the Los Angeles riots and the Rodney King beating, the arrest and trial of Simpson was an event made for mass communications. Yet the catapulting of the Simpson case into a cultural obsession – a compelling drama that mixed sexual violence and racial difference with murder – was an outcome of media reporting that was quite unanticipated. That is to say, the media events and media realities surrounding the Simpson case at once magnified and distorted the non-mediated reality of the murder of

Nicole Brown Simpson. Seen in this light, the Simpson case was, in a very powerful sense, a product of mass communication technology: radio, television, cable, magazines, books, the information super-highway – all facilitating the worldwide diffusion of information. For example, television coverage of the police chase of Simpson's white Ford Bronco along southern California freeways was viewed by an estimated 93 million people on networks across America. Similarly, both the preliminary hearing and the trial of Simpson were covered live by many television stations, and were repetitively billed as 'The Trial of the Century'. As an indication of the market's appetite for things Simpson, seven books were published about the case in the USA, and that was actually prior to the trial itself. Inspired by the contemporary notion of free and open information, the mass media influenced, and were also influenced by, this fever of interest in Simpson.

How are we to understand the power of mass communication in reshaping the Simpson case? As a sign of the commodification of celebrity to the nth degree? As an indication of a society obsessed with entertainment? Or perhaps as a dispersal of culture into that of 'hyperreality'? Such ideas are certainly not without some merit, in so far as they draw attention to the simultaneous mediatization and globalization of contemporary social life. But where these perspectives fail to identify what is truly significant about this media coverage of Simpson lies in the avoidance of the fears and anxieties which have engaged people most intimately. For the sheer diversity of this media coverage, from daily news updates through to Internet electronic scrutiny, provides compelling evidence of the conflictual emotions and political differences which the Simpson case has galvanized. The Simpson case clearly touches on powerful political and cultural issues, of which race, gender, sexuality and justice are some of the most salient. Since my focus here concerns the context of changing relations between technology and culture, I shall not attempt to analyse these political currents in any detail. Instead, in what follows, I shall concentrate mainly on certain aspects of the restructuring of culture and technology, reflexive scanning and media, in people's working through of the Simpson case.

One way of charting that working through is to look briefly at the interactive nature of the Internet and other computer-based on-line information services. Such technologies allowed people around the globe to explore certain repressed political and social issues, such as those of race, gender and sexuality, provoked by the Simpson case; to question social attitudes and psychological stereotypes; and to transform received social meanings into more open-ended and reflective cultural concerns. Consider, for instance, the role of Internet technology in response to the 'blackening' of Simpson's skin colour for the cover of an edition of *Time* magazine. This alteration of Simpson's photograph was seen by many as an effort to racialize and criminalize his identity. As John Fiske observes, 'the familiar O.J. was hardly recognizable, but that was not [the] point: what was perfectly recognizable was the even more familiar figure of the Black-male-criminal'.[16] Significantly, the picture created by *Time* generated angry debate on an Internet African American bulletin board. Contributors proposed and attacked various theories of racism, of the nature of criminalization in the sphere of race relations, as well as considering the potential trial consequences of what was termed the 'niggerizing' of Simpson.

So too in the formal institutional domain, the Simpson case evoked containing environments by which American society sought to reflect on the kinds of political and social conditions bound up with, and in some sense responsible for, such an eruption of racist and sexist ideologies. At Harvard Law School in 1994, for example, many first-year law undergraduates enrolled in a new course, 'Cyberlaw: A course in skills of mind and practice'.[17] The course focused exclusively on the Simpson murder trial, and students undertook research projects relating to different aspects of the case, such as whether DNA evidence should be admitted at the trial. Of particular interest, however, was the use of the information superhighway: students and faculty conducted research into the Simpson case using new technologies, primarily through the communications system Counsel Connect, which permitted access to Lexis and Westlaw programs. This technology not only involved the building of electronic data-bases relating to individual research projects. It also formed a techno-logical backcloth for interactive computer communications and conferencing. Participants were able to retrieve hourly news reports, follow daily court transcripts, debate the imbalances of gender and race in the American legal system, and even analyse the impact of new technology and media upon the Simpson trial. This transfer of information, as electronic memos travelled back and forth among the participants, can be viewed as a containment and elaboration of intersubjective psychic states. It is a containment in so far as this technology allowed individuals a space to come to terms with, and think about, issues that many found deeply unsettling as regards the Simpson case.

What I am suggesting here is that the use of such new technologies does not merely function as culturally all-determining or all-fragmenting, as critics often allege. On the contrary, there is an opening out to our psychological and cultural modes of sense-making, a questioning of our access and perception of reality. As a postmodern containing environment, communication technology functions in part to deepen our reflexive scanning of unconscious anxieties and political differences, and thereby offers the possibility of unlocking the pre-existing categories by which we make sense of social experience. In the Simpson case, the Internet and related technologies opened a path for tolerating confusion, for proceeding without absolute guidelines, and a holding space against the rentless modernist drive to wipe out all chaos and otherness. This is not to say that the opening of such a path led all its inhabitants successfully to tolerate ambiguity, ambivalence and uncertainty. But it did mark a point in which people could attempt to think, seriously and passionately, about the conflicts of the case.

Against the claims of liberal humanists, however, it must be stressed that postmodern containing environments are not a neutral medium of information. Rather, as the Simpson saga demonstrates, the space for thinking generated by new technology is bound up with deep and persistent cultural issues of race, gender, sexuality, rights, ethics and justice, issues that are already in social circulation. Nonetheless, what is on offer through technology is a potential space for holding things in mind as well as the possibility for thinking otherwise.

Living with catastrophic change

The climate of catastrophe surrounding the contemporary world is deeply marked by technoscientific rationality and the modes of representation to which it gives rise. Global communication, whilst implicated in the rationalization of the world, brings alive the very destructive, and particularly painful, experiences of torture and mass death that humanity has undergone recently. Bosnia, Rwanda, East Timor, Haiti, Iraq, Beijing: these very contemporary histories of torture are regularly presented before our eyes, although actually to grasp it requires a reflexive involvement with self and world of considerable strain. This strain arises since the barbarous force of States torture has become a core condition of our time (Amnesty International estimates that more than half the governments of the world – many of which are signatories to the United Nations Conventions Against Torture – now practise torture upon their citizens.) As such, torture is also a condition that defines our relation to the future.

Knowledge of torture disturbs, profoundly. It festers in the mind, at once making and breaking the interdependence of the political and personal spheres. Even at a geopolitical distance, torture exerts power over us; it generates fear, despair, terror. Images of torture, regularly displayed in the mass media, have the power to translate such fear into avoidance. We unconsciously turn away from the dread of cruelty, taking flight in panic, the apprehension of catastrophe.

The terror induced by images of State cruelty and torture can, however, sometimes lead to reflection and involvement rather than despair and withdrawal. *The Politics of Cruelty,* by Kate Millett, offers such a starting point for thinking through the more general meanings and shocks provoked by this century of torture and mass death. Millett's analysis is especially interesting in the present context, since she proceeds to analyse torture from the inside, the subjective reactions to State-inflicted pain and humiliation. Her prime focus is the shattering of selfhood and identity in the face of horrific media spectacles of executions and beatings. As Millett writes of this self-dislocation:

> Perhaps, first of all, I must deal with the very fact of my reaction: is it too strong, in some way embarrassing? One's own fault, a weakness, sentimentality, a kind of stupidity, literal mindedness? What even occurs in this flashtide of feeling, this flush – for blood may rush to the face, one experiences a fever, sensation buzzes and scintillates, the stomach responds as it does in panic, an adrenaline response. A fear-or-flight reaction? There is a terrible apprehension of vulnerability.
>
> There is also a blinding experience of shame, of being shamed, even personally shamed, not the grand rational manner of finding human behaviour utterly repellent and confusing – how could people do such a thing, it makes one ashamed of one's species, etc. Another shame – deeper, personal, one's own. A remembrance and accumulation: the shame of being laughed at, degraded, made a spectacle of, giving way slowly to the sting of insult . . . But everything resides in that subtle shift, the difference between despair and anger, that fine line which culture and conditioning have blurred and confused.[18]

Shock, ambivalence and confusion, Millett points out, are often displaced by overpowering feelings of shame. In an age of the technology of mass extermination, the remembrance of cruelty is intolerable. It is psychologically easier, or more comfortable, to turn off. Or so it seems.

Yet the reflexive engagement with such anxieties is possible, under certain social conditions. From this angle, something deep within the self, something deeply shaming, needs to be acknowledged for grasping the pain and humiliation of others. Some unknown aspect of one's own reality needs to be discovered, and this implies putting on hold what it is we think we actually know about ourselves, other people and the social world. Working these unknown aspects of our feelings and experiences through can lead to a greater capacity for confronting otherness, at once personal and political. Provided an individual can tolerate moments of what Bion calls 'catastrophic change', it will be possible to think about what has happened politically, historically and culturally. Here the capacity to tolerate the unknown, to 'go with' uncertainty, is vital to thoughtfulness and critical questioning. Beyond the black and white dichotomy of paranoid-schizoid ideology, to know doubt and ambiguity is to be immersed in the pluralism, difference and spontaneity of postmodern social conditions. Ambivalence, however, should not necessarily be seen as an obstacle to political knowledge and action. The capacity to tolerate feelings of confusion and anxiety is essential to reflective political thinking and judgement. The danger of trying to short-circuit ambivalence, as Millett suggests, is that such a strategy plays into the hands of a culture that already jerks its knee at the very mention of ambiguity.

Afterword: the politics of imagination

An enormous contradiction surrounds the question of the profoundly imaginary dimensions of self and society in contemporary theory. Broadly speaking, the human imagination is recognized as central to defining and regulating selves, identities, cultures and societies in accordance with the interplay of impulse and sexuality in its various forms of rapture and pain, security and danger, hope and despair. This much of Freud is tried and tested: we may forget about the identity of humanity, since the principle of identity is self-contradictory, transfigured always as a condition of desire, and fragmented by the primary processes of displacement and condensation. Paradoxically, however, this dislocation or dispersal of identity is no sooner spoken than forgotten, only to be suppressed by the persistence of structuralist or functionalist 'explanation' in which an archaic yearning for certitude is given free rein. Fearing that the decentring of the subject will translate into a fully blown disintegration, contemporary critics proceed to disown the representational energies by which desire is facilitated, and also to deny the imagination of and for human selves in the name of such abstract classifications as power, difference, body and text. The location of imagination in contemporary theory is thus one of perpetual deferral, at once recognized and disowned, no sooner isolated as central to creativity and self-actualization than locked into a deathly repetition of the self-same.

The significance of the discourse of modernity and postmodernity in this context is that it returns us with full force to the question of the imaginary dimensions of self and society. Here, the central role of the imagination – and, specifically, fantasy – is uncovered in the positing of a compulsive modern drive for order, transparency and uniformity on the one hand, and of a postmodern embracement of plurality, ambivalence and uncertainty on the other. Modern and postmodern cultural forms, I have argued throughout this book, are inconceivable without the specific psychic modalities of desire, anxiety and repression in which such experience and meaning are generated. The nature of fantasy is thus located at the level of the energetic signals, in the form of representation, in which identity and society are constituted. It is not simply that there is a reversal in that strange forgetting by which society institutes itself; even though such a reversal is central to the advent of postmodernity. Rather, contemporary society is split in its modes of affectivity, deploying both modern and postmodern fantasies in the framing of social and cultural life.

Yet the contemporary articulation of cultural differences is insistently identified with recognizing the damaged and traumatized nature of human subjectivity and social communities. Beyond the mirror-image of modernist, imperialist ideologies that oppose self and other, postmodernity takes its stand on the shifting margins of ambivalence and uncertainty, tolerating confusion, and taking risks to affirm the emotional need for autonomous human relationships and social solidarity. This is the chance of postmodernity, a chance beyond the politics of identity to the political future of ourselves.

Notes

FOREWORD

1   Hannah Arendt, *Men in Dark Times* (New York: Harcourt Brace & Company, 1983), pp. viii-ix.
2   Ulrich Beck, *Risk Society* (London and Thousand Oaks: Sage, 1992), p. 21.
3   Dany-Robert Dufour, "Les Désarrois de L'Individu-Sujet," *Le Monde diplomatique*, February 2001, pp. 16–17.
4   Beck, *Risk Society*, p. 137.
5   Pierre Bourdieu, *La Misère du Monde* (Paris: Seuil, 1993), pp. 1449–1554.

INTRODUCTION TO 2ND EDITION: PSYCHOANALYSIS, MODERNITY, POSTMODERNISM

1   Douglas Kirsner, *Unfree Associations: Inside Psychoanalytic Institutes* (London: Process Press, 2000).
2   Julia Kristeva, *Revolt, She Said* (Cambridge, MA, and London: Semiotext (e), 2002), p. 67.
3   Nikolas Rose, *Governing the Soul: The Shaping of the Private Self* (London and New York: Routledge, 1989), pp. 253–54.
4   Rose, *Governing the Soul*, p. 193.
5   Vivien Burr and Trevor Butt, "Psychological Distress and Postmodern Thought" in *Pathology in the Postmodern*, ed. D. See (London and Thousand Oaks: Sage, 2000), p. 194.
6   Burr and Butt, "Psychological Distress and Postmodern Thought," p. 194.
7   Julia Kristeva, *Hannah Arendt* (New York: Columbia University Press, 2001), p. 230.
8   Julia Kristeva, *Hannah Arendt: Life Is a Narrative* (Toronto: University of Toronto Press, 2001), p. 64.
9   Zygmunt Bauman, "The Re-Enchantment of the World, Or, How Can One Narrate Postmodernity?" in *The Bauman Reader*, ed. P. Beilharz (Oxford: Blackwell, 2001).

INTRODUCTION 1ST EDITION: FANTASY, MODERN AND POSTMODERN

1   Sigmund Freud, "A note upon the 'mystic writing-pad'" 5, *The Standard Edition of the Complete Psychological Works of Sigmund Freud,* hereafter SE, trans. J. Strachey (London: Hogarth Press, 1935–74), XIX, p. 230.
2   Jacques Derrida, "Freud and the scene of writing," in *Writing and Difference* (Chicago: Chicago University Press, 1978). pp. 196–231.
3   Zygmunt Bauman, *Modernity and Ambivalence* (Cambridge: Polity, 1990), p. 272.

CHAPTER 1 THE AMBIVALENCE OF IDENTITY: BETWEEN MODERNITY AND POSTMODERNITY

1   Max Weber, "Science as a vocation." in H.H. Gerth and C.W. Mills (eds), *From Max Weber: Essays in sociology* (New York: Free Press, 1974), p. 155.
2   Claus Offe, "Modernity and modernization as normative political principles," *Praxis International*, 7. 1. April. 1987, pp. 2ff.

3 Max Horkheimer, "Rise and decline of the individual." in *The Eclipse of Reason* (New York: Seabury Press, 1974), pp. 128–61.
4 Christopher Lasch, *The Culture of Narcissism* (London: Abacus, 1980) and *The Minimal Self* (New York: Norton, 1984).
5 Jürgen Habermas, *The Theory of Communicative Action* (Cambridge: Polity, 1987).
6 Cornelius Castoriadis, "The retreat from autonomy: Post-modernism as generalized conformism," *Thesis Eleven*, 31, 1992, pp. 21–3.
7 Marshall Berman, *All that is Solid Melts into Air* (London: Verso, 1982).
8 Ibid., p. 24.
9 Ibid., p. 15.
10 Theodore Roszak, *Person-Planet: The creative destruction of industrial society* (London: Gollancz, 1979).
11 Stephen Frosh, *Identity Crisis: Modernity, psychoanalysis and the self* (London: Macmillan, 1991), pp. 19–20.
12 Herbert Marcuse, *Eros and Civilization: A philosophical inquiry into Freud* (London: Ark, 1956).
13 Anthony Elliott, *Social Theory and Psychoanalysis in Transition: Self and society from Freud to Kristeva* (Oxford and Cambridge, Mass.: Blackwell, 1992).
14 Sigmund Freud, *The Interpretation of Dreams*, SE, V, p. 507.
15 Jacques Derrida, "Freud and the scene of writing." *Yale French Studies*, 48, 1972, pp. 96–7.
16 Sigmund Freud, "A difficulty in the path of psycho-analysis," SE, XVII, p. 143.
17 See Jacques Derrida, *Of Grammatology*, trans. G. Spivak (Baltimore: Johns Hopkins University Press, 1976) and *Writing and Difference*, trans. A. Bass (Chicago: University of Chicago Press, 1978); Michel Foucault, *The Order of Things* (New York: Vintage, 1973) and *Power/ Knowledge: Selected interviews and other writings 1972–77* (New York: Pantheon, 1980); Jean Baudrillard, *Mirror of Production*, trans. M. Poster (St Louis: Telos, 1975) and Mark Poster (ed.), *Jean Baudrillard: Selected writings* (Cambridge: Polity, 1988); and Jean-François Lyotard, *The Postmodern Condition: A report on knowledge* (Minneapolis: University of Minnesota Press, 1984) and *The Differend: Phrases in dispute* (Minneapolis: University of Minnesota Press, 1988).
18 Jean Baudrillard, *Simulations* (New York: Semiotext(e), 1983), p. 146.
19 Fredric Jameson, *Postmodernism, or The Cultural Logic of Late Capitalism* (Durham: Duke University Press, 1991), p. 25.
20 Zygmunt Bauman, *Intimations of Postmodernity* (London: Routledge, 1991), p. 35.
21 Zygmunt Bauman, *Modernity and Ambivalence* (Cambridge: Polity, 1990), p. 98.
22 Zygmunt Bauman, *Postmodern Ethics* (Oxford: Blackwell, 1993), p. 245.
23 Jürgen Habermas, *Knowledge and Human Interests* (London: Heinemann, 1972), chapters 10 and 11.
24 D.W. Winnicott, *Collected Papers: Through Paediatrics to Psychoanalysis* (London: Tavistock, 1958).
25 It should be underlined that Winnicott's notion of the "true self" is an ideal type, relied upon to track disturbances in relating to self, to others and to culture. As Winnicott puts this, "there is but little point in

formulating the concept of a True Self, because it does no more than collect together the details of the experience of aliveness', in D.W. Winnicott, *The Maturational Process and the Facilitating Environment* (New York: International Universities Press, 1965), p. 148.

26 Wilfred Bion, *Learning from Experience* (London: Maresfield, 1962), p. 36.

27 Ibid., p. 98.

28 See Cornelius Castoriadis, 'Logic, imagination, reflection', in A. Elliott and S. Frosh (eds), *Psychoanalysis in Contexts: Paths between theory and modern culture* (London and New York: Routledge, 1995), pp. 17–49.

29 Anthony Elliott, 'The affirmation of primary repression rethought', in Elliott and Frosh (eds), *Psychoanalysis in Contexts*, pp. 36–52.

30 Julia Kristeva, *Strangers to Ourselves* (London: Harvester, 1991), p. 189.

31 Ibid., p. 187.

32 Stephen Mitchell, *Hope and Dread in Psychoanalysis* (New York: Basic Books, 1993), p. 21.

33 Jean Baudrillard, 'On nihilism', *On the Beach*, 5, Winter, 1984, p. 24.

34 Jameson, *Postmodernism*, p. 15.

35 See in particular Gilles Deleuze and Félix Guattari, *Anti-Oedipus: Capitalism and schizophrenia* (New York: Viking, 1977) and Jean-François Lyotard, *Economie libidinale* (Paris: Minuit, 1974). I discuss the limitations of the theories of schizo-analysis and libidinal economy in my *Psychoanalytic Theory: An introduction* (Oxford and Cambridge, Mass.: Blackwell, 1994), pp. 144–61.

36 On this point, see James M. Glass, *Shattered Selves: Multiple personality in a postmodern world* (Ithaca: Cornell University Press, 1993).

37 See Bion, *Learning from Experience*; Donald Meltzer, *Sexual States of Mind* (Perthshire: Clunie, 1973) and *Studies in Extended Metapsychology: Clinical applications of Bion's ideas* (Perthshire: Clunie, 1986). Thomas Ogden suggests that psychic creativity arises in and through a dialectical relation between the paranoid-schizoid position and the depressive position. Paranoid-schizoid turbulence breaks up the structuration of integration and ambivalence reached in the depressive position, as depression serves to balance the psychic turbulence of pure loving and pure hating. This interplay will be discussed more fully in chapters 3 and 5. See Ogden, 'The dialectically constituted/decentred subject of psychoanalysis II. The contributions of Klein and Winnicott', *International Journal of Psychoanalysis*, 73, 4, 1992, pp. 613–26.

38 Kristeva, *Strangers*, p. 189.

CHAPTER 2   CONTRADICTIONS OF THE IMAGINATION: FREUD IN THE
STREAM OF MODERNITY

1   Jacques Barzun, *A Stroll with William James* (Chicago: University of
Chicago Press, 1984), p. 25.
2   Lancelot Law Whyte, *The Unconscious before Freud* (London:
Tavistock, 1962).
3   Malcolm Bowie, *Psychoanalysis and the Future of Theory* (Oxford and
Cambridge, Mass.: Blackwell, 1993), pp. 118–19.
4   The current scientific controversy surrounding Freud is highly complex,
and it has had a profound impact both within the psychoanalytic world
and outside it. The point I am seeking to make here is perhaps marginal,
but (as Freud has taught us to see) the marginal often has a way of
dislocating what is regarded as central: attacks on the scientific status of
psychoanalysis on the basis that its propositions, interpretations and
observations can be neither demonstrated nor refuted actually work
within, and serve to reproduce, the guiding spirit of modernity, a spirit
which aims for certitude and transparency. Yet Freud's discovery of
psychical imagination and fantasy, uncovered as a disruptive and relentlessly critical potential of modernity (and one, in my view, that is fully
embraced only in postmodernity), renders implausible the idea of de-
ducing formal reason or knowledge that is free from the contradictions
of subjectivity, sexuality and desire. The key reference points in this
tiresome polemic are Adolf Grünbaum, *The Foundations of Psychoanalysis* (Berkeley: University of California Press, 1984); and, more
recently, Fredric Crews, 'The Freudian way of knowledge', *New Crite-
rion*, 2, 1984, pp. 7–25. The best recent critique of these positions is
Charles Spezzano, *Affect in Psychoanalysis: A clinical synthesis*
(Hillsdale, NJ: Analytic Press, 1993), chapter 1.
5   Freud's 'Project for a scientific psychology' was first published in 1950
as *Aus der Anfängen der Psychanalyse* (London: Imago, 1950). It was
translated into English in 1954 in Ernst Kris, *The Origins of Psychoanalysis* (New York: Basic Books, 1954). References to the text in this
chapter are to the SE, I.
6   Freud, 'Project', SE, I, p. 295.
7   For a brief discussion of the influence of Helmholtz and Herbart on
Freud, see Paul Ricoeur, *Freud and Philosophy: An essay on interpretation* (New Haven: Yale, 1970), pp. 72–3.
8   Richard Wollheim, *Freud* (London: Fontana, 1971), p. 45.
9   Freud, 'Project', p. 318.
10   See Frank J. Sulloway, *Freud: Biologist of the mind* (New York: Basic
Books, 1979), chapter 4; and Wollheim, *Freud*, chapter 2.
11   Wollheim, *Freud*, p. 46.
12   Ibid., p. 48.

13   Jeffrey M. Masson (ed.), *The Complete Letters of Sigmund Freud to Wilhelm Fliess, 1887–1904* (Cambridge, Mass.: Harvard University Press, 1985), p. 146.

14   Sigmund Freud, *Outline of Psychoanalysis*, SE, XXIII, p. 182.

15   Ricoeur's critique of the 'Project' makes a good deal of this point, highlighting that Freud cannot give a mechanistic explanation of how the threat of unpleasure leads to a non-cathexis of quantities stored in the ego. See Ricoeur, *Freud and Philosophy*, p. 80.

16   Susan Isaacs, 'The nature and function of phantasy', in P. King and R. Steiner (eds), *The Freud–Klein Controversies 1941–45* (London: Routledge, 1991), p. 96.

17   Sigmund Freud, 'Letters to Fliess', SE, I, p. 247.

18   Masson, *Complete Letters*, pp. 264–5.

19   John Toews, 'Historicizing psychoanalysis: Freud in his time and for our time', *Journal of Modern History*, 63, September 1991, pp. 504–45, at p. 513.

20   Philip Rieff, *Freud: The mind of the moralist* (New York: Harper and Row, 1961), p. 36.

21   Sigmund Freud, *The Interpretation of Dreams*, SE, V, p. 525.

22   Anthony Elliott, *Psychoanalytic Theory: An introduction* (Oxford: Blackwell, 1994), pp. 17–18.

23   Jeffrey Masson, *The Assault on Truth: Freud's suppression of the seduction theory* (New York: Farrar, Straus and Giroux, 1984), p. 144. Perhaps this is also the place to note that I accept Masson's point concerning the sterility of psychoanalytic therapy, or at least of its failings when practised reductively. However, against Masson, I locate the reasons for this in the growing psychologization of culture and the transformation of psychoanalysis into an expert-system of specialized knowledge. As such, the undoing of such psychologization involves grasping the constitutive role of fantasy in subjectivity, culture and society; it requires a postmodern turning back of fantasy upon itself. Such an undoing would involve, *contra* Masson, more fantasy not less; or, at least, more of a critical appreciation of the structuring role of fantasy in personal and cultural life. My view on this issue is set out in greater detail in the following sections of this chapter.

24   Jeffrey Prager, 'On the abuses of Freud', *Contention*, 4, 1, Fall, 1994, p. 214.

25   Philip Rieff, *The Triumph of the Therapeutic* (New York: Harper and Row, 1966) and *Freud: The mind of the moralist* (Chicago: University of Chicago Press, 1979).

26   Rieff, *Triumph*, p. 56.

27   Anthony Giddens, *Modernity and Self-Identity* (Cambridge: Polity, 1991).

28   Sherry Turkle, *Psychoanalytic Politics* (London: Free Association, 1922), p. 49.

29   Michel Foucault, *The History of Sexuality*, published in three volumes,

of which volume 1: *An Introduction* (Harmondsworth: Penguin, 1981) is especially relevant to the concerns of this chapter.

30 Ibid., p. 154.
31 Ibid., pp. 110–11.

CHAPTER 3   THE EPIC OF MASTERY: MODERNIST EDGES OF FANTASY

1 Ulrich Beck, *Risk Society: Towards a new modernity* (London: Sage, 1992), p. 36.
2 Ibid., p. 24.
3 Ulrich Beck, 'Self-dissolution and self-endangerment of industrial society: what does this mean?' in U. Beck, A. Giddens and S. Lash, *Reflexive Modernization* (Cambridge: Polity, 1994), p. 174.
4 Anthony Giddens, *The Consequences of Modernity* (Cambridge: Polity, 1990), p. 38.
5 Anthony Giddens, *Modernity and Self-Identity* (Cambridge: Polity, 1991), p. 28.
6 Anthony Giddens, 'Living in a post-traditional society', in Beck, Giddens and Lash, *Reflexive Modernization*, p. 59.
7 See Scott Lash and John Urry, *Economies of Signs and Space* (London: Sage, 1994), chapter 3.
8 Ulrich Beck, 'Self-dissolution', in *Reflexive Modernization*, p. 174. Perhaps this is also the place to note that I am aware of Beck's insistence on the differences between 'reflection and reflexivity' as regards social autodynamism. My criticisms are, however, directed towards his notion of reflexivity as self-reflection in both the personal and institutional spheres. My thanks to Andrew Newton for discussion on this point.
9 Giddens, *Modernity and Self-Identity*, p. 39.
10 Anthony Elliott, *Psychoanalytic Theory: An introduction* (Oxford: Blackwell, 1994), pp. 71–5.
11 Michael Rustin, 'Incomplete modernity', *Radical Philosophy*, 67, Summer, 1994, p. 10.
12 Jacques Ellul, *The Technological Society* (London: Cape, 1965), p. 89.
13 Cornelius Castoriadis, *Philosophy, Politics, Autonomy* (Oxford: Odeon, 1991), p. 272.
14 Ibid., p. 249.
15 Marko Prelec, 'The Western response to the war in Bosnia: a house built on sand', in Rabia Ali and Lawrence Lifschultz (eds), *Why Bosnia?* (Connecticut: Pamphleteer's Press, 1993), p. 194.
16 *The Sunday Times*, 16 August 1992, part 2, p. 3.
17 Christopher Lasch, *The Minimal Self* (New York: Norton, 1984), p. 111.
18 Julia Kristeva, *Strangers to Ourselves* (Hemel Hempstead: Harvester

Wheatsheaf, 1991), p. 13.

19 Sigmund Freud, *Civilization and its Discontents*, SE, XXI, pp. 135–6.

20 Theodor Adorno, *Negative Dialectics* (New York: Seabury, 1973), p. 371.

21 Rabia Ali and Lawrence Lifschultz, 'In plain view', *Why Bosnia?*, p. xviii.

22 As the press reported, the cost–benefit analysis was itself a cynical exercise designed to get the thumbs-down from Congress: *The Sunday Times*, 16 August 1992, p. 10.

23 Ali and Lifschultz, *Why Bosnia?*, p. xxviii.

24 The UN General Assembly voted to lift the arms embargo against Bosnia in December 1992, requesting the Security Council to authorize 'all means possible' to preserve Bosnia's territorial integrity. See Ali and Lifschultz, *Why Bosnia?*, p. xxviii.

25 See Stjepko Golubic, Susan Campbell and Thomas Golubic, 'How not to divide the indivisible', in Rabia Ali and Lawrence Lifschultz, *Why Bosnia?*, pp. 209–32.

26 Renata Selecl, *The Spoils of Freedom* (London: Routledge, 1994), p. 16.

27 Slavoj Žižek has powerfully underlined this element in Western media discourses on Bosnia. As he observes, 'examples of "compassion with suffering in Bosnia" that abound in our media illustrate perfectly Lacan's thesis on the "reflexive" nature of human desire: desire is always desire for a desire. That is to say, what these examples display above all is that compassion is the way to *maintain the proper distance* towards a neighbour in trouble', *The Metastases of Enjoyment* (London: Verso, 1994), p. 221.

28 Marko Prelec, 'A house built on sand', in Ali and Lifschultz, *Why Bosnia?*, p. 195.

29 The Frankfurt School critic Theodor Adorno was, of course, acutely sensitive to the politicobureaucratic tendency to reinscribe human subjectivity within destructive, pathological fantasies of mastery and omnipotence. In *Minima Moralia* (London: Verso, 1987) Adorno writes: 'the pattern of all administration and "personnel policy" tends of its own accord, and in advance of any education of the political will or commitment to exclusive programmes, towards Fascism. Anyone who has once made it his concern to judge people's suitability sees those judged, by a kind of technological necessity, as insiders or outsiders, as belonging or alien to the race, as accomplices or victims' (p. 131).

30 See Jürgen Habermas, *The Philosophical Discourse of Modernity* (Cambridge: Polity, 1987).

31 John Dunn, *Rethinking Modern Political Theory* (Cambridge: Cambridge University Press, 1985), p. 153.

32 Cornelius Castoriadis, 'The state of the subject', *Thesis Eleven*, 24, 1989, p. 27.

CHAPTER 4 POSTMODERN CONTEXTS, PLURAL WORLDS:
THE POSSIBILITIES AND PRESSURES OF SOCIAL CHANGE

1 Marike Finlay, 'Post-modernizing psychoanalysis/psychoanalyzing postmodernity', *Free Associations*, 16, 1989, pp. 43–80.
2 Ibid., p. 49.
3 Jean-François Lyotard, *Peregrinations* (New York: Columbia University
   Press, 1988), pp. 31–6.
4 The best recent discussion of mass communication is Nick Stevenson,
   Understanding Media Cultures: Social theory and mass communication
   (London: Sage, 1995).
5 See Joshua Meyrowitz, *No Sense of Place: The impact of electronic
   media on social behaviour* (New York: Oxford, 1985).
6 Susan R. Brooker-Gross, 'The changing concept of place in the news', in
   Jacquelin Burgess and John R. Gold (eds), *Geography, the Media and
   Popular Culture* (London: Croom Helm, 1985), p. 63.
7 Jacques Lacan, *Le séminaire Livre II: Le moi dans la théorie de Freud et
   dans la technique de la psychanalyse* (Paris: Seuil, 1977), p. 286.
8 Zygmunt Bauman, *Postmodern Ethics* (Oxford: Blackwell, 1993), p.
   198.
9 Cornelius Castoriadis, *The Imaginary Institution of Society* (Cambridge: Polity, 1987), p. 287.
10 Anthony Elliott, 'The affirmation of primary repression rethought', in
   A. Elliott and S. Frosh (eds), *Psychoanalysis in Contexts: Paths between
   theory and modern culture* (London and New York: Routledge, 1995),
   pp. 36–52.
11 Didier Anzieu, *The Skin Ego* (New Haven: Yale University Press, 1989),
   p. 57.
12 Ibid., p. 105.
13 Christopher Bollas, *Being a Character: Psychoanalysis and self experience* (New York: Hill and Wang, 1992), p. 51.
14 Ibid., pp. 52–3.
15 Wilfred Bion, *Learning from Experience* (London: Heinemann, 1962),
   p. 6.
16 Ibid., p. 7.
17 Ibid., p. 84.
18 Ibid., pp. 84–5.
19 Wilfred Bion, *Second Thoughts* (London: Marsefield, 1967), p. 89.
20 Wilfred Bion, 'Differentiation of the psychotic from the non-psychotic
   personalities', in Elizabeth Bott Spillius (ed.), *Melanie Klein Today*
   (London: Routledge, 1988), p. 64.
21 Bion makes a distinction between normal and abnormal experience
   generated in the paranoid-schizoid mode, and the forms of projective
   identification deployed. He speaks of projective identification as both a
   form of communication and a way to evacuate and fragment mental

content. In projective identification as communication, internal objects become available as a mechanism for communication between the unconscious of one person and that of another. The processing of a projective identification thus involves an intersubjective restructuring, a passing back-and-forth until modified, of those unconscious contents which are experienced as intolerable and unmanageable. In projective identification as evacuation, intersubjective communication is severely hampered because thought and meaning are attacked and destroyed. For further discussion, see the essays by Bion, Meltzer, Rosenfeld and Joseph on projective identification in Spillius, *Melanie Klein Today*.

22 Bion, 'Differentiation', in Spillius, *Melanie Klein Today*, p. 65.

23 Hanna Segal, 'Notes on symbol formation', *International Journal of Psycho-Analysis*, 38, 1957, pp. 339–43.

24 Paul Hoggett, 'The culture of uncertainty', in B. Richards (ed.), *Crises of the Self* (London: Free Association, 1989), p. 31.

25 Fredric Jameson, *Postmodernism, or The Cultural Logic of Late Capitalism* (Durham: Duke University Press, 1991), p. 375.

26 Jean Baudrillard, *Les stratégies fatales* (Paris: Grasset, 1983), p. 9.

27 Ibid., p. 271. A recent assessment of Baudrillard's call to side with the object can be found in Douglas Kellner, *Jean Baudrillard: From Marxism to postmodernism and beyond* (Cambridge: Polity, 1989), pp. 154–65.

28 Winnicott suggests that fear of breakdown is not an anxiety projected into the future, but a fear relating to an earlier experience of the individual, and is thus something which is pivotal to the organization of experience in the present. D.W. Winnicott, 'Fear of breakdown', *International Review of Psycho-Analysis*, 1, 1974, pp. 103–7.

29 Jameson's concept of 'cognitive mapping' is certainly complex and contradictory, if only because he has argued that it applies to both processing and blockages in thinking. At a minimum, however, it seems clear that he intends by it all 'attempts to span or coordinate, to map, by means of conscious and unconscious representations', *Postmodernism*, p. 416. My point is that the concept should not simply be projected into the future, as a prefigurative image of utopia, but rather should be understood to exist in a dialectical relation to the internal deformations or fragmentations promoted by postmodernity. From this perspective, such mappings are continually lived and experienced as part of self-existence, even if they contain material which is unthinkable on a conscious psychical plane. Significantly, such an understanding allows us to grasp cognitive, and crucially affective, mapping as arising from a failure of defensive organization. That is to say, the evacuation of pain through the defensive use of anti-thought exists in a complex interplay with thinking and the containment of experience. (To add affective and emotional capacities to the cognitive as characteristics of mapping extends the reach of this concept, I believe, in ways which are more

personally and culturally differentiated.) In postmodern conditions which disturb and terrify, then, denial and discontinuity may certainly become more prevalent in the organization of experience, but there is always some mapping or scanning of that experience generated in a paranoid-schizoid mode which is *stored* for later thinking. This issue will be discussed in detail in chapter 5.

30 Thomas H. Ogden, *The Primitive Edge of Experience* (New Jersey: Jason Aronson, 1989).

31 Ibid., quotations from pp. 218 and 219.

32 Arlene Kramer Richards, 'A romance with pain: a telephone perversion in a woman?', *International Journal of Psycho-Analysis*, 70, 1989, pp. 153–64.

33 Ibid., quotations from pp. 153–4, 159, 156, 160.

CHAPTER 5 POSTMODERNITY, OR MODERNITY IN REVERSE: REFLEXIVE SCANNING, STRANGENESS, IMAGINATION

1 Zygmunt Bauman, *Modernity and Ambivalence* (Cambridge: Polity, 1991), p. 98.

2 Christopher Bollas, *Being A Character: Psychoanalysis and self experience* (New York: Hill and Wang, 1992), p. 27.

3 Ibid., p. 60 and following quotation, p. 59.

4 See Christopher Bollas, *The Shadow of the Object: Psychoanalysis and the unknown thought* (New York: Columbia University Press, 1987).

5 George Atwood and Robert Stolorow, *Structures of Subjectivity: Explorations in psychoanalytic phenomenology* (Hillsdale, New Jersey: The Analytic Press, 1984), pp. 88–9.

6 Betty Joseph, 'Transference: the total situation', *International Journal of Psycho-Analysis*, 66, 1985, p. 447.

7 Sigmund Freud, 'Negation', SE, XIX, p. 237.

8 Sigmund Freud, 'The uncanny', SE, XVII, p. 241.

9 Thomas Ogden, *The Primitive Edge of Experience* (New Jersey: Jason Aronson, 1989), pp. 29–30.

10 Walter Benjamin, 'The work of art in the age of mechanical reproduction', in *Illuminations*, ed. and intro. by Hannah Arendt, trans. Harry Zohn (London: Fontana, 1969), p. 238.

11 A full-scale encounter with Benjamin's account of experience would be out of place in this study. However, it is relevant to question the extent to which Benjamin's notion of experience connects and contrasts with that of Bion. Benjamin's dialectical notion of experience is developed out of that hermeneutic interplay which Wilhelm Dilthey called 'inner lived experience' and 'outer sensory experience'. Blending the realms of concrete immediacy and conceptual reflection, Benjamin came to view experience as a learning process – established through shock and disorientation – over time. Bion shares this basic emphasis on disorienta-

tion, yet unlike Benjamin views the fundamental co-ordinates of possible experience as a process of unconscious transformations. For an excellent discussion of Benjamin's account of experience, see Martin Jay, 'Experience without a Subject', *New Formations: The Actuality of Walter Benjamin*, 1994, pp. 145–57.

12 Terry Eagleton, *The Ideology of the Aesthetic* (Oxford: Blackwell, 1990), p. 327.

13 Horst Moebius and Barbara Michel-Annen, 'Colouring the grey everyday: the psychology of the Walkman', *Free Associations*, vol. 4, part 2, no. 32, pp. 570–6. Quotations from pp. 572 and 576.

14 Julia Kristeva, *Tales of Love* (New York: Columbia University Press, 1987), p. 55, and also for the following quotation.

15 Bollas, *Character*, p. 59.

16 John Fiske, *Media Matters: Everyday culture and political change* (Minneapolis: University of Minnesota Press, 1994), p. xvi.

17 Dorothy Zinberg, 'O.J. mania catapults trial into cyberspace', *The Australian Higher Education*, 30 November 1994, p. 37.

18 Kate Millett, *The Politics of Cruelty* (New York: Viking, 1994), p. 159.

Index

Index